Hannah Ryggen

Supported by
NORLA Norwegian Literature Abroad
with Sparebankstiftelsen DNB

Der Traum in uns
Frankfurter Buchmesse 2019 Ehrengast Norwegen

Hannah Ryggen
Woven Manifestos

Marit Paasche, Esther Schlicht (Eds.)

SCHIRN
KUNSTHALLE
FRANKFURT

Prestel
Munich · London · New York

Contents

Foreword

The Schirn has taken Norway's appearance as the Guest of Honour of this year's Frankfurt Book Fair as an opportunity to dedicate a large solo exhibition to the textile artist Hannah Ryggen. However, simply wanting to present her as a "Norwegian" artist falls somewhat short of the mark. Ryggen was born in Sweden in 1894 but lived in Norway from 1924 until her death in 1970; she once described herself as Swedish, but her art, in contrast, as Norwegian. What is, in fact, manifested in her extraordinary work, however, is the noble position of a cosmopolitan—indeed, of a citizen of the world, beyond any concept of nation states.

Ryggen is undoubtedly one of the most important Scandinavian women artists of the twentieth century. Trained as a painter, she abandoned painting in 1923 in order to turn to weaving. In her monumental tapestries, she took up fundamental topics of human existence and society: the cruelties of war, abuse of power, reliance on nature, and the bonds with family and fellow human beings. Many of her works deal with the events and political conflicts in Europe in the 1930s and 1940s, from Mussolini's invasion of Ethiopia to the occupation of Norway by the German National Socialists. After the Second World War, from a small, self-supporting farm in the northwest of Norway, she continued to position herself vis-à-vis contemporary issues such as nuclear armament and the Vietnam War. In her work, she thus combined the influences of the European avant-garde with elements of folk art in a unique way, and pressing political concerns with mythological motifs or topics from day-to-day life.

Following the presentation of selected works from Ryggen within the framework of dOCUMENTA (13) in Kassel in 2012, the exhibition in Frankfurt provides an in-depth view of her oeuvre for the first time in Germany. At the same time, our presentation ought not to be viewed as a late assessment of an artist who has hitherto been ignored. During her lifetime, Ryggen was indeed present in a number of important solo and group exhibitions in European countries as well as in the United States, and she represented Norway at the 32nd Venice Biennale in 1964. It was only after 1970 that her artistic legacy, which she always vehemently defended as fine art, was increasingly categorized within the field of arts and crafts and thus never, as with most works created on the loom, truly penetrated the art-historical canon. In the past few years, however, the reception of Ryggen's political tapestries has morphed anew and they have been receiving increasing attention within the context of contemporary art. This is due not only to the revision of European modernism currently occurring on a broader level but also to the fact that, in a contemporary climate characterized by growing inequality, nationalism, and populism in politics, Ryggen's uncompromising oeuvre truly has an unsettling topicality.

My heartfelt gratitude goes to the Nordenfjeldske Kunstindustri-museum, the National Museum of Decorative Arts and Design, in Trondheim, which houses the most important collection of works by the artist, and in particular to its director, Åshild Adsen. The exhibition would not have been possible in this form without her willingness to cooperate and to generously support the project with important loans. Steffen Wesselvold

Holden, the curator of the museum's collection, also dedicated himself to this project unconditionally in various respects. I express my warmest thanks to him, too.

All the other institutional lenders are sincerely thanked for their willingness to be temporarily separated from significant works. They have thus made a significant contribution to the success of our project. Within Norway, my thanks go to: Petter Snare of KODE – Art Museums and Composer Homes in Bergen; in Oslo, the office of the Prime Minister of Norway, Anne Wiland of the DNB Art Collection and the Telenor Art Collection, Karin Hindsbo and Elsebet Kjerschow of the National Museum of Art, Architecture, and Design, and Eivind Furnesvik of STANDARD (OSLO); and, in Trondheim, Johan Börjesson and Randi Thommessen of the Trondheim kunstmuseum. Within Sweden, my thanks go to Nina Due and Josefin Kilner of the Röhsska Museum of Design and Craft in Göteborg, Kirse Junge-Stevnsborg, Sara Rydby, and the former director Cecilia Widenheim of the Malmö Konstmuseum, as well as Ann-Charlotte Backlund and Andreas Nordh Hansson of the City Museum of Stockholm. I also express my gratitude to private lenders in Norway and Sweden who do not wish to be mentioned by name. Furthermore, I would like to thank NTNU University Library in Trondheim for their assistance with image research.

Additionally, my heartfelt thanks go to NORLA, Norwegian Literature Abroad, for its backing for and outstanding collaboration on this project. Early confirmation of its considerable support for our project made the exhibition at the Schirn possible in the first place. We are very pleased that an additional sponsor could be obtained as a result of NORLA's commitment with the Sparebankstiftelsen DNB, which also made a substantial contribution to the realization of the project. I thank in particular Margit Walsø, the director of NORLA, Halldór Guðmundsson, Project Manager for the Guest of Honour 2019 presentation, and Marit Ingvill Sande, the coordinator of the Guest of Honour cultural programme for the Frankfurt Book Fair 2019, for their extensive personal dedication and indispensable support in the planning, preparations, and realization of the exhibition. I would also like to express my gratitude to the Royal Norwegian Embassy in Berlin for its dedicated support in communications for the exhibition.

As always, I am extremely grateful to the City of Frankfurt for its valuable, ongoing support for our work at the Schirn, and, representatively for all the decision-makers, Lord Mayor Peter Feldmann and Ina Hartwig, Deputy Mayor in charge of cultural affairs.

My special gratitude goes to the curators of the exhibition, Marit Paasche and Esther Schlicht, who jointly developed and realized it in a very compelling way. Esther Schlicht, Deputy Director and curator of the Schirn, initiated the project, and I am very pleased that she was able to obtain Marit Paasche, undoubtedly the best expert on the work of Hannah Ryggen, as a guest curator. Johanna Laub supported them with great dedication as a curatorial assistant; I would like to thank her very much for the splendid support in the preparations for and realization of the exhibition.

I sincerely thank Marit Paasche for her enriching text contribution to the catalog. With her essay and the texts accompanying the exhibited works, she provides in-depth insights into Hannah Ryggen's impressive oeuvre as well as into the historical and political circumstances that significantly influenced the artist. My gratitude also goes to Ingar Dragset for the intriguing interview with Esther Schlicht, to Marie Luise Knott for her enlightening essay, and to Johanna Laub for the comprehensive chronology, which provides a valuable overview of Ryggen's biography and the political and historical backgrounds. Amy Klement and Katia Stieglitz are thanked for their sensitive translations of the texts into English. My gratitude goes to Sarah Quigley for the attentive copyediting. I would also like to express my special thanks to Prestel Publishing for its close collaboration on this publication, in particular Katharina Haderer and Antje Eszerski. For the outstanding design of this catalog, I thank Sibylle Ryser, Basel, as well as Alexandra Papadopoulou and Marie Schoppmann from VERY, Frankfurt, for the extraordinary exhibition design.

Without the dedicated team at the Schirn, this impressive exhibition and the accompanying publication would not have come about. I would like to express my heartfelt gratitude to all the employees: I thank Karin Grüning, Elke Walter, and Luise Leyer for coordinating the transportation as well as the installation and de-installation of the exhibited works, Christian Teltz and Oliver Taschke for the technical support, and Anna Noll as assistant to the exhibition management. Furthermore, my gratitude goes to Andreas Gundermann and the installation team as well as to the restorer Christine Stührenberg. Luise Bachmann, Heike Stumpf, Hannah Ruiz, and Elena Schmidt are thanked for the marketing and the design of the campaign. I would like to thank Johanna Pulz, Julia Bastian, Elisabeth Pallentin, and Isabelle Hammer for their press and public relations work. In addition, I thank Antonia Lagemann along with Anuschka Berthelius for coordinating and supervising the publication as well as for editing the Schirn Magazine. For the accompanying education program, my gratitude goes to Chantal Eschenfelder along with Simone Boscheinen, Laura Heeg, Irmi Rauber, Olga Schaetz, and Anna Haag. My thanks go to Ute Seiffert and Lena Sobczinski for developing and coordinating the events. I thank Julia Lange and Miriam Werner for the sponsorship and for assisting our partners and patrons. My gratitude is also due to Heike Berndt, Claudia Kroh, Tanja Stahl, and Anna Schulmeyer in the administration of the Schirn, as well as to Daniela Becker for her assistance in numerous tasks. Finally, I would like to thank the messengers Stefan Schell and Lukas Müller, Rosaria La Tona and the cleaning services team, Bettina Beyermann, Vilizara Antalavicheva, and Josef Härig at reception as well as all the other Schirn staff members who were involved in the realization of this extensive project.

Philipp Demandt
Director
Schirn Kunsthalle Frankfurt

Blod i gresset (*Blood in the Grass*), 1966
Tapestry woven with pile in wool and linen, 240 × 290 cm

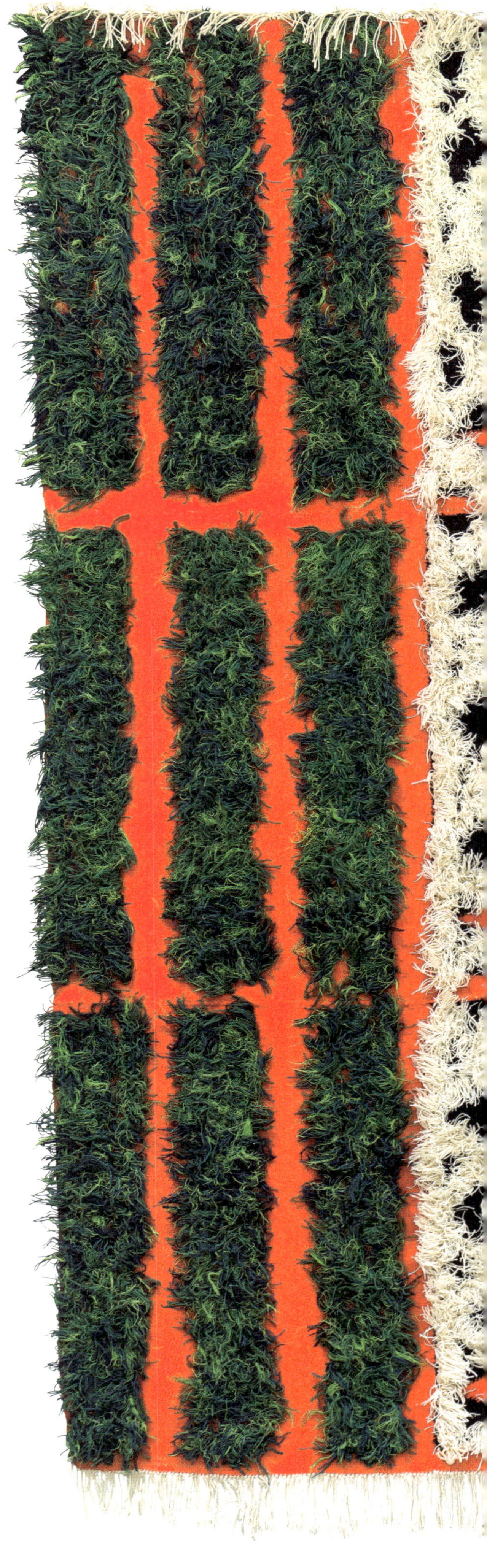

Hannah Ryggen was seventy-two years old when she sat down at the loom and wove *Blood in the Grass*, a shockingly vital protest against the United States' warfare in Vietnam. This is also the first and only work in which she used artificially dyed wool, notable in the blood-red gullies that run through the lush green Vietnamese landscape. The U.S. president, Lyndon B. Johnson, is portrayed in a cowboy hat with his famous and often photographed dog. Two blue bands contain missiles being fired in the direction of communist North Vietnam. One of these bands goes across Johnson's body, and the work's title is woven directly under it: "Blod i gresset." On March 21, 1966, Ryggen wrote a letter which makes clear her opinion of the Americans' conduct: "This evening they said that the South Vietnamese were to pay $300 million to [the US]. That's great, the people pay for the United States to spread poisons over 20 million acres of land so that food cannot be produced on that soil. Those poor folks will pay with money, blood, and tears. I cannot fathom that lousy president in the Land of Freedom and Lincoln. But most people agree with them because they believe that the United States is going to save them from communism. Yes—the world is no better than it was before."[1]

1 Hannah Ryggen, in a letter to her cousin Lisa Nilsson in Copenhagen, 21.3.1966, NTNU University Library, Trondheim.

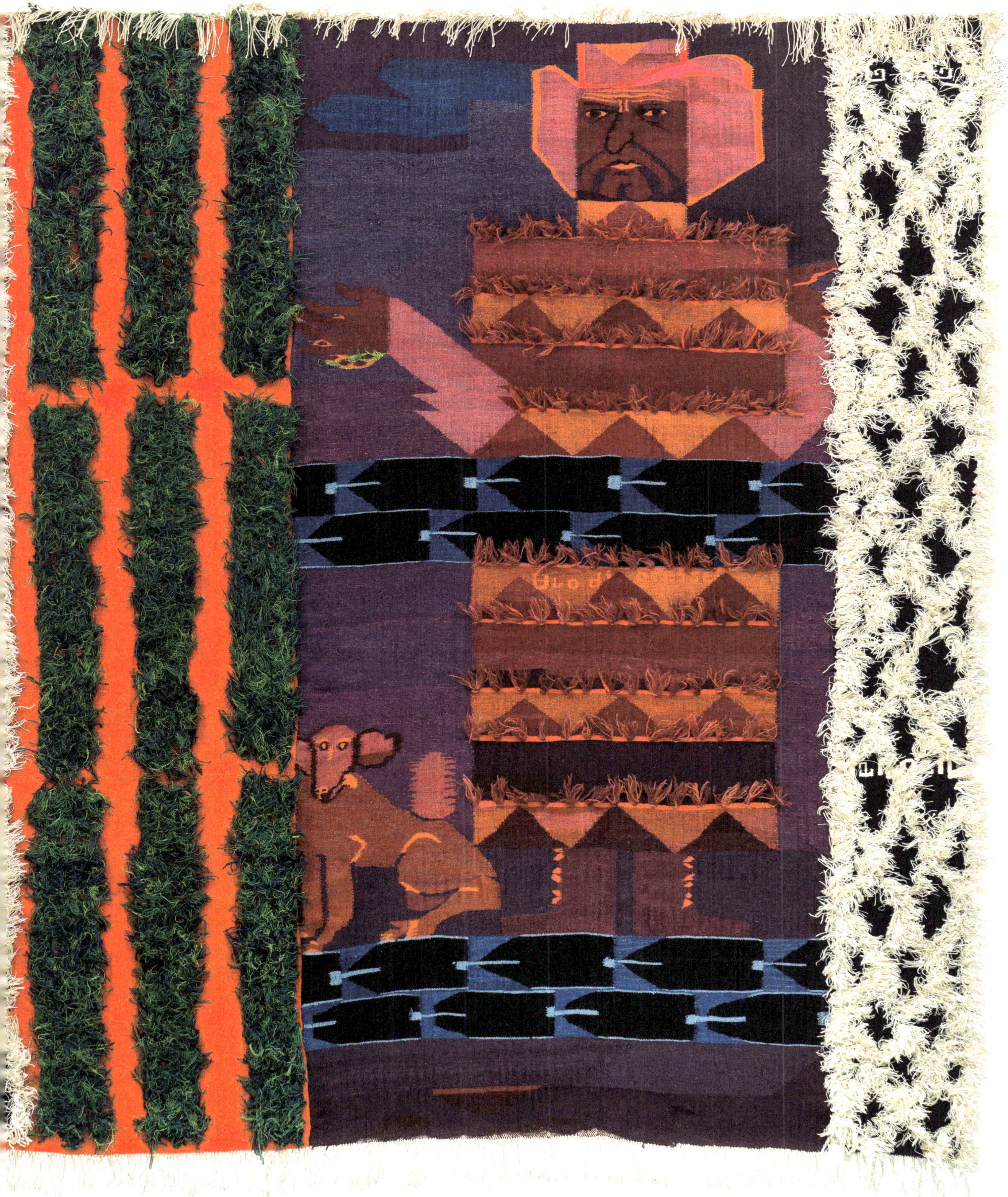

Marit Paasche

Unfolded. The Monumental Tapestries of Hannah Ryggen

Throughout her entire life as an artist, Hannah Ryggen actively used her works as statements to society. She never considered the task of responding to events occurring around her to be anyone else's obligation; she shouldered the responsibility herself. She took stock of her own life, and questioned generally held views about the role of women in society, poverty, economic injustice and inequality, and international conflicts caused by the rise of the National Socialists and fascism in Europe. In this essay, some of the material and art-historical prerequisites for Ryggen making her works will be explored, for perhaps the activist aspect of her art can best be understood from the context of a discussion about the function of art and the position that monumental painting and murals occupy in Norwegian art.

To Hannah Ryggen, art was an interface with existence. It spanned everything from the most intimate realms in her life, such as her love for her husband Hans and their daughter Mona, to her rage over Mussolini's invasion of Ethiopia in 1935 and the United States' role in the Vietnam War in the 1960s. Ryggen's prodigious output suggests that her loom was seldom idle.[1] She shifted constantly between producing small and large works. The smaller ones were often witty commentaries on varied topics: they could be portraits, observations on nature, or tokens of esteem.[2] In general, her small-format works were reserved for the purpose of barter—used as payments for services or for others lending a helping hand. Some were also made as gifts, while others served as tests for difficult elements in motifs that required practice before being executed in a larger format. In this exhibition, we have chosen to concentrate on the monumental works, because it was these works in particular that Ryggen addressed to the public, and these she considered important for the world to see.

Ryggen held her works up as banners, using them as 'moveable murals.' They were frequently exhibited, and sometimes also censored. She trusted art infinitely and had unwavering confidence in its power. Such faith in the significance of art is contagious. Experiencing Hannah Ryggen's art brings to mind the Finnish-Swedish poet Elmer Diktonius' reaction after reading his colleague Edith Södergran's poetry: "It gleams. I am still aglow with it, shall always be."[3]

Early years and the *Baltic Exhibition*

Hanna Josefina Maria Jönsson came into the world in Malmö, Sweden, in 1894; she died in Norway in 1970.[4] She was born into a working-class family with a strict mother who had strong convictions about the education of her children. FIG. 1 As a result, both Hannah and her sister Agda became primary school teachers, while her brother Erik gained employment in a bank. Hannah was clever at school and received high marks—with the exception of one subject: pedagogics. She was neither good with children nor adept at giving instruction, but the teaching profession gave her economic independence, as well as offering long summer holidays.

In 1914 she discovered art in earnest when the major *Baltiska utställningen* (*Baltic Exhibition*) opened in Malmö. The exhibition, which ran from May 15 to October 4, was like a Nordic edition of the World's Fair in which the countries surrounding the Baltic Sea participated, and it had

1 There were only a few periods in her life when Ryggen did not touch the loom, and these were due either to illness or extremely difficult circumstances.

2 Frequent motifs here were wine glasses or goblets; Ryggen enjoyed raising a glass with good friends.

3 Eva Ström, *Edith Södergran,* Stockholm: Natur & Kultur, 2002 (e-book).

4 Hanna Josefina Maria Jönsson changed her first name to Hannah quite early on, although during the 1920s she still alternated between signing her name Hanna or Hannah.

two primary themes: art and industry.[5] In addition to presentations of technical and industrial innovations, there were large exhibits of Russian, German, Danish, and Swedish contemporary painting. To qualify for selection, the artworks had to have been created by still living artists and after 1897. Another criterion was that the art, whether in the form of paintings, drawings, sculptures, printed matter, or decorative and utilitarian objects, had to have been made by the artists themselves.

Hannah Jönsson and her cousin Emil Nilsson, with whom she was quite close, purchased discounted admission cards that were valid for the entire duration of the exhibition, so they both spent much time there. They saw intense, vibrantly colorful paintings by the Russian artists Wassily Kandinsky and Alexej von Jawlensky, and German radical and expressionist painting from the informal collective known as Die Brücke. The exhibition also featured contemporary art in which the distinction between art and craft was not so strictly drawn. This was a clear European trend, manifested in the Arts and Crafts movement in England, the Wiener Werkstätte in Austria, and somewhat later the Bauhaus in Germany. Norway had the Lysakerkretsen (Lysaker Circle). In all of these movements, weaving was a important medium, as it had been, too, in the *Baltic Exhibition.*

Dresden, art history and the Flemish loom

It was during the summer of 1914, after the *Baltic Exhibition* had opened and the First World War had broken out, that Hannah Jönsson decided she would pursue art. She took a brief drawing course, and two years later, in 1916, she began studies with the German-Danish artist Fredrik Krebs (1845–1925). Krebs gave private lessons at the technical college in Lund (today the Faculty of Engineering at Lund University) to a select group of students—mainly men, but a few women as well. Jönsson did not have the means to quit her job, so she continued teaching in Malmö by day, in the afternoons taking the train to Lund to study there, six days a week. Under Krebs, who considered Rembrandt the greatest of all artists, she learned the practical aspects of painting: grinding and mixing pigments, rendering perspective, drawing freehand and painting from the model. Krebs also gave his students an introduction to the classics of art and cultural history. This was essential for those students who, like Jönsson, came from poor, working-class environments.

Hannah Jönsson studied with Krebs from 1916 to 1922, interrupted only by demanding periods at the school where she taught, and the long summer holidays during which she traveled and drew all manner of things, as evidenced by sketchbooks filled with studies of working women, houses and streets, landscapes and portraits. She was quick to learn, but the combination of the Rembrandt-esque palette and classical realism favored by Krebs, along with genres considered appropriate for women at the time—interiors, portraits, and still lifes—did not ignite her interest. FIGS. 2–5

In 1922 Krebs recommended that Hannah take a study trip to Dresden. She departed at the start of the summer holidays with the objective of studying the Old Masters so admired by Krebs in the Gemäldegalerie Alte Meister. The museum housed works from the early Renaissance through

5 Due to the outbreak of the First World War that year, the scale of the exhibition was somewhat reduced, and Russia and Finland were included only on a quasi-official level.

FIG. 1

Hannah Ryggen in Malmö, undated

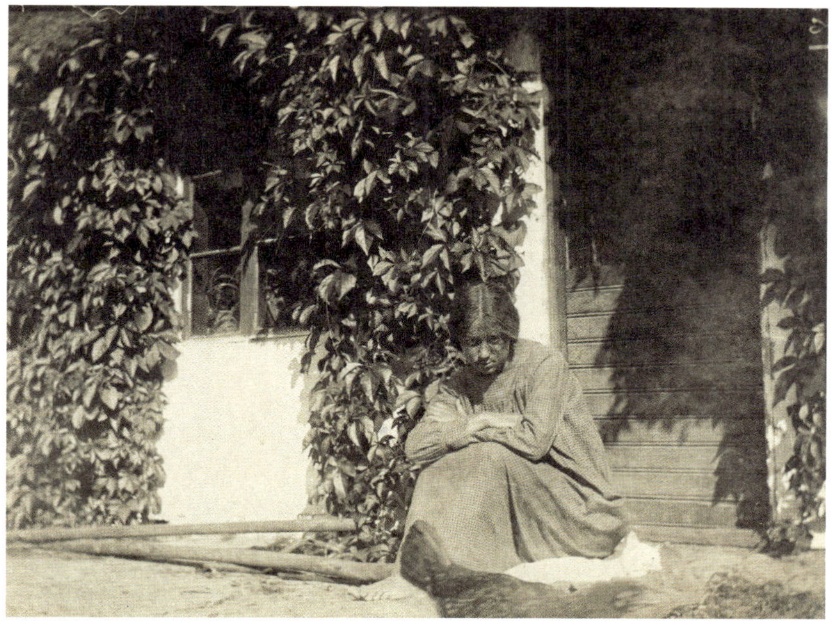

FIG. 2

Hannah Ryggen, portrait of a farmer's wife named "Boel Fröls," drawing on paper, dated July 21, 1920

FIG. 3

Hannah Ryggen, portrait of a fisherman from Bedinge, Sweden, drawing on paper, dated July 7, 1919

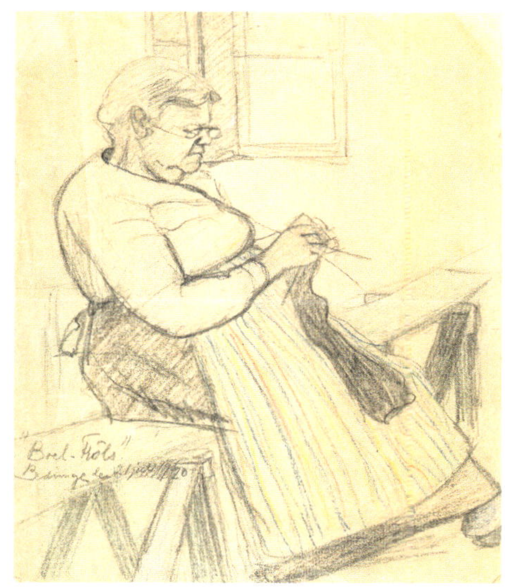

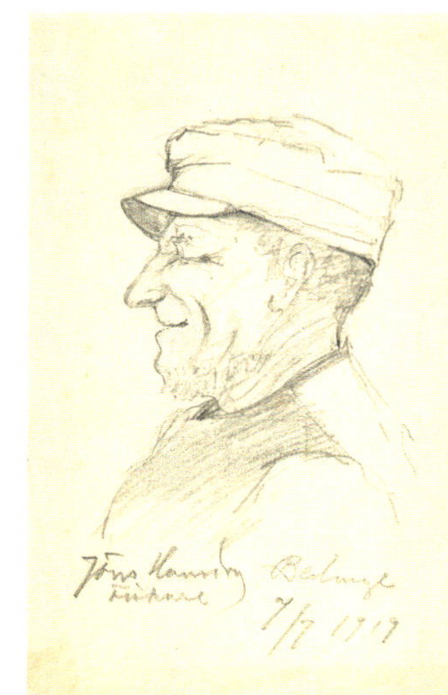

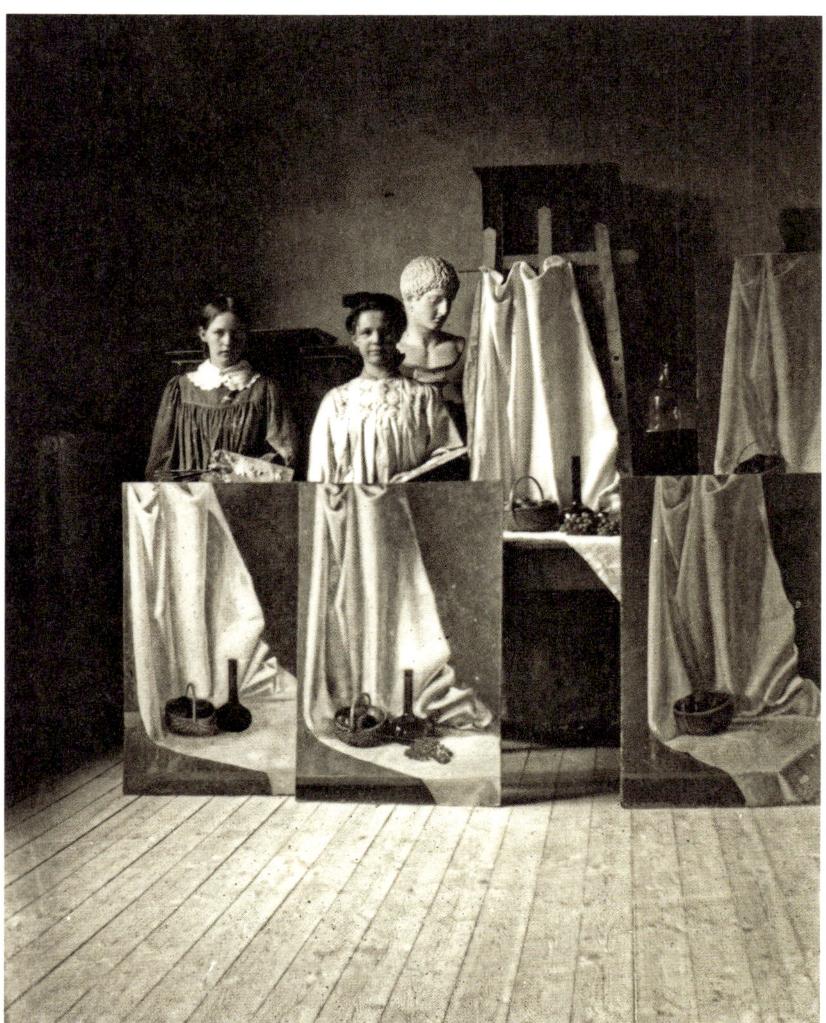

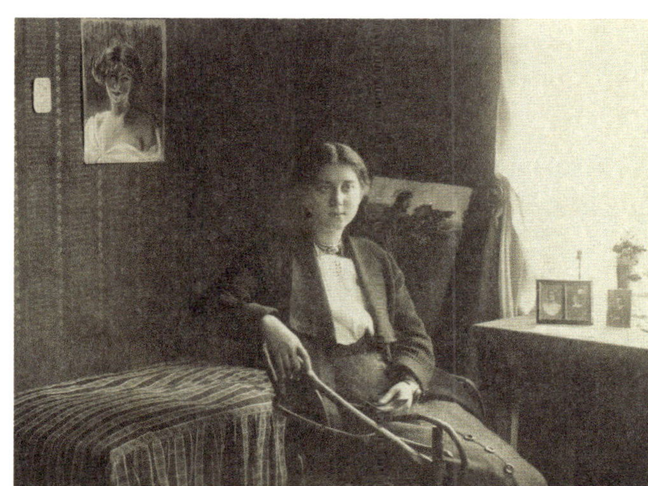

FIG. 4

Hannah Ryggen in her room in Malmö, undated

FIG. 5

Fredrik Krebs' female art students posing with their still lifes, undated

the Baroque by artists including Raphael, Albrecht Dürer, Jan van Eyck, Hans Holbein the Younger, Peter Paul Rubens, Rembrandt van Rijn, Jan Vermeer, Diego Velásquez, and Nicolas Poussin. Many of them made a strong impression on her, as we see from certain motifs she incorporated into her works during the 1950s and also in 1968, including Vermeer's *The Procuress* (1656). She also talked about these artists; in an interview with Møller Nielsen in the Danish newspaper *Social-Demokraten* in 1946, for example, she described Vermeer and Francisco de Goya as superlative painters:

> Vermeer from Delft. Now there was a painter... or Goya! You know the picture with those Spanish royals, where those three meatheads stand simpering and tittering and snickering. They are dressed in glittering silks and brocade robes. And there the three buffoons stand putting on airs and unaware, that all of posterity for hundreds of years sees how they are in all their grinning hideousness—bloodsuckers, living off other people's needs and privations.—Now that is what I call painting.[6]

Dresden is also where Hannah Jönsson met the Norwegian painter Hans Ryggen (1894–1956), the man who would become her husband and confidant in both art and life. Hans was studying in Dresden with other Norwegian painters, and he had the German Expressionist Otto Lange (1879–1944) as a private teacher. Lange was a contemporary of the Die Brücke artists, but he had a different orientation; he had begun at the Dresdner Kunstgewerbeschule (Dresden School of Arts and Crafts) and came relatively late to fine art.[7] There is much to suggest that Otto Lange also knew Hannah; Hans exclaimed, at any rate, that he was jealous of Lange in a letter to Hannah in 1923. It is possible that she had met the German artist somewhat earlier. In 1920, two years before the trip to Dresden, Lange had participated in a major exhibition, *Tysk och Österrikisk Konst* (*German and Austrian Art*), held at the Lunds Universitets Kunstmuseum (Art Museum of the University of Lund).[8] The exhibition focused on graphic works and included leading artists such as Erich Heckel, Käthe Kollwitz, Max Liebermann, Gustav Klimt, Emil Nolde, Felix Müller, Egon Schiele, and Max Pechstein. Considering Krebs' status in Lund, it is reasonable to assume that he and his students visited and discussed the exhibition thoroughly. And if Otto Lange was in Lund in connection with its opening, it is also overwhelmingly likely that he had occasion to meet Krebs, Jönsson, and the other students. FIGS. 6, 7

We will never know whether Hans' jealousy was warranted or not, but it is interesting that, in addition to painting, Lange designed interiors and made textile samples and handicrafts, and in 1925 he was appointed as a professor at the Staatliche Kunstschule für Textilindustrie (National Academy for Textile Industry) in Plauen. The possibility that he may have influenced Hannah's decision to switch from painting to weaving cannot be dismissed. In any case, upon her return to Malmö in 1922, she purchased a small Flemish loom. She struggled with this loom, however, as is apparent in another interview in the *Social-Demokraten* from September 1946:

6 *Social-Demokraten,* August 6, 1946.

7 See *Mit Leidenschaft ins Holz gerissen: Der Dresdner Expressionist Otto Lange (1879–1944),* Städtisches Kunstmuseum Spendhaus Reultingen, 2011.

8 That Ryggen saw the exhibition is highly likely, as a copy of the exhibition catalog was in her possession.

Are you familiar with this?—No?—It is an instrument of torture, I can tell you. I had to teach myself to weave. The warp was too narrow and I fussed and yanked at the threads and beams. [...] And by the time I'd woven just four small tapestries, I was exhausted. [...]—Then I got to know Hans, and we moved to Norway. Hans is a creative genius. Everything I need, he invents, you know. He built me a loom—the world's greatest loom, which I could operate with my feet and work much more easily with. I have had it for 23 years and have woven all my large tapestries on it.[9]

The four small works Ryggen refers to, *Evas datter* (*Eve's Daughter,* 1922), *Nøkken* (*The Water Sprite,* 1923), *Høst* (*Autumn,* 1924) and *De tre gratier* (*The Three Graces,* 1925), reveal an artist who has not yet mastered the medium, nor found her voice with respect to the content. All this would change with the new custom loom that Hans built for her.

The significance of color and the myth of the primitive

When their stays in Dresden were over, Hans returned to Ørlandet, in central Norway, and Hannah to Malmö and her teaching job. Hans was *odelsgutten* (first in line to inherit a family's land), and he dreaded the estate issue that awaited him back home at Ørlandet; it involved what was for him an impossible choice—to follow life as an artist or as a farmer. The actual resolution was a kind of third path: he passed his right of succession onto his younger brother and decided to build a little house for himself and Hannah on his grandfather's property. In this way, he believed, he would be able to combine his artistic career with his deep connection to the land and nature.

The terrain at Ørlandet is flat, and the winters can be severe, with gusting winds and heavy rain and snow. Hans did not downplay the harsh climate. In a letter to Hannah he described how the soil had become too loose, as it had not tolerated the excessive rainfall in November; the roots of the grass had frozen in the night, and the fields lay like "one black desert." When at last the new season arrived in the barren winter landscape, Hans described it in similar detail:

And now the ground begins to swell, like it's growing out of some substance underneath, a substance so succulent and clear in color, it is still hidden from view by the withered straw [...] that kind of color—growing from nothing to a swelling, intoxicating—I would very much like to delve into it. I will never abandon nature, I want it to be the foundation of everything I do.[10]

This intimacy with and love for the natural environment that Hans describes in his letters is something Hannah came to share, as is especially evident in the incredible wealth of color she was able to extract from it. FIGS. 8–10

It took roughly a decade of trial and error for Hannah Ryggen to master all aspects of weaving—techniques, motif, format—and not least, it took time to determine what she wanted to convey. In addition, there was the labour of dyeing. The goal was to extract as many hues as possible from her natural surroundings, and gradually the attic of 'Fønnan' (as they dubbed their little house) was filled with dyed skeins of wool in countless shades

9 Johan Møller Nielsen, "En Protest, en Skampæl, en flammende Saga" (A Protest, a Stain of Shame, and a Flaming Tale), *Social-Demokraten,* September 1946.

10 Letter from Hans to Hannah Ryggen, 22.03.1923, Trondheim Norges teknisk-naturvitenskapelige universitet (NTNU University Library, Trondheim).

FIG. 6

Otto Lange, *Tanz um das Goldene Kalb* (*Dance around the Golden Calf*), 1918, color lithography, 51×38.5 cm, Collection Friedbert Ficker, Kunstsammlungen Zwickau Max-Pechstein-Museum

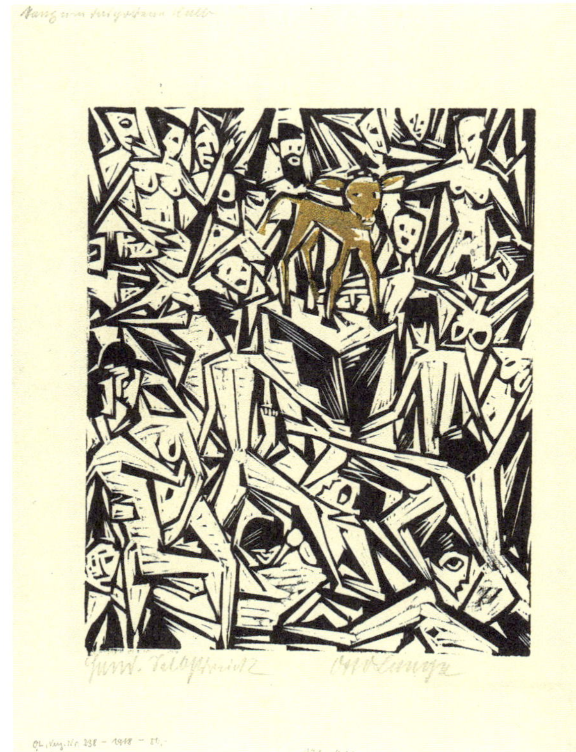

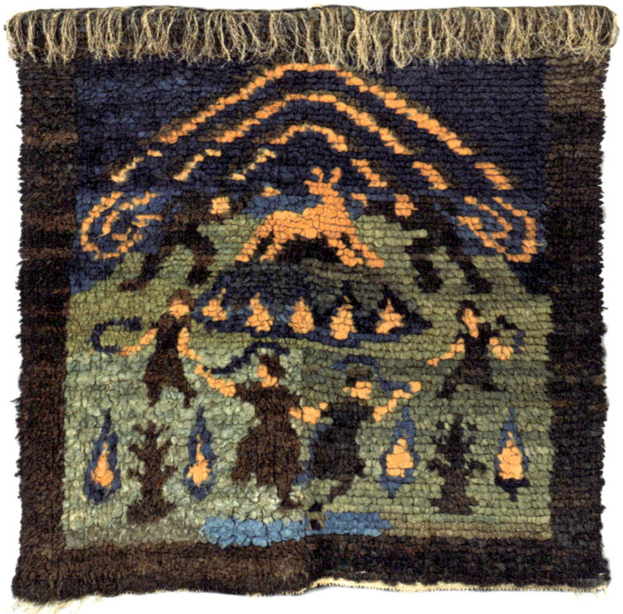

FIG. 7

Hannah Ryggen, *Dansen rundt gullkalven* (*Dance around the Golden Calf*), 1930, tapestry woven with high pile in unwashed wool, 146×135 cm, Nordenfjeldske Kunstindustrimuseum (National Museum of Decorative Arts and Design), Trondheim

FIG. 8

Mona Ryggen in the attic of their house at Ørlandet, with hanging yarn, undated

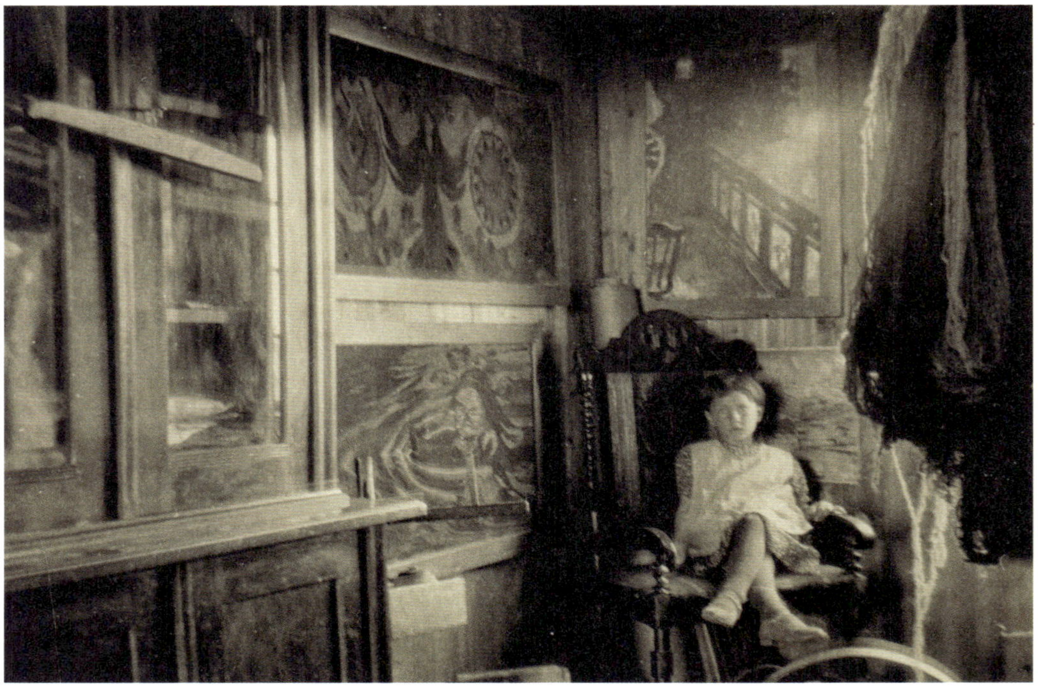

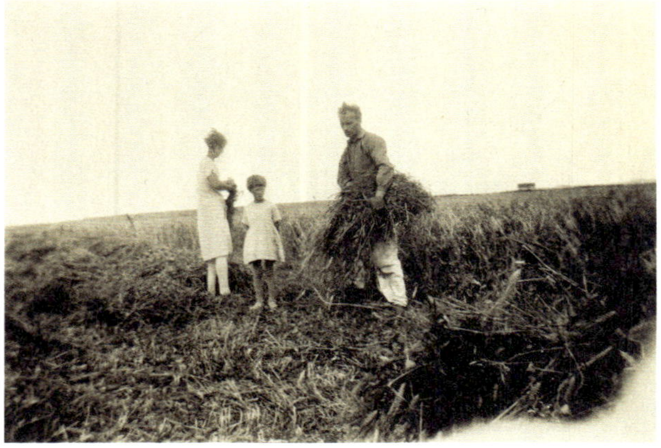

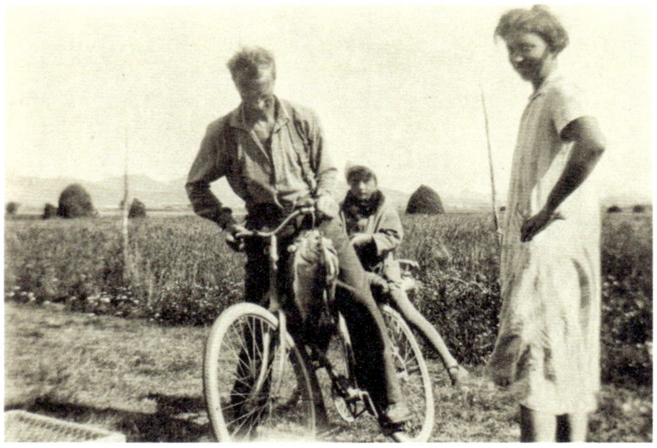

FIG. 9

Hans, Mona, and Hannah Ryggen by the hay racks at Ørlandet, undated

FIG. 10

Hans, Mona, and Hannah Ryggen at Ørlandet. Hans and Mona are returning from a fishing trip, undated

created from goat willow bark, bird cherry, haircap moss, birch leaves, heather, common lichen, Scots pine bark, *granskjegg* (a hanging lichen), juniper, northern bedstraw, *korkje* (a stone lichen), herb-paris, and more.[11] Every nuance of color corresponded to a specific entity in nature. Through the creation of color, she took her immediate surroundings out into the greater world, and by her choice of subject matter, the world at large came closer to them. The wool and linen that she used were also pure products of her environment.

In the dyeing process there are many variables that have to be coordinated and controlled. In a memo on dyeing with the flower known as devil's-bit scabious, Ryggen wrote in her rambling way: "The leaves are boiled in water with the yarn, then it's taken up and laid on grassy turf and sprinkled with cold ashes and turf is placed on top with the grassy side down. Can also become green by putting the yarn directly on the grass with ashes."[12] And about dyeing yarn yellow with the roots of dock plants: "The yarn is cooked in whey along with the roots, placed hot in a tub and poured over with urine. Rinsed in cold water and hung warm in the shade. Can also be boiled with birch leaves."[13] She had painstakingly acquired a fairly advanced knowledge of chemistry.

The dyeing process could also be influenced by the light, the time of year plants were picked, and the quantity of yarn per batch of dye. And while light, through the plants used, gave the tapestries their colors, light also weakened the colors' intensity over time. There is much indication, however, that Ryggen considered this fading to be beneficial. The dyes were deliberately made as concentrated as possible because she knew the colors would become subdued over time. She regarded fading as nature's way; to a certain extent, therefore, changes should be viewed as a part of the works' fundamental conception. Immutability is unnatural, and Ryggen's tapestries *are* nature.

Hannah Ryggen's signature color, pot-blue (*potteblått*), is worth mentioning here as well. Pot-blue, or pee-blue (*pissblått*) as it was also called, was a favorite topic with the journalists because of how it was made. A key ingredient is, in fact, urine, and preferably urine from men who have been drinking. Ryggen often referred to another secret ingredient; in some places it was orange peel, in others birch leaves. In a letter to her daughter Mona, who also wove, she imparted the following recipe, this time without either orange peel or birch leaves:

> Pot-blue I don't think you can make in the space you have. You know it 'smells.' The sun is the best even heat for what you collect [urine]. When the pot is full, it needs to stand for a few days. I grind the indigo fine and add what looks to be about ½ hg and upwards. You stir it every day (it cannot get cold) add a coffee cup's worth of fresh urine every now and then. On a hot sunny day you test whether it's ready. You put in a clean dry wool thread and leave it for about three hours. When you take it out it should be as green as grass and become blue in the air. If it's not, leave the pot to sit and try again in another few days. If the yarns do not turn green, it's a bad batch and there's nothing to be done about it. This summer I have been lucky: I dug two big holes in the ground. Hans cut the grass

11 Hannah Ryggen wrote extensively about dyeing in her journals, NTNU University Library, Trondheim.

12 Undated note, Nordenfjeldske Kunstindustrimuseum (henceforth referred to as NFKIM).

13 Undated note, NFKIM.

and we pressed the cuttings into the holes when the grass got warm [due to composting] I made a hole in the middle and there I put the urine jar with tar paper over and stones on top. On days when it was sunny I took from the pot. It got a nice even heat and I could just dye and dye endlessly.[14]

Even though Ryggen's ability to extract pigments attests to an advanced and sophisticated understanding of nature, her works have often been described in ways that evoke entirely different associations. Frequently used adjectives include primitive, naive, simple, and rustic, in addition to terms such as witchcraft, hex, black magic, and sorcery.

The Norwegian art historian Albert Steen is among those guilty of such patronizing formulations, as for example: "Any direct influence of primitive peoples' art is difficult to prove in Hannah Ryggen's tapestries, but her creativity has similarities with what we find in children's or uncultivated peoples' art." Steen also maintained that Ryggen "had it in her blood, perhaps inherited from the peasant women down there on the plains of Skåne," i.e. rather than something gained through systematic and determined hard work.[15] Steen was far from alone in this regard. Academics, journalists, and critics collectively created an image of Ryggen as a colorful artist-type who fulfilled a pedestrian and persistent romantic idea of the female artist as a child of nature (literally, an infantilizing expression): a sensitive, impulsive, and expressive soul who mainly just wanted to express herself in a medium that belonged to the female realm. Factors relating to the political, the intellectual, and the artistic, such as her art-historical references, training as a painter, and knowledge of international contemporary art, were given a negligible amount of attention in the literature about Ryggen's work.[16]

This is misleading, for Hannah Ryggen was both well-read and informed about politics and contemporary art. She received a steady supply of fiction and books about artists such as Paul Gauguin, Pierre Bonnard, Vincent van Gogh, Édouard Manet, Paul Cézanne, Henri Matisse, Edvard Munch, and others. She held Pablo Picasso in high regard, and like him, she borrowed freely from art history, contemporary art, folk art, and news images, in addition to relying on her own imagination.

A crossroads

In their first years living in Rønnan, the Ryggens subsisted on their livestock, grains, and other foodstuffs they cultivated, and they planted a garden with herbs and flowers that they both adored. But daily life there was hard. Rønnan had no running water, electricity was not installed until 1944, and much of the day was spent laboring. The family's self-sufficiency formed the bedrock of Hannah Ryggen's political orientation: the belief that everyone ought to be able to support themselves and their families, and no one should be above another:

Every man and woman, rich or poor, ought to be raised capable of two things: producing their own food and supporting themselves. It is unjust that some serve others. Everyone should work, no one should be above another. Equality for all mankind. We are all flesh and blood, just the same.[17]

14 Letter from Hannah Ryggen to Mona Ryggen Granholm, May 1955, NTNU University Library, Trondheim.

15 Albert Steen, *Hannah Ryggen – en dikter i veven* (*Hannah Ryggen – A Poet by the Loom*), Oslo: Kunstindustrimuseet/Aschehoug, 1986, 44, 18.

16 The gender-biased reception and aspects of the literature on Hannah Ryggen are discussed in greater detail in my doctoral dissertation *Forhandlinger med historien* (*Negotiations with History*), NTNU (2018). (Available in Norwegian only.)

17 Letter from Hannah Ryggen to Andreas Schjoldager, 26.03.1942, NFKIM.

Self-sufficiency and equality are themes in several of the first monumental works that Ryggen made, including *Fiske ved gjeldens hav* (*Fishing in the Sea of Debt,* 1933), *Vi og våre dyr* (*Us and Our Animals,* 1934), *Ugift mor* (*Unwed Mother,* 1937) and *En fri* (*A Free One,* 1948). These works also introduced a new formal idiom and an uncompromising approach to the function of art.

Hannah Ryggen was in the process of becoming a skilled painter before she moved to Ørlandet, but she sought a different palette and a more modern style than those Krebs had favored. "Suddenly there awoke in me the need to do something with my hands," she wrote. "I could not paint like Krebs and still be myself. It suddenly occurred to me that I would weave pictures [...]."[18] Abandoning painting in favour of the loom, as she announced in a letter to Hans at the end of January 1923 shortly before arriving—in a late stage of pregnancy—at Ørlandet, must have made it simpler for her to free herself. Also, tapestry's strong roots in folk art and handicraft may have been important from a political perspective, and the slow working process certainly suited her temperament better, but perhaps the greatest incentive offered by weaving was the possibility of working in large formats. This afforded her entree into the arena of monumental painting and at the same time provided an escape from the prevailing inclination to disparage female painters. FIGS. 11, 12

It was some time, however, before Ryggen attempted the large format. Until about 1933, she created many household objects. The Nordenfjeldske Kunstindustrimuseum in Trondheim today houses many examples of sketches for cushion cover designs, table runners, and even wallpaper: an indication that Ryggen was just as versatile as Lange. But she greatly disliked making things after patterns, and she was not concerned with technique per se. In 1933 she was invited to exhibit at Trondhjems Kunstforening, and *Fishing in the Sea of Debt* was among the tapestries she showed there. The work received very positive reviews, and the reception of this exhibition may have influenced her subsequent radical decision: to quit making handicrafts, and to concentrate on major, monumental works that would be sold only to public institutions.[19] To Ryggen, the tapestries were public statements that ought to be available to everyone.

Considering the small family's precarious financial situation, Ryggen's decision seems both uncompromising and risky. The large-format works were time-consuming to make, and for a long time they were just another expense. Documentation shows that in the fourteen years from when Ryggen made *Synderinnen* (*The Sinner*) in 1926 until 1940, she earned about 3000 Norwegian kroner from her tapestries. By way of comparison, the average salary in Norway in 1930 was approximately 2500 kroner per annum. Yet she was resolute, and in a letter to her friend Andreas Schjoldager in 1937, she wrote:

> I can't conceive of earning a living from the tapestries I weave. *Tendens* [art in Norway in the 1930s with a political agenda] tapestries for rich people, that's a joke. But when I mull it over, I think if I lived in a true workers' state, at best my tapestries would adorn schools and community centers. I wouldn't be paid huge sums for them, but I'd have had food for my hard work and maybe a couple

18 Hannah Ryggen's undated notes addressed to Dyre Vaa, and donated to Nordenfjeldske Kunstindustrimuseum by Thora Vaa in 1990.

19 Just five of the large, famous works by Hannah Ryggen are in private collections today—*Fiske ved gjeldens hav* (*Fishing in the Sea of Debt*), *Gullammet Iselin* (*The Golden Lamb Iselin*), *Livet glir forbi* (*Life Slides By*), *Freiheit* (*Freedom*), and *Schweden* (*Sweden*)—and three of them are owned by the same family. Sale of these works was due to extraordinary circumstances associated with Ryggen's daughter Mona's illness and their living conditions.

of free trips a year, electric lights and a bath! I think so. As it is now, I'd have starved if it hadn't been for our little patch of land and the cow. Now artists like me are totally superfluous, and why should it be otherwise, art is just luxury seen from that perspective.[20]

Hannah Ryggen's notion of art as an important, democratic, social benefit did not just exist in her own mind, it was part of a larger tradition. The idea of abandoning the bourgeoisie's gilt-framed paintings and charging art with other, more important functions was prominent on many levels in the European art world. In Norway, there were two main directions, one after the painter Christian Krohg (1852–1925), who clearly communicated the value of art's social commitment, and the other following the Lysaker Circle's more nationalistically oriented line.[21]

Albertine and the Lysaker Circle

Christian Krohg had strong ties to France and he became particularly interested in French naturalism.[22] He also played an active role in what is often described as the 'modern breakthrough' in Scandinavia: a literary movement that combined politics, aesthetics, and ethics in an attempt to bring about changes in society. Henrik Ibsen, August Strindberg, Georg Brandes, and Bjørnstjerne Bjørnson were among the others involved in this movement. In an article from 1888 entitled "Om det ene fornødne i kunsten" (On the only necessity in art), Krohg insisted that the artist must create for the many, the masses. For if art is to be important for democracy and is to function as a vital element in cultural development, the artist must take part in his own time:

[It is] imperative that the artist and that which he creates are not only children of the times in which they live, but practically of the day in which they live. Not that the motif needs only to be taken from the previous day's events, but [...] the same heartbeat that is common to all of this great life we call the present: that is what must be sensed in an artwork, if it is to be of any consequence for our era.[23]

Krohg also demonstrated art's ability to influence public discourse with his painting *Albertine i politilegens venteværelse* (*Albertine to See the Police Surgeon,* 1885–1887) and his novel *Albertine* (1886). Albertine is a poor young woman who has been raped by a policeman, and is subsequently accused of prostitution and sent to the police doctor for a humiliating gynaecological exam. Although prostitution was illegal, there was nevertheless a regulatory authority that, among other things, ensured that prostitutes were tested for venereal diseases. The state's approach to prostitution was thus, at best, characterized by a double standard, and this is precisely what Krohg attacked and criticized by taking up Albertine's cause. In this monumental painting FIG. 13 Krohg depicts Albertine after the rape, when she is forced to show up at the police doctor's surgery to be checked for venereal disease—just like the prostitutes—and is thus branded one. Both the painting and the book created a sensation, and the latter was outlawed and impounded.

20 Letter from Hannah Ryggen to Andreas Schjoldager, dated "Ørlandet's holy three kings" (indicating the beginning of January), 1937, NFKIM. The Norwegian painter Reidar Aulie, who was also a critic, wrote in the Norwegian newspaper *Arbeiderbladet* (February 3, 1939): "*Tendens* art's primary and greatest difficulty is that it should be able to clarify, illustrate, and be literary without losing its own artistic value. At the same time, it should address pressing current issues and be able to draw viewers out into the timeless world that is called art. Hanna [sic] Ryggen manages this in a way one seldom or never sees."

21 Christian Krohg was responsible for the establishment of the National Academy of Art in Oslo in 1909 and was the academy's first professor. Hans Ryggen was, for a time, one of his students.

22 For a thorough analysis of Krohg's relation to naturalism, see Øystein Sjåstad, *Christian Krohg's Naturalism,* Seattle and London: University of Washington Press, 2017.

23 Published in the Danish journal *Kunstbladet. Nordisk tidsskrift,* no. 14 (July 31, 1888): 168–171.

FIG. 11

Hannah Ryggen by the loom in Malmö, 1922

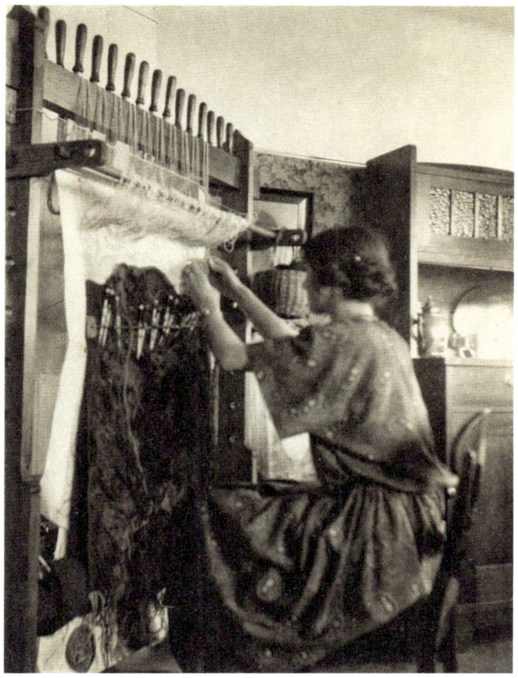

FIG. 12

Hannah Ryggen, *Fiske ved gjeldens hav* (*Fishing in the Sea of Debt*), 1933

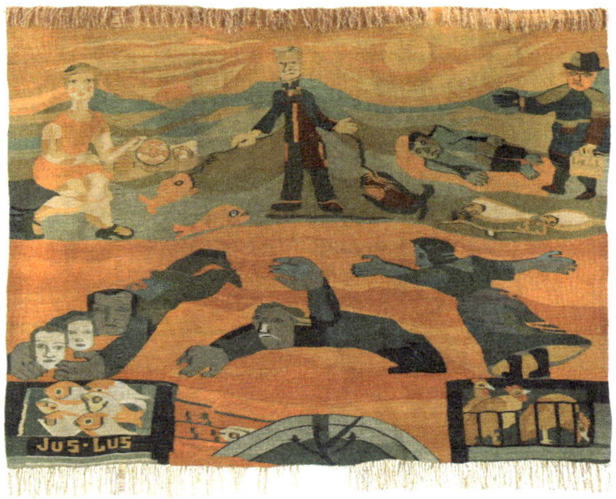

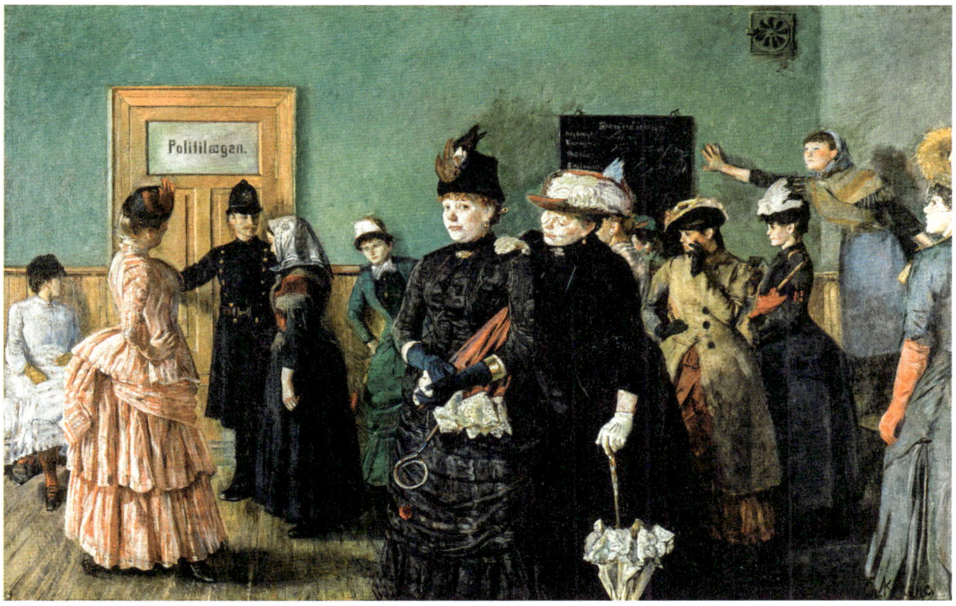

FIG. 13

Christian Krohg, *Albertine i politilegens venteværelse* (*Albertine to see the Police Surgeon*), 1885–1887, oil on canvas, 211 × 326 cm, National Museum of Art, Architecture and Design, Oslo

FIG. 14

Edvard Munch, *Arbeidere i snø* (*Workers in Snow*), 1913–1915, oil on canvas, 163 × 200 cm, Munchmuseet, Oslo

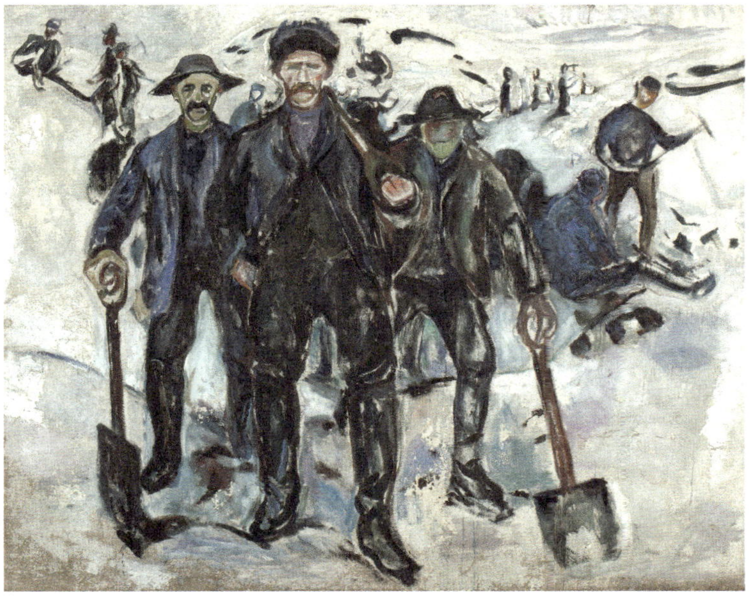

Edvard Munch (1863–1944) may not have been quite so radical as Krohg, but he, too, sought a reckoning with the art of the bourgeoisie, as described by the Norwegian art historian Gerd Woll in her book *Edvard Munch – Monumentale prosjekter 1909–1930* (Edvard Munch – Monumental Projects 1909–1930). Munch strove for a long time to create a frieze devoted to workers, in which the motif of *Arbeidere i snø* (*Workers in Snow,* 1913–1915) was to have been included FIG. 14, but unfortunately the frieze was never realized. Munch had strong connections to Germany as well as many close German friends, including Harry Graf Kessler, whose journals are a rich source of information about German society during this period. In 1919, after a dinner with good friends, among them Ludwig Justi, then director of the Nationalgalerie Berlin, Kessler made the following notes:

> In the evening we had dinner in Zehlendorf with the Minister of Finance, Simon, who resigned today, along with his colleague Südekum, the director of the Nationalgalerie Jusit, Dr. Käsbach and Dr. Hübner. Much talk about art, little about politics. Unanimity that a transformation in German art from the bourgeois to the popular had already arrived prior to the revolution. A transformation from Impressionism, which in easel paintings offers an intimate, bourgeois art, to Expressionism, which commands an audience: large spaces, monumental commissions, effect on broad masses, pathos and rhetoric. The differences are akin to those between a causerie in a Paris salon and a public address at Berlin O or Schwabing. Käsbach and Justi want to open a gallery for this modern, expressionistic art.[24]

Ten years later, in 1929, Munch dimly echoed Kessler's words in a letter drafted to a Swedish friend in connection with an exhibition in Stockholm: "The small format [...] with its pretty, often large frames, is now an art dealer's art—it is bourgeois and came about after the [...] French revolution—Now it is the workers'. What if art were to become common property, as it was in antiquity—in public buildings and on the street? Frescos?"[25] Munch then marked his disavowal of the bourgeoisie's art with a transition to monumental painting, which could be everyone's property.

The other main direction was spearheaded by the Lysaker Circle, an informal association of artists and intellectuals who used literature, research and art to create a 'Norwegian identity.' Their activity has to be viewed in light of Norway's struggle for independence, which led to secession from the union with Sweden in 1905 and Norway's establishment as an independent nation. The Lysaker Circle's objective was to establish Norway as a modern European and independent cultural nation by forging a distinct idiom with colors and symbols derived from Norwegian folktales. Within the visual arts, concepts of 'Norwegian colors,' 'Norwegian motifs,' and a decorative style with its origins in folk art were launched. In this context, tapestry held a unique position by virtue of its long tradition in Norway, which is much longer than painting's; there are large and comprehensive collections of tapestries in Norway, beginning with the *Baldisholteppet* (Baldishol Tapestry) from the 1100s.

24 Journal entry dated 04.01.1919. *Harry Graf Kessler, Tagebücher 1918–1937,* ed. Wolfgang Pfeiffer-Belli, Frankfurt a. Main: Im Insel Verlag, 1979 [1961], 91.

25 Draft of a letter to Ragnar Hoppe, MM N 41, 1929, Munchmuseet, Oslo. In another note from roughly the same time, Munch states in a similar vein: "One has painted little pictures sold in gold frames to adorn the bourgeoisie's walls for so long {...} that one begins to believe painting is an ordinary trade—like making shoes—a factory—I have never considered painting to order." Munchmuseet, MM N 40.

The decorative, the ornamental and 'moveable murals'

The need for an art directed toward the general public, art that could strengthen national identity, in conjunction with the growing need to construct national buildings and institutions, led to a revitalization of an old European tradition in Norway: monumental painting or the mural.[26] Beginning with the interior decoration of the Bergen stock exchange in 1911 and Munch's frieze for the University of Oslo's auditorium in 1916, and lasting until the completion of the Oslo City Hall in 1950, many monumental paintings were executed in public buildings. Arne Nygård Nilssen, an authority on this genre in Norway, states in his 1928 book *Moderne norsk veggmaleri* (*Modern Norwegian Mural Painting*) that once modern painting, exemplified by Matisse and Cubism, broke with the principles of naturalistic rendering, the way was paved for wall painting to make use of the new styles in contemporary painting, such as the composition and modulation of color in Cézanne or the decorative and flat, expansive approach to color in Gauguin, as well as a distinct use of line. From van Gogh and Munch, one could find inspiration in the concentration and exaggeration of the expression.

According to Nilssen, this allowed for a fundamental renewal of architectonic painting.[27] Wall painting was able to simultaneously harken back to tradition and further its own present. That "the new decorative art had a partiality for the abstract, the mathematical, the beautiful and the decorative in choice of color—in short, the ornamental" was of great importance.[28] Nilssen's summary of the ornamental is vague, but it is worth noting the extent to which he emphasized the expressive, the colors and the exaggeration. These features can also be recognized in a more radical form in Ryggen than in those who are considered the champions of the mural in Norway: Alf Rolfsen (1895–1979), Axel Revold (1887–1962), and Per Krohg (1889–1965), also known as *freskobrødrene* ("the fresco brothers"). FIGS. 15–18

If we look at the tapestries housed in the Oslo City Hall and other public buildings from the 1950s and later, the majority of them have a purely decorative quality and are portable; they can be moved without much disturbance to their surroundings. They were in essence far more practical than a fresco, which is physically attached to the architecture. The renowned French architect Le Corbusier drew this connection between tapestry, murals, and the nomadic in our age printed in the magazine *Zodiac* in 1960:

> [...] we change apartments as our families grow or shrink; we are changing our conditions constantly [...]. We cannot have murals painted on the walls of our apartments. The woolen wall that is tapestry can be detached, rolled up, carried under one's arm, be taken to be hung elsewhere. That is why I have named it *Muralnomad*.[29]

In the Norwegian context, tapestry for these purposes was in general defined as handicraft; it was solely intended to be decorative: that is, with use made of stylized line, color fields, and ornament. Like many of the monumental paintings and murals, tapestry tended toward design.[30]

26 This development occurred not only in Norway but also in the other Nordic countries, and to a certain extent in Germany with, among others, Ferdinand Hodler's Jena works from 1909.

27 Arne Nygård Nilssen, *Moderne norsk veggmaleri* (*Modern Norwegian Mural Painting*), Oslo: Gyldendal, 1928, 13.

28 Op. cit., 16.

29 Le Corbusier, "Tapisseries Muralnomad," *Zodiac,* no. 7, 1960: 57.

30 The etymology of the word *decorative* is worth an article in itself. I use it here in the general, prevailing sense of the term in Norway at that time, which includes stylized use of line, pure color fields and use of ornament. Jan Askeland maintains that for Gerhard Munthe—who was a central figure in the Lysaker Circle—and his generation, the expression 'decorative art' was used about both handicrafts and interior décor. See Askeland, *Freskoepoken 1918–1950* (*The Age of Fresco, 1918–1950*), Gyldendal: Oslo, 1965, 18.

FIG. 15

Alf Rolfsen, *Okkupasjons-frisen* (Occupation Frieze), 1947–1950, mural painting, Oslo City Hall, art collection of Oslo municipality

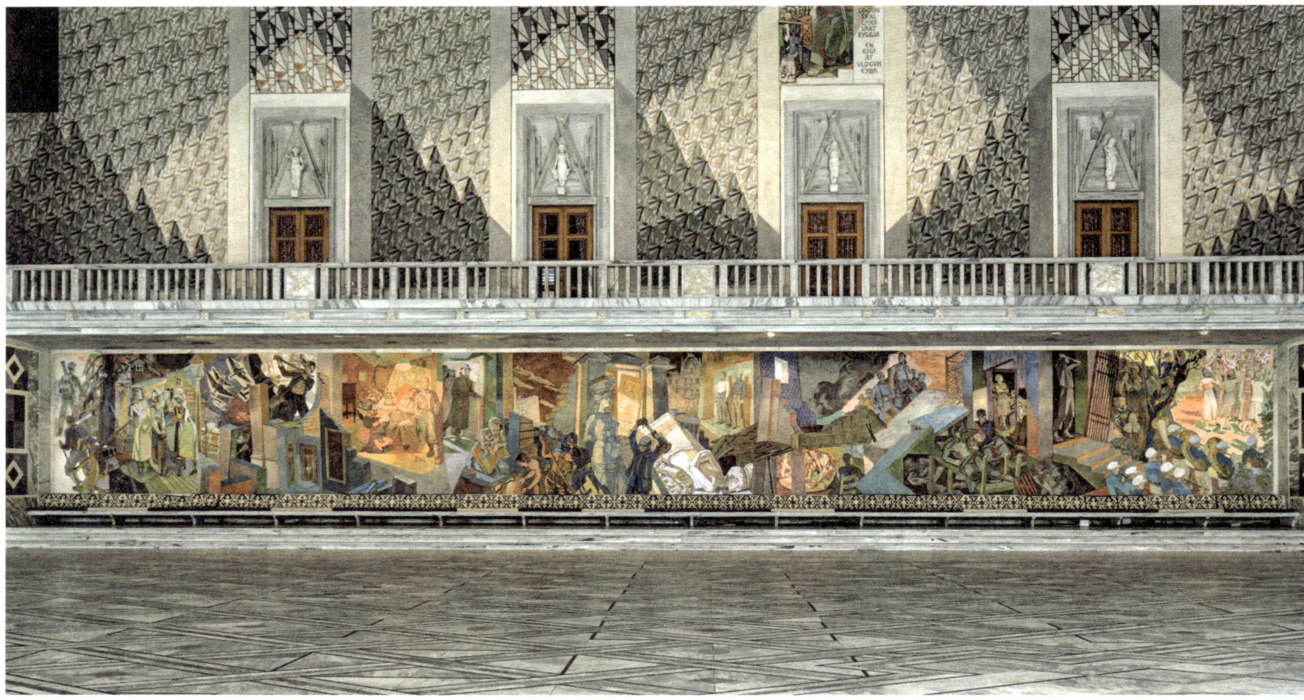

FIGS. 16, 17

Alf Rolfsen, *Okkupasjons-frisen* (Occupation Frieze), details

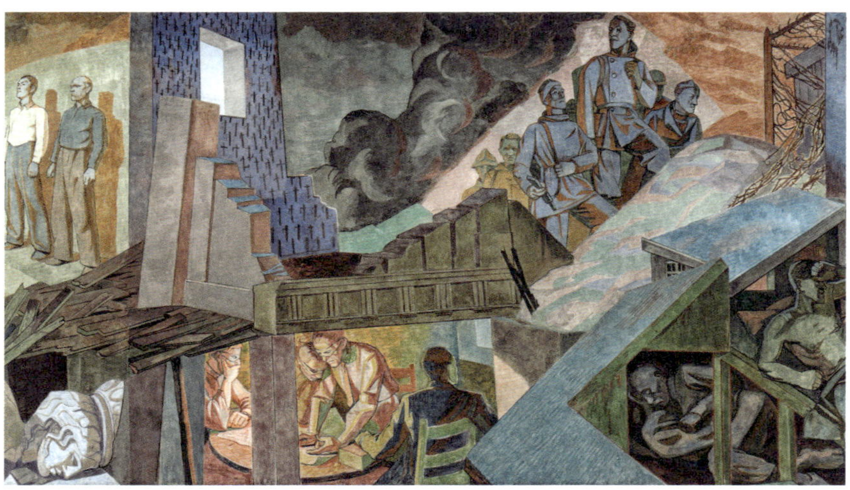

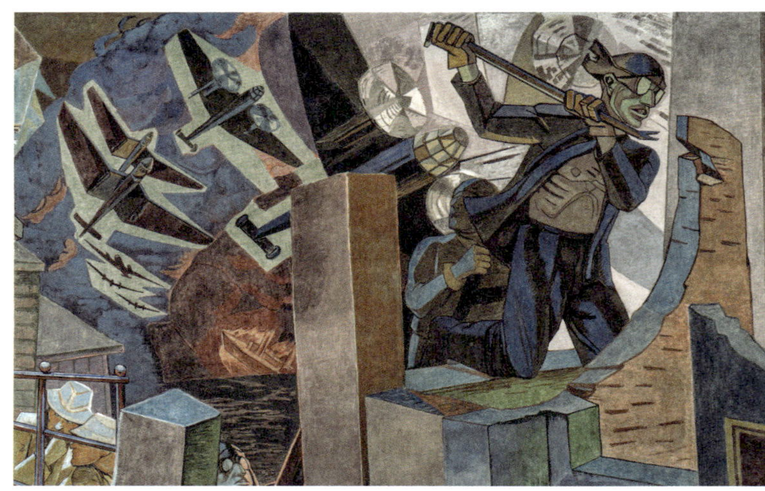

FIG. 18

Axel Revold and Ulrikke Greve, *Harald Hardråde grunnlegger Oslo* (*Harald Hardråde Founds Oslo*), 1937, tapestry woven in wool and silk, 126×226 cm, art collection of Oslo municipality

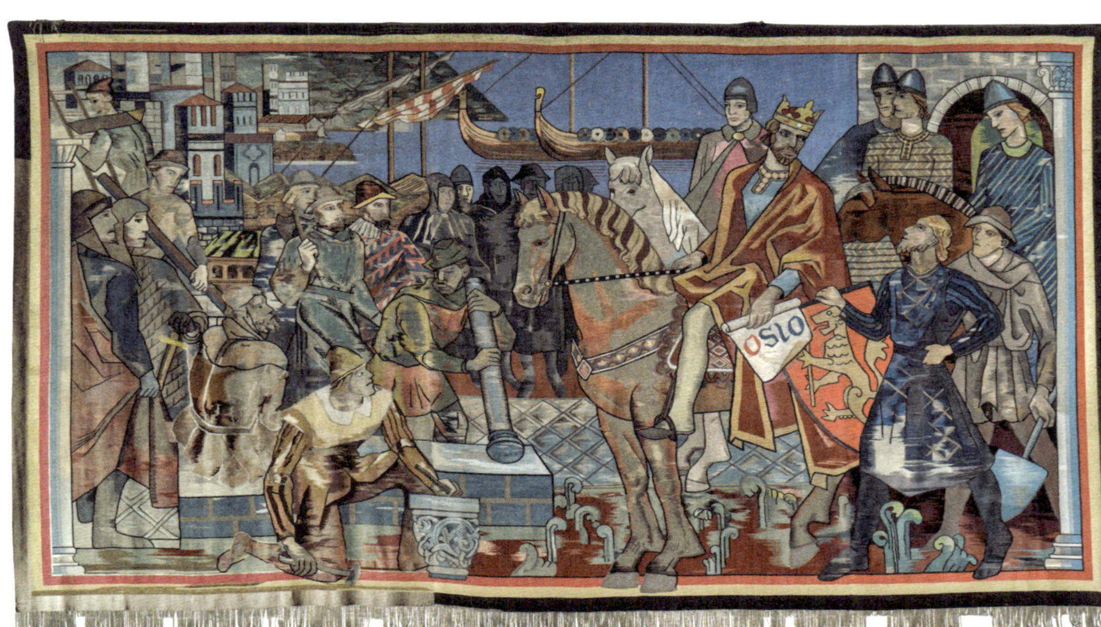

If we compare the use of ornament in Rolfsen's frieze about the German occupation (in the Oslo City Hall) with Ryggen's, we find obvious similarities. However, elements employed for 'decorative' purposes in Rolfsen are clearly much more often meaningful in Ryggen. In *Drømmedød* (*Death of Dreams,* pp. 38/39), at first the ornamentation appears to be a seemingly neutral pattern created from strictly ordered, repetitive geometric forms in brown and gray. It takes a bit of time before one realizes that swastikas appear and disappear as the gaze shifts between the gray and the brown. The swastikas (the ornament) thus comprise both foreground and background: partly camouflaged, but always numerous.[31]

In *Trojansk hest / Picassoteppet* (*Trojan Horse / Picasso Tapestry,* pp. 98–103), ornament is used to bind together the different time periods as well as the new and old art, while *En fri* (*A Free One,* pp. 96/97) displays much of what is distinctive about Ryggen's style: her use of the picture plane and her combination of figures and ornament. The rendering of "the gray ones" is especially striking. They are reduced to heads and hands integrated into a constraining structure consisting of pronounced, broad stripes in a light golden-brown. The stripes run through large areas of the tapestry and are only absent around the couple at the top of the social hierarchy and around the poet.

Each figure's degree of visibility or status in the society is expressed by how completely they have been rendered. This is the means by which Ryggen conveys a hierarchy among the figures. The slaves, the gray ones, are visible only as hands and as faces, or fragments of faces. The social climbers are depicted in a pink hue and have more distinct bodies, and they are grasping the blue column that bears the state. One of the climbers' hands is clenched, the other raises a hand, probably signaling his desire to move upward. There is also a notably amorphous pink area that culminates in a blue hand right of center in the tapestry's uppermost edge. This blue hand looks as though it is about to clasp the woman's hand. Blue blood—nobility—implies that privileges and rights are inherited and therefore difficult to attain by other means.

The broad golden-brown bands running diagonally from left to right hold the figures in place. Being bound signifies never being able to break free from the society of which one is a part. Each and every one of us contributes to—and is responsible for—the development of society, and it is upon this responsibility that freedom is established.

Hannah Ryggen recognized as early as the 1930s the radical political potential in tapestry as movable murals and in contrast to many of her colleagues, she deliberately distanced herself from the decorative. In numerous letters, interviews and journal entries, she emphasized that pure design—and she included abstract painting in this category—is not for her. Without the human presence, as represented by the figure, form and color were just decoration to her. As late as 1969 she wrote: "They are preaching now that art should not be figurative. But what is a theater with an empty stage?"[32]

Ryggen realized her desire to create an art for everyone, owned by everyone. She also heeded Krohg's words about taking part in one's own time by making a "life's frieze" (*livsfrise*) in which major political conflicts

31 For a more detailed discussion of ornamentation, see Paasche, *Hannah Ryggen: Threads of Defiance,* London: Thames and Hudson, 2019, ch. 10.

32 Hannah Ryggen, journal entry, 09.01.1969, NFKIM.

were juxtaposed with important themes in her own life. Her life's frieze, however, was in the form of a tapestry: a medium that had both a long tradition and a strong position in Norway, partly due to the Lysaker Circle's efforts. Hannah Ryggen could also, as opposed to the Norwegian mural painters, take her works out into the world.

Censorship and the stage

Etiopia (*Ethiopia,* 1935, pp. 50–53) was one of the first works Ryggen exhibited outside of Norway. There is a specific history behind this work. In October 1935, Italy, under the fascist dictator Benito Mussolini, invaded defenceless Ethiopia, and the League of Nations neither defended nor supported Ethiopia and its Emperor Haile Selassie. Ryggen was so outraged that she wove *Ethiopia* in one furious stretch, finishing it in one month. In the tapestry's righthand corner she depicts an Ethiopian driving a spear through Mussolini's severed head and holding it up as a gruesome warning. Directly below is the abbreviation "hr. M."

Ethiopia was displayed in the Norwegian pavilion at the Paris World's Fair in 1937. In a neighboring pavilion, that of Spain, Picasso's famous anti-war painting *Guernica* (1937) was on display. Picasso's work garnered enormous attention, and its format (351 × 782 cm), approach to color, and installation all combined to give the impression of a cross between a news photo and a mural.[33] But it was Ryggen's *Ethiopia* that came to be censored in 1937. The arrangers feared offending the Italian representatives and therefore folded over the portion of the tapestry that showed Mussolini's head, an action that clearly demonstrated the work was not only about a conflict—its antagonizing presence also instigated action and conflict.

After *Ethiopia,* Ryggen made a series of anti-Nazi and anti-fascist works addressing events outside and within Norway's borders. Both the number of large works and their dimensions attest to a capacity for work that is extraordinary—in 1936 she followed up with not one but *three* works: *Death of Dreams, Morgengry* (*Dawn*), and *Gru* (*Horror*). The first of these is about the fate of Carl von Ossietzky and Nazism's grip on society, while *Horror* and the later work *Spania (La hora se approxima)* (*Spain (The Hour is Approaching)*) from 1938 criticize Franco's slaughtering of civilians during the Spanish Civil War. This war was a subject of great concern and discussion in the Norwegian media. Likewise, the Nazis' arrest and beheading of the German communist and mother Liselotte Herrmann—whom Ryggen portrayed in the tapestry *Liselotte Herrmann halshuggen* (*Liselotte Herrmann Decapitated,* 1938, pp. 40/41)—aroused intense political engagement on the part of women in Norway and Europe. With these timely, topical works, Ryggen signaled her unambiguous political position.

Between these strongly anti-fascist and anti-Nazi tapestries, Ryggen made a work entitled *Ugift mor* (*Unwed Mother,* 1937) in which she continued her exploration of themes taken up in *Gullammet Iselin* (*The Golden Lamb Iselin,* 1935) and *The Sinner;* namely, how women's positions in society are subordinate to power structures created by men, and how women

33 James Attlee provides a thorough and fascinating depiction of the making of *Guernica* and the history of this work in *Guernica. Painting the End of the World* (London: Head of Zeus, 2017). In the book, Attlee relates Dora Maar's comment about viewing *Guernica* as if it were a photograph, and he describes how replicas were made in tapestry form as a solution to problems of wear-and-tear and transportation, the first one in 1955, followed by others. One of the replicas was ordered by Nelson Rockefeller and loaned indefinitely to the United Nation's press room. When Colin Powell, then secretary of defence in the US, held a press conference there just prior to the Iraq War in 2003, it was decided that the famous image should be covered (Attlee, 172–75). In other words, both *Guernica* and *Ethiopia* have been censored, but at different times.

are subjected to double standards and social sanctions that are especially associated with sexuality. *Unwed Mother* can also be seen as a continuation of the motif previously introduced by Krohg with *Albertine* and by the other Nordic authors who were considered part of the 'modern breakthrough.'

In *Unwed Mother* Ryggen places a woman who has had a child out of wedlock in the tapestry's central panel, as if she is on a stage. FIG 19 Being an unwed mother was shameful in itself, and it was no small feat to provide for children alone. For women in cities, working in a factory was a possibility, but then someone else had to take care of the child. Taking in work as a seamstress, a common, low-paying women's job at this time (and one that was often associated with prostitution), was one of the few ways to care for children and work at the same time.

Albertine was a seamstress, and Krohg painted *Trett* (*Tired*) in 1885—that is to say, in the same period as *Albertine to See the Police Surgeon.* There are striking differences in the depiction of women in Krohg's and Ryggen's works. In Krohg's painting, the woman has fallen asleep, exhausted, by the sewing machine, although the light from the window next to her suggests that it is daytime. FIG 20 In Ryggen's version, the seamstress is hard at work on a piece of delicate pale pink fabric, probably for a skirt. On the chair to the left hangs a finished jacket in the same material. The woman behind the sewing machine holds up a scrap of fabric to a happy and pleased little toddler beside her. In both of the side panels it is night, and men emerge from different patterns. What transpires in these areas is unclear, but it is nevertheless subsidiary to the woman and child, who are imbued with both pride and dignity. With this depiction, Ryggen underscores that no shame should be associated with being an unwed mother or fending for oneself and one's children.

The motif is framed by a border around the entire tapestry, while two blue columns create a triptych-like structure. The religious allusion is not coincidental. In *The Sinner* (pp. 68/69), Ryggen also makes use of a biblical figure, the woman who allegedly committed adultery and whom a group of Christian men were about to stone to death before Jesus intervened and prevented her punishment by remarking: "He that is without sin among you, let him first cast a stone at her."[34] Ryggen places the woman in a procession of clergymen with a mix of faces and clothing from both the present and earlier eras. In this way she emphasizes that female sexuality is still, as then, often met with condemnation and double standards. As in *Unwed Mother,* men could call on women covertly, and then chastise them in public.

The urge to tell a story and the successive form of presentation that Ryggen made use of in both *Unwed Mother* and *Us and Our Animals* (pp. 36/37) are also characteristic of the monumental painting or mural tradition from this period. In addition there is a scenic or theatrical element in several of Ryggen's compositions that evinces the kinship with Norwegian monumental painting. The theatrical is particularly notable in *The Golden Lamb Iselin* (pp. 70/71), where the beautiful young Iselin towers imposingly on a tiled floor, framed by two drapes that are raised and tied like a stage curtain.[35] From behind the drapery on the left, an older man appears, seated

34 The Bible, John 8:7.

35 The drawn stage curtain is repeated in Ryggen's *Marie Antoinette* (1939). It can be tempting to imagine that Rafael's *Sistine Madonna* (1512/1513), which hangs in the Gemäldegalerie Alte Meister in Dresden, might have been a source of inspiration. Another interesting feature of this painting is the rendering of the sky, filled with faintly visible faces; multiple faces grouped on the surface recur in very many of Ryggen's works.

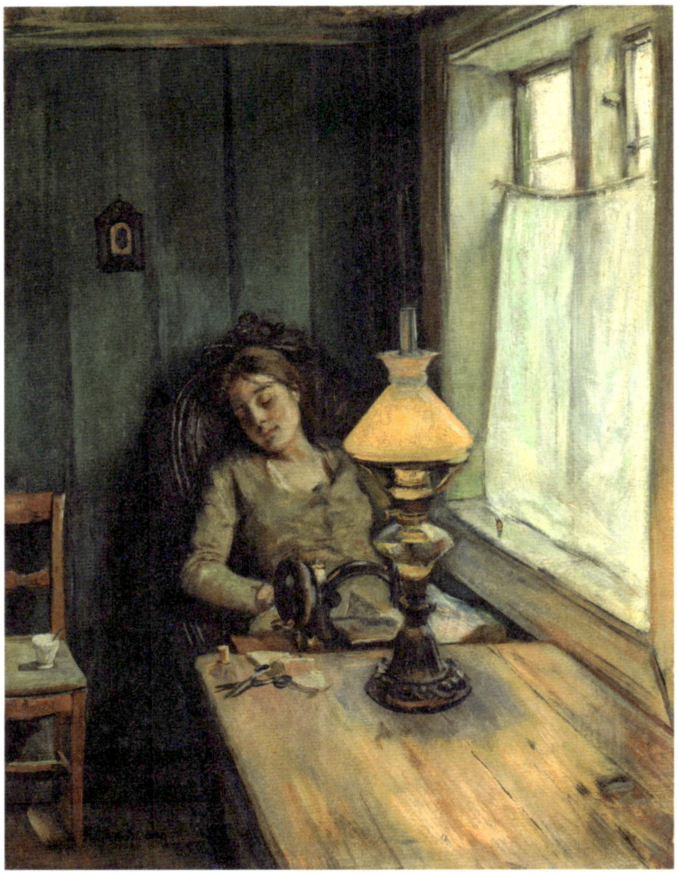

FIG. 20

Christian Krohg, *Trett* (*Tired*), 1885, oil on canvas, 80.2 × 61.5 cm, National Museum for Art, Architecture and Design, Oslo

FIG. 19

Hannah Ryggen, *Ugift mor* (*Unwed Mother*), 1937

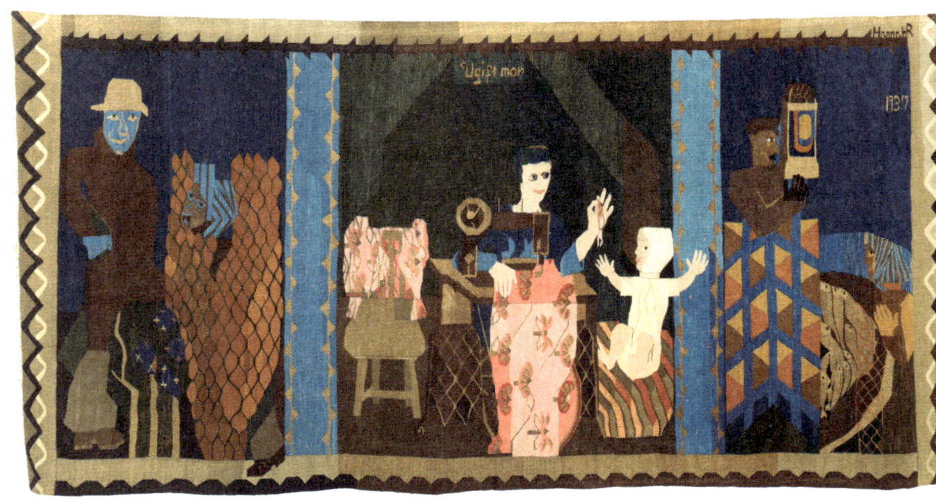

FIGS. 21, 22

Hannah Ryggen, *Vi lever på en stjerne* (*We Are Living on a Star*), 1958, total view and detail

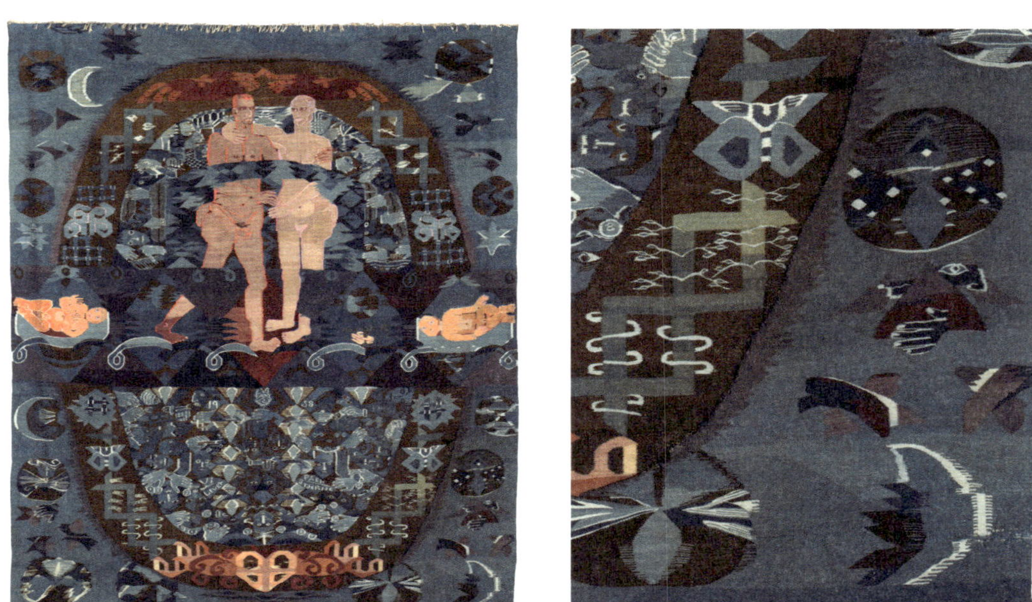

and in pyjamas, with a furrowed drawn face, smoking a cigarette. The work *6. oktober 1942* (*6 October 1942,* 1943, pp. 42–45) also has a scenic construction, one in which Ryggen juxtaposes actual and imaginary events and historical figures; so, too, does *Schweden* (*Sweden*, 1946, pp. 48/49), in which she gathers Swedes who were prominent during the Second World War within the same space. The title—the German word for Sweden—alludes to the dual role the country had during the war. Sweden was officially neutral, yet it helped the Nazis by making its railways, among other things, available to them, rather than aiding its neighboring countries.

In addition to playing on aspects of monumental painting, Ryggen also borrows quite freely from other trends and effects in contemporary art. For example, spaces between figures consist of monochrome areas or patterns that are not contiguous, a device used to link different events within one pictorial area. In this way the space is unfolded onto the picture plane, as in many of Ryggen's motifs. She also employs collage-like techniques: in *Sweden* she has 'pasted' the face of the Swedish king, Gustav V, onto the figure of Mor Svea (the personification of Sweden, with a dress in the colors of the Swedish flag, blue and yellow). Gustav V was sympathetic to the Nazis, and with this device Ryggen shows how Sweden was divided: it gave with one hand and took with the other.

Collage as a technique was developed in the 1920s by artists such as Hannah Höch, Kurt Schwitters, and John Heartfield. By rearranging the pictorial elements the artist could disrupt meaningful connections between persons, time, and space, create new combinations and lines of connection, and stretch time. There are many parallels in Höch's and Ryggen's work: the utilization of elements from news photos, the treatment of the picture plane like a stage, and an affinity for the absurd and the satirical. Both also drew on tradition, with past and present melding into each other, not just in terms of content but also in terms of the visual language.

Thus it is wrong to limit Hannah Ryggen's works solely to a decoding of historical symbols and figures, as the work is then quickly reduced to passive representation and becomes something that belongs to the past. Such an approach is in fundamental conflict with what Ryggen was trying to achieve—indeed, with what she succeeded in achieving—both visually and in terms of content. By emphasizing the picture plane, and using ornament and pattern to link the various elements in a single composition, she allows the motif to hover between an actual moment in time and all time, thus freeing it from a specific space. The subject matter in *Sweden*—how power is administered—is both specific and universal. Thus Ryggen's art also preserves its activist impulse.

We Are Living on a Star: a message in motion

For the Nordic exhibition at Liljevalchs in Stockholm in 1948, an entire room was devoted to Hannah Ryggen, and eleven works were on display. In his critique of the exhibition, Gotthard Johansson emphasized Ryggen's connection to monumental painting: "There is little in Nordic monumental painting that has such a large and simple form and yet also has such a rich visual and timely content as this weaver's poems from the loom."[36]

36 *Svenska Dagbladet,* October 6, 1948.

Ryggen actively applied herself towards the monumental tradition. She believed *Us and Our Animals* was suitable for the interior of the Oslo City Hall and sent it for consideration. The work was not accepted, however, and she was incensed by its rejection. She speculated about the causes and in the end, in *Hjemlige guder* (*Homely Gods,* 1951, pp. 84/85), formulated her own commentary about the powers that determine who is given a chance and who is not. In this work we see the Norwegian artist Henrik Sørensen standing farthest to the left with his model, his right hand resting on the City Hall. Edvard Munch hovers in the background, while his wealthy patron Rolf Stenersen holds the reins to the chariot with all the money. As a sarcastic retort Ryggen depicts Sørensen and Stenersen as Tor and Odin, the two most important gods in Norse mythology: the two men advised in matters regarding the decoration of the City Hall. Sørensen had also made a central fresco in the building (and used the largest atelier in one of its towers for many years), although the newspaper *Dagbladet* and a unified art world argued that Munch ought to have received a commission in the City Hall.[37] She mocked all the fuss and felt there should be a limit to how much room these men were allowed to occupy in the matter.

Ryggen would, however, eventually succeed in obtaining a major public commission. FIGS. 21, 22 In 1955 she received a request from architect Erling Viksjø to make a work for the main entrance hall of the government headquarters known as 'the Highrise' (*Høyblokka*) in the newly planned government quarter in Oslo. It was to become one of her most iconic works: *Vi lever på en stjerne* (*We Are Living on a Star,* 1958). In this tapestry, she carries to conclusion the themes already raised in *Livet glir forbi* (*Life Slides By,* 1939, pp. 94/95) and revisited in *Dikt av T. S. Eliot* (*Poem by T. S. Eliot,* 1952, pp. 108/109): how do we, as human beings, steward time and love, and what role should art have in our relationships with others and the world?

In December 1956, Hannah Ryggen's husband Hans died. To Hannah, the loss was as though the bearing wall in existence had collapsed. Color drained from the world. *We Are Living on a Star* became her way of learning how to live again.[38] It took her half a year to dye all the wool for this tapestry, and another thirteen months to weave it. The same oval—the fabric of life—that appears in *Poem by T. S. Eliot* is repeated here but in a vertical position, and is used to define an area around the two lovers. This area separates the earth and the surrounding cosmos. Children come sailing in towards the couple from each side of the blue band—time—and this band also entwines the man and the woman. Time unites and divides. Within this band Ryggen also inserted her own signature and a shuttle, because time is also what is formed in her hands, in her art.

The couple in the oval are surrounded by faces and hands holding various tools. As in *A Free One,* they labor and expend their time. In the lower portion of the oval, red hues blaze, reminiscent of the fire in *Poem by T. S. Eliot*. The warm, deep-red glow of love appears in the area where the man and woman are standing, and hovers above their heads. The nude couple are a symbol of life's continual regeneration, but the work is also about life as a battleground, about the unwavering red flame and the eternal blue moment. *We Are Living on a Star* emphasizes the fellowship of humankind

37 The situation was certainly not made better when, in 1950, *Dagbladet* ran a double-page spread about two female weavers from the handicrafts milieu who had executed a work with historical motifs after a pattern by a male artist. This tradition was in part what Hannah Ryggen emphatically rebelled against when she began to weave. She wanted to control the entire process herself, and used neither patterns nor sketches. See "Fra Baldisholteppet til Kaare Mikkelsen Jonsborgs Rådhusteppe" (From the Baldishol Tapestry to Kaare Mikkelsen Jonsborg's Tapestry in the City Hall), *Dagbladet,* March 1, 1950.

38 For a more in-depth analysis of this work, see Paasche, *Hannah Ryggen. Threads of Defiance,* ch. 11.

through a formal composition in which the ornamental pattern draws the figures towards each other, linking them to past, present, and future, and to the unremitting progression of time.

We Are Living on a Star hung in the entrance hall of the Highrise until July 22, 2011: the day that the Norwegian right-wing extremist and terrorist Anders Behring Breivik detonated a car bomb just in front of the building. Behring Breivik then drove to the island of Utøya, about an hour outside of Oslo, where, dressed as a policeman, he shot and killed sixty-nine participants of the Labour Party's youth organization's summer camp, most of them teenagers.[39]

The tapestry withstood the explosion because it is so pliant and relatively light. It received a gash in the lower right corner, which conservators have repaired. That this tapestry, which so powerfully proclaims faith in love as a personal and political force, should be struck in the first major attack on Norwegian society since the Second World War is now manifested by a trace, a scar in the bottom right corner. The scar is a reminder that no political struggle is ever concluded; these battles must be fought again and again.

The concept of the independent free individual is central in Hannah Ryggen's art, yet it is also an integral part of the fabric of society and the natural world. Ryggen's work combines idealism—faith that the world can be a better place—with a belief in the function and value of art as both idea and action, and as a 'moveable mural.' Her tapestries can be admired for the power of their beauty, but they can also be borne like banners. Hannah Ryggen understood well how to weave the political into a monumental format that was bound neither to a specific place nor an architectonic framework. She also deliberately chose—at great sacrifice—not to sell the largest works to private collectors, so that these works would remain accessible to the general public. This is one of the reasons why Schirn Kunsthalle Frankfurt is able to exhibit the full spectrum of Hannah Ryggen's art today.

39 According to the judgment in the case against Behring Breivik, the motivation for the terror attack was his belief that "[a]ll the parties in Parliament (Storting), but in particular the Labour Party" were complicit in a political agenda that had transformed Norway "into a multicultural state, one in which the Norwegian indigenous population is in the process of being exterminated." See https://lovdata.no/static/file/1282/toslo-2011-188627-24-eng.pdf for the official English translation of the Oslo District Court judgment dated August 24, 2012.

Fiske ved gjeldens hav (*Fishing in the Sea of Debt*), 1933
Tapestry woven in wool and linen,
145×185 cm

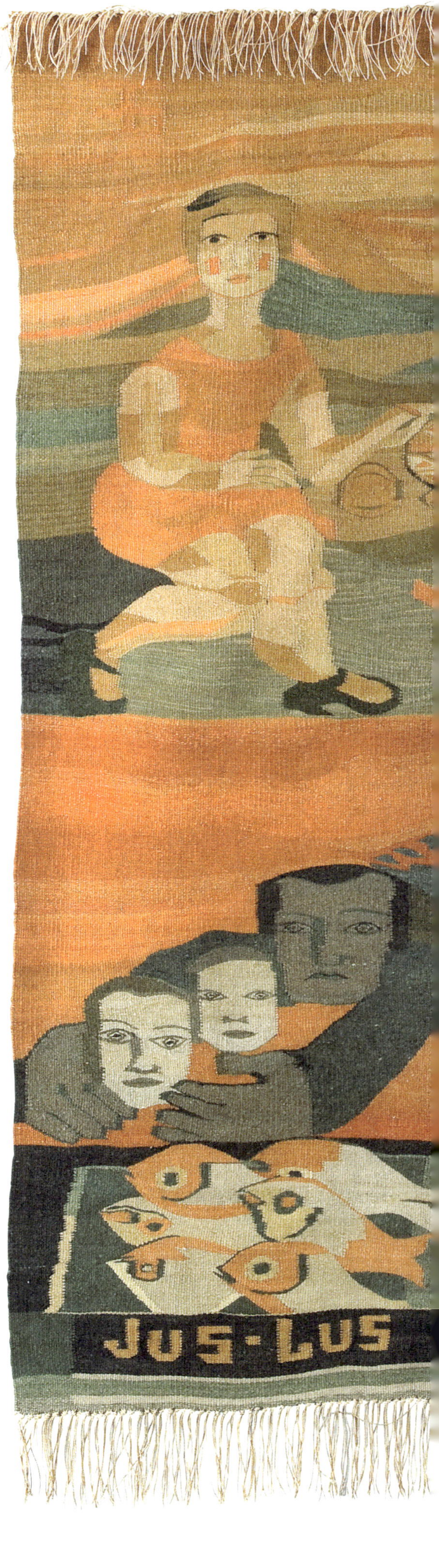

The great economic crisis that characterized the early 1930s also struck Scandinavia. Industrial production fell, and unemployment figures rose dramatically. In Norway, the worst year of the crisis was 1933. Many were devastated by overwhelming debt, and the many fishermen in Ørlandet, where Hannah and Hans Ryggen lived, were among the hardest hit.
That same year, Ryggen wove *Fishing in the Sea of Debt*. The tapestry depicts the banks' debt collectors fishing in the bloody waters of financial ruin. A boat has just capsized, and three adults and two children are floating in the sea. One of the men is struggling to keep the two small children's heads above water, while the woman to the right has already drowned; her body is sinking to the bottom. The woman's chickens, her only source of income, have been sold to meet interest payments. The man to her left has his mouth and nose barely above the surface of the water. The fish depicted in front of him can no longer provide him with enough income to support himself. On land, a man lies dead on the ground. A doctor attending to his body greedily snatches one last coin. To the left, the banking commissioner's wife sits at an amply laden table observing the scene, seemingly unmoved by the tragedy that is unfolding in front of her.
In *Fishing in the Sea of Debt*, Ryggen revives the mediaeval way of composing in color fields, while also drawing on modernist painting and her own skills as a painter. She also, in her characteristic and expressionistic way, includes aspects of her private life in her treatment of public issues. Ryggen had personally experienced having the last of her egg money taken by the mortgage commissioner, so she knew what it felt like to be burdened by debt.

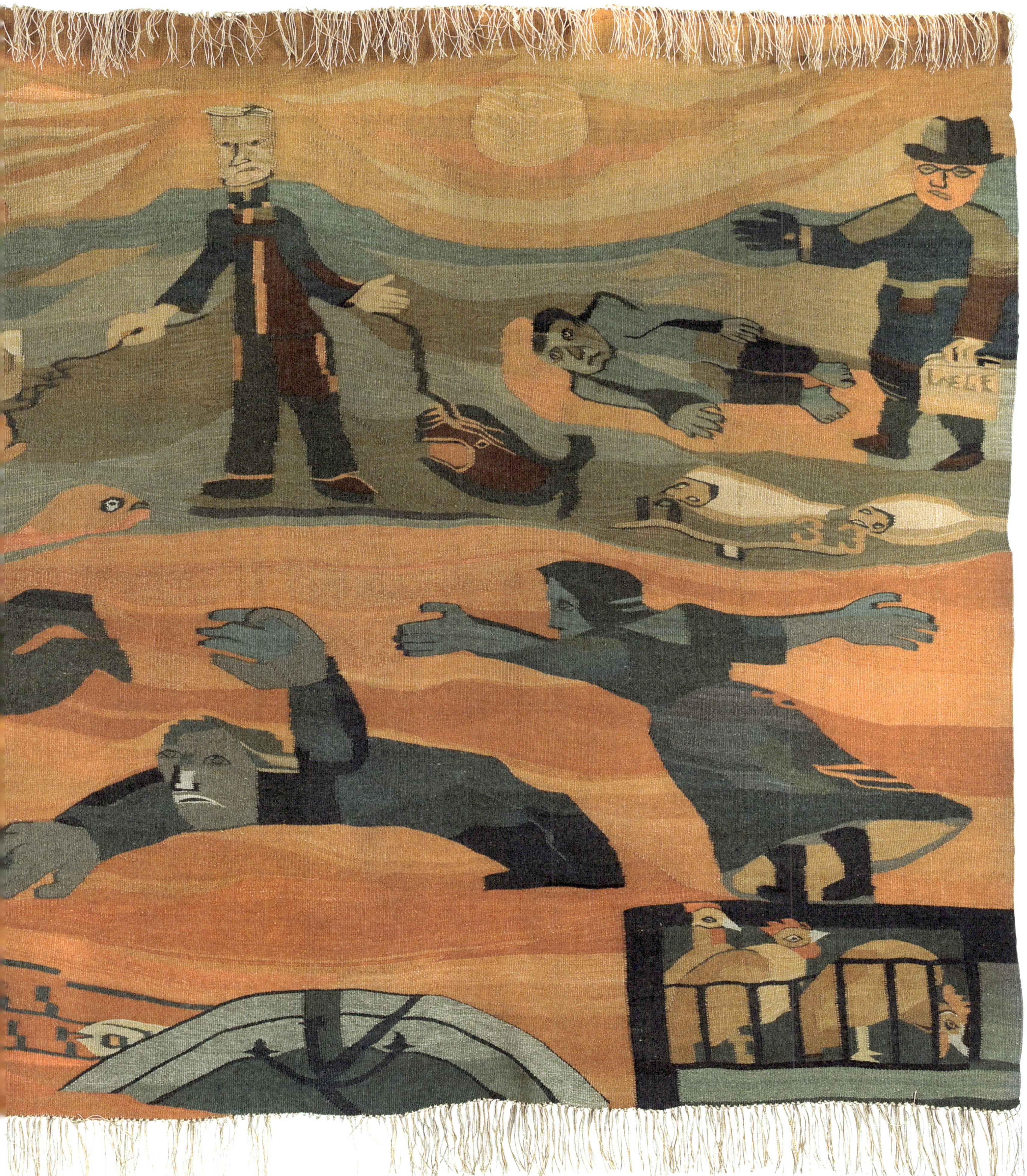

Vi og våre dyr (*Us and Our Animals*), 1934
Tapestry woven in wool and linen, 187.5 × 491 cm

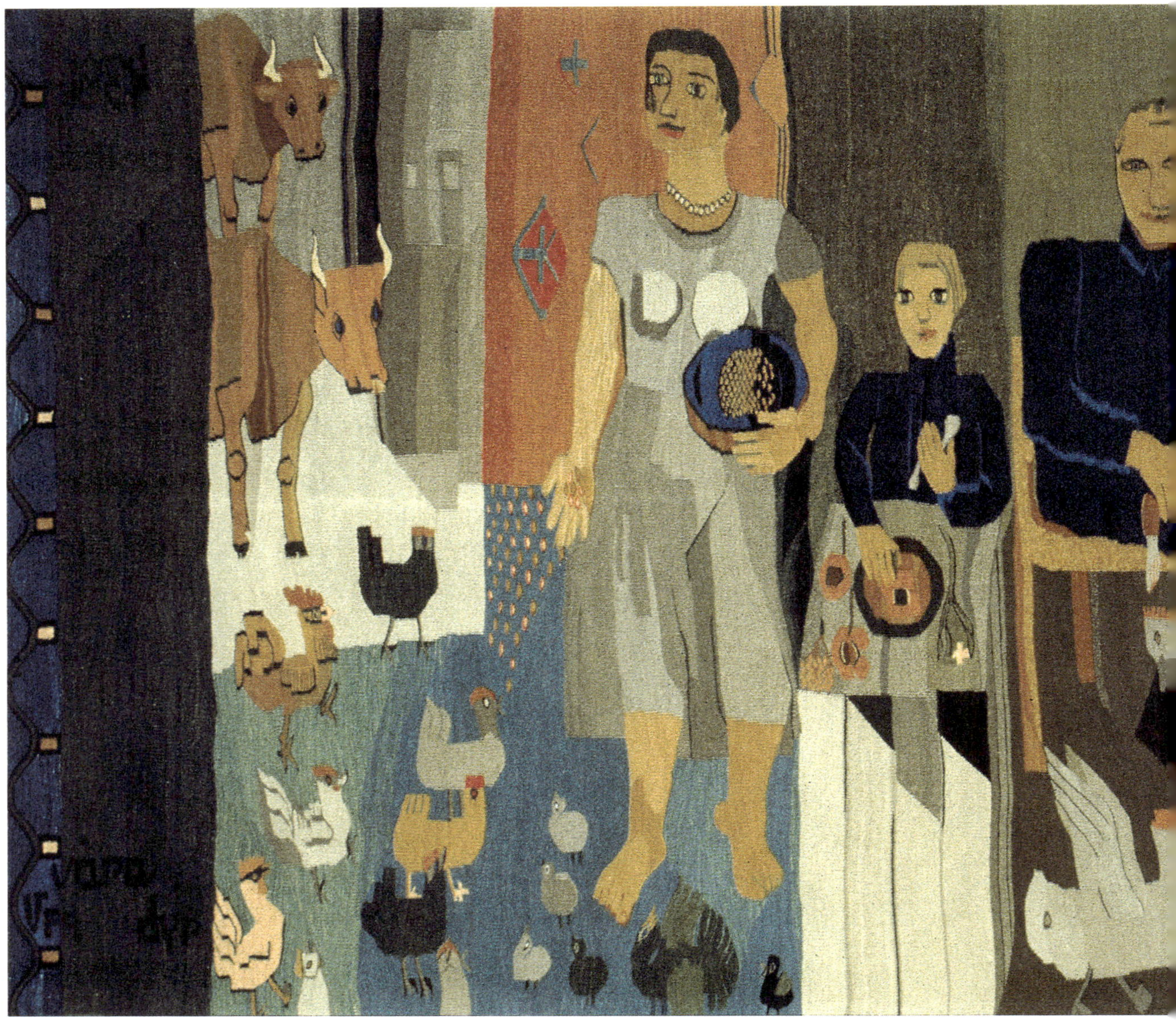

The Industrial Revolution had enormous consequences for both urban development and living conditions, and it fundamentally altered the way human beings related to nature and the production of objects. When Hannah Ryggen wove *Fiske ved gjeldens hav* (*Fishing in the Sea of Debt*) in 1933, in solidarity with debt-laden workers, it was an overt political act. The following year she wove the monumental *Us and Our Animals,* which portrays the Ryggen family on their farm with their animals.

Ryggen was very fond of the animals and considered them part of the family. She was in torment whenever one of them had to be slaughtered, as we see depicted in the middle section, where a headless goose wanders aimlessly in front of the dinner table. Both *Fishing in the Sea of Debt* and *Us and Our Animals* are experience-based works. The former is explicitly political, but *Us and Our Animals* also conveys a political message, albeit somewhat less emphatically: By thematicizing the core conditions of the family, the work questions a fundamental aspect of humanity's existence: namely, our relationship to nature and how to subsist from it without doing harm. Hannah Ryggen's respect for and love of nature was all-encompassing. Today, the self-sustainability of nature's ecosystems is under massive attack, and the precarious situation has sparked renewed interest in the eco-philosophical themes and ideas behind *Us and Our Animals.*

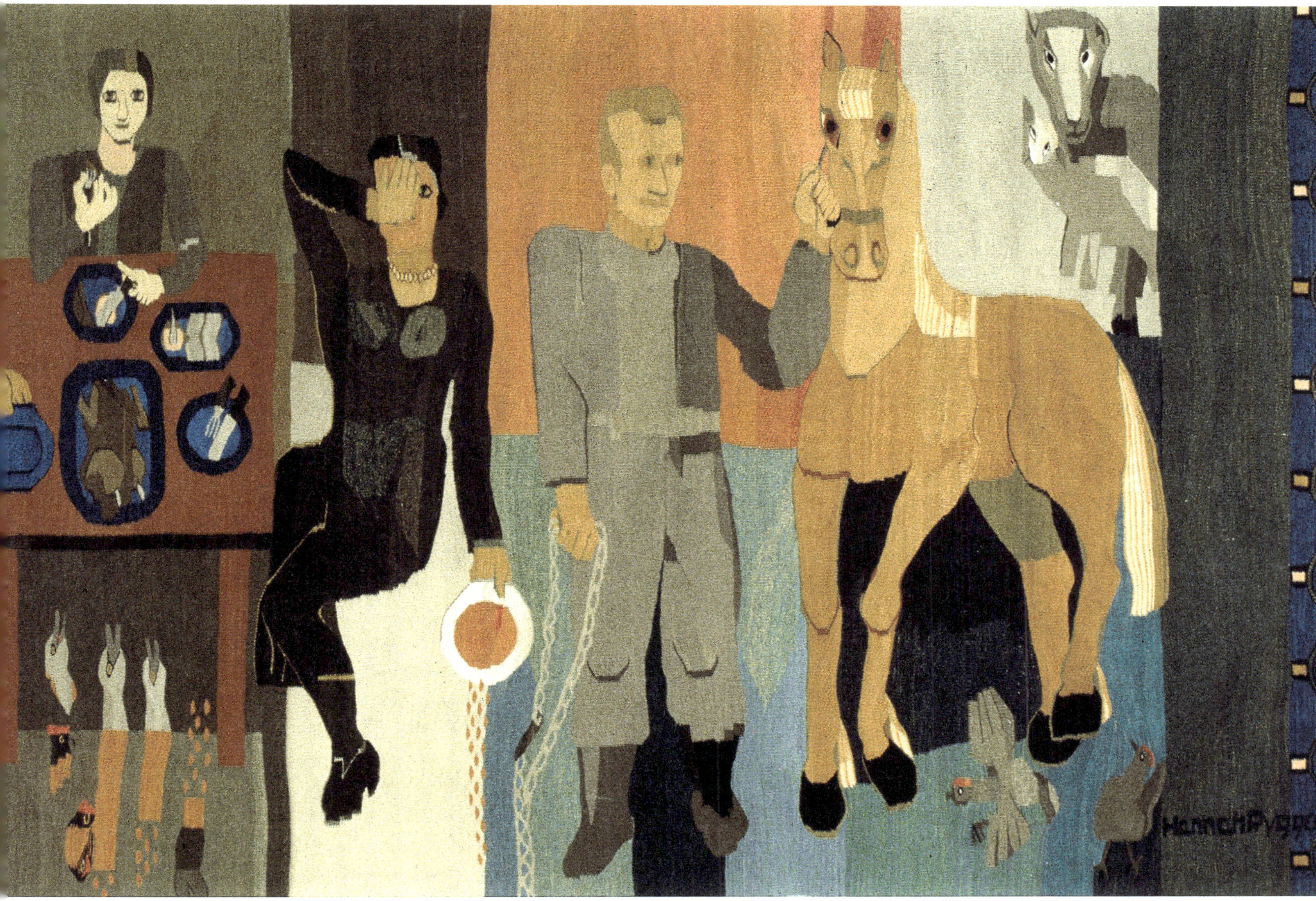

Drømmedød (*Death of Dreams*), 1936
Tapestry woven in wool and linen,
235 × 273 cm

The motivation for *Death of Dreams* was the case of Carl von Ossietzky, a German writer and pacifist. As international affairs editor for the newspaper *Berliner Volks-Zeitung,* Ossietzky disclosed the German military's plans for a coup at the beginning of the 1920s. In 1931, by which time he had become editor of *Die Weltbühne,* Ossietzky was indicted on charges of treason and espionage, and sentenced to eighteen months in prison for his disclosure of Germany's re-armament efforts, a breach of the Treaty of Versailles. He was arrested again on charges of treason the day after the Reichstag fire in Berlin in 1933 and died in prison in 1938, the same year as Liselotte Herrmann (whom Ryggen also portrayed, see pp. 40/41). Ossietzky was a polarizing political symbol in Norway. Ryggen completed *Death of Dreams* in May 1936. It was exhibited soon thereafter and caused a sensation. This was a period during which cultural statements were largely judged according to political orientation. The tapestry was both a commentary in the context of the ongoing debate and a personal opinion about how the world would look under Nazi control. Ryggen wrote: "Woven in the year 1936, three years after Hitler came to power. I called it 'Death of Dreams' because now all dreams would die." [1]

Ossietzky is behind bars, handcuffed. To his right, Joseph Goebbels, Hermann Göring, and Adolf Hitler form a triumvirate, supported by swastikas. Their faces and hands are woven in an intense shade of purple with traces of crimson. Goebbels clasps his hands around the throat of a prisoner who hangs helplessly in his grip. On the right is another group, this one behind bars. The main person here is Albert Einstein, standing with a violin in his hand. Einstein was a prominent opponent of the Third Reich, and as early as 1933 he renounced his German citizenship in protest against the Nazis' persecution of the Jews. In front of this group the bars of the cell are broken in places. The area below the figures is restricted to two main colors: brown and gray. The ornamentation, with its seemingly neutral yet highly disciplined and repetitive geometric forms, is extremely effective. Swastikas emerge and dissolve, depending on whether one looks at the light gray or the brown. The legs and feet of the lifeless prisoner in Goebbels' clutch hang over the lower field, and the gray prison uniform melds with the gray of the ornamentation.

1 Exhibition card written by Hannah Ryggen in 1946. Archives of Designmuseet, Copenhagen.

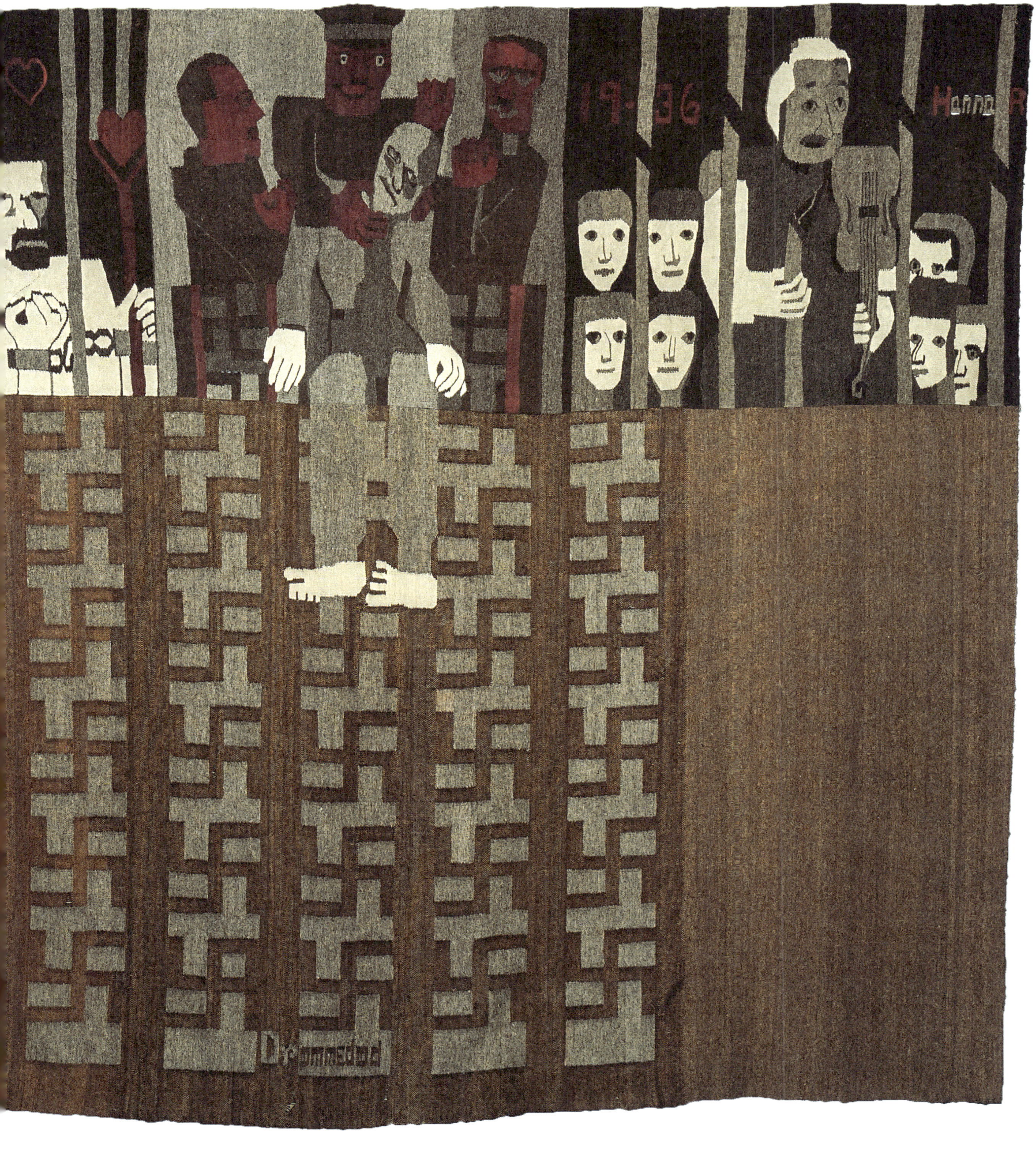

19·36
Hanna R
Drømmedød

Liselotte Herrmann halshuggen (*Liselotte Herrmann Decapitated*), 1938
Tapestry woven in wool and linen, 187.1 × 154 cm

Liselotte Herrmann was politically active in the Red Student League (Roter Studentenbund) and was a member of the Communist Party (KPD) in Germany. In 1933 she signed a manifesto 'Defence of Democratic Rights and Freedoms,' and as a result was expelled from university. In 1934 she gave birth to a son, Walter. She continued to work illegally against the Nazis, and on December 7, 1935, she was arrested for treason. Despite being tortured, Hermann disclosed no information and was classified as *Unverbesserliche* (incorrigible).

In Ryggen's tapestry we see Herrmann seated with her child on her lap in an idyllic garden-like setting. The way in which she is holding the child is almost identical to her pose in a photograph printed in the Norwegian newspaper *Dagbladet* on March 5, 1938. Yet the path from happiness to imprisonment was very short, visualized by a single footprint in the direction of the cell. She was imprisoned for nineteen months before her case was heard by a so-called People's Court (*Volksgerichtshof*), during which time her son Walter lived with his grandparents. In 1937 Hermann was sentenced to death. When she asked to say goodbye to her son, her request was refused; instead, according to the newspapers, the prison guards threw Walter's clothes into her cell. Despite intense international protest Liselotte Herrmann was guillotined on June 20, 1938.

In this tapestry, the tragedy unfolds in succession, as in folk art weavings, early Christian decorative traditions, or the more modern photo reportage from this time. The subject is clearly inspired by the classical motif of the Madonna in the rose garden. The development of events can be read in a progression that moves from left to right, and from top to bottom: first the scene with mother and child, then the red-hued executioner in the upper right corner, to the blood-red footprint in the lower part of the weaving, and lastly to the prison cell where Hermann clasps baby clothes spun from soft *geiteragg,* a goat fibre Ryggen had not used before, nor would again. The cruciform structure provides a taut composition that functions extremely well against the rich coloration.

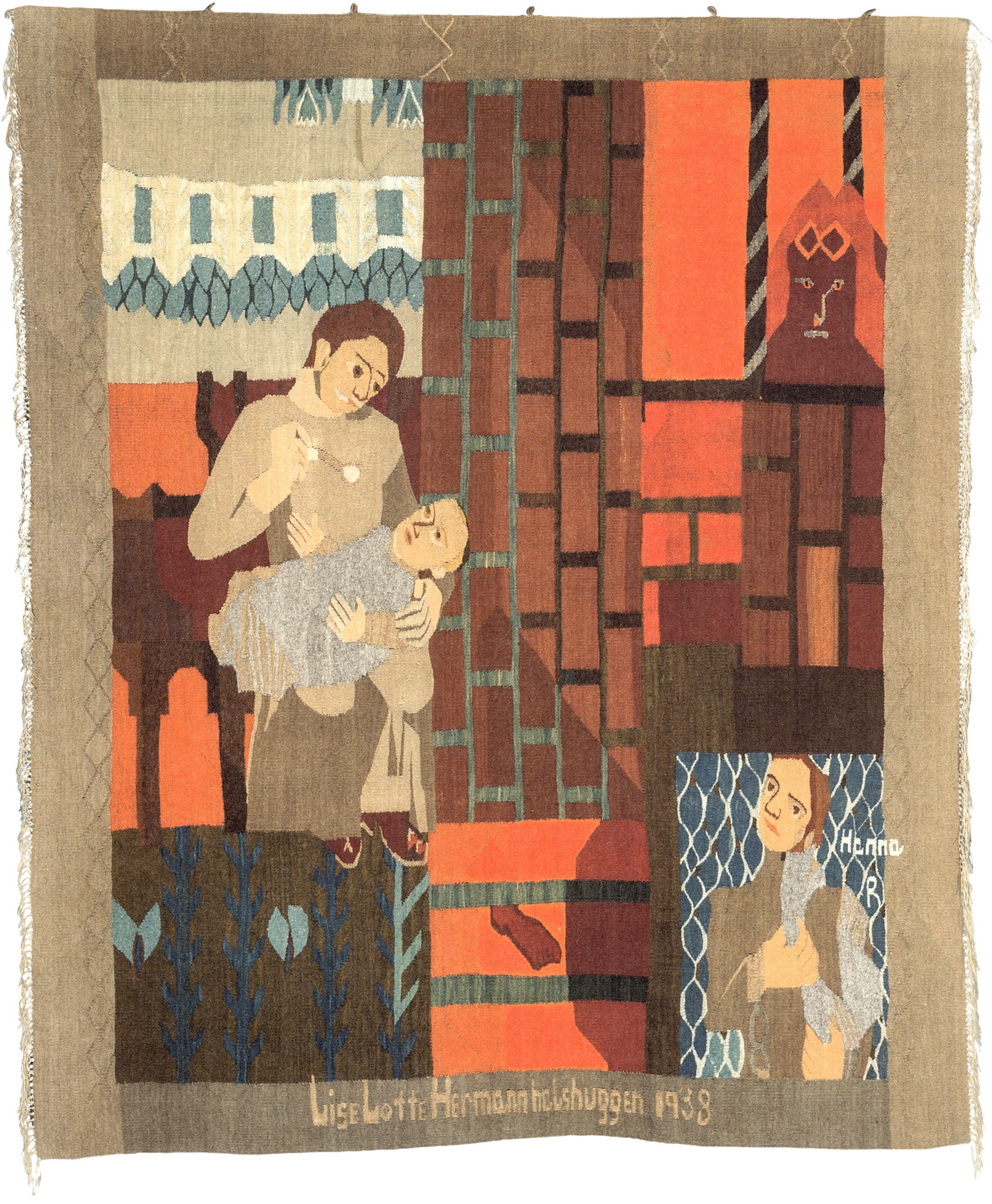

Hanna
R
LiseLotte Hermann halshuggen 1938

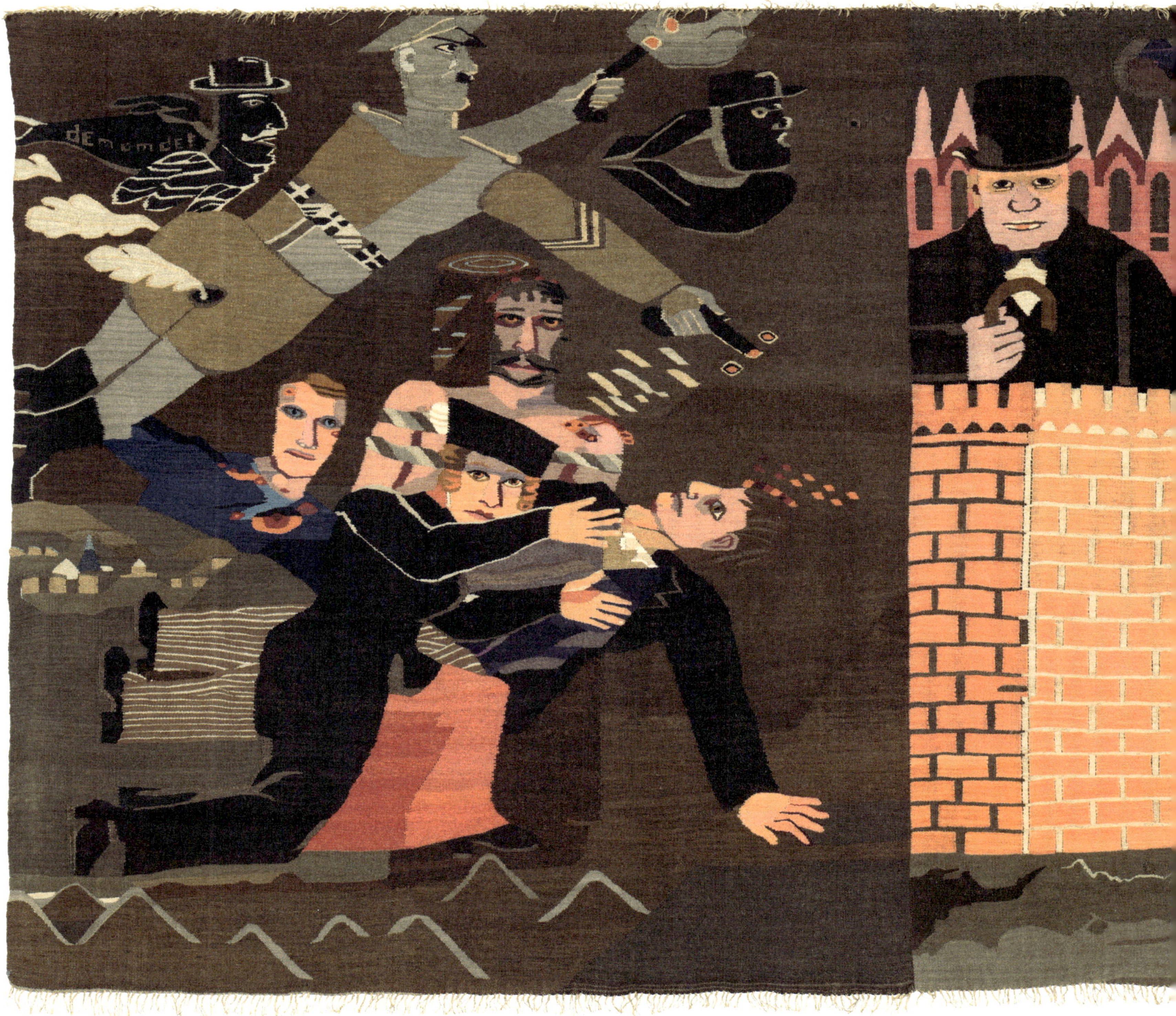

6. oktober 1942 (*6 October 1942*), 1943
Tapestry woven in wool and linen,
175 × 419.5 cm

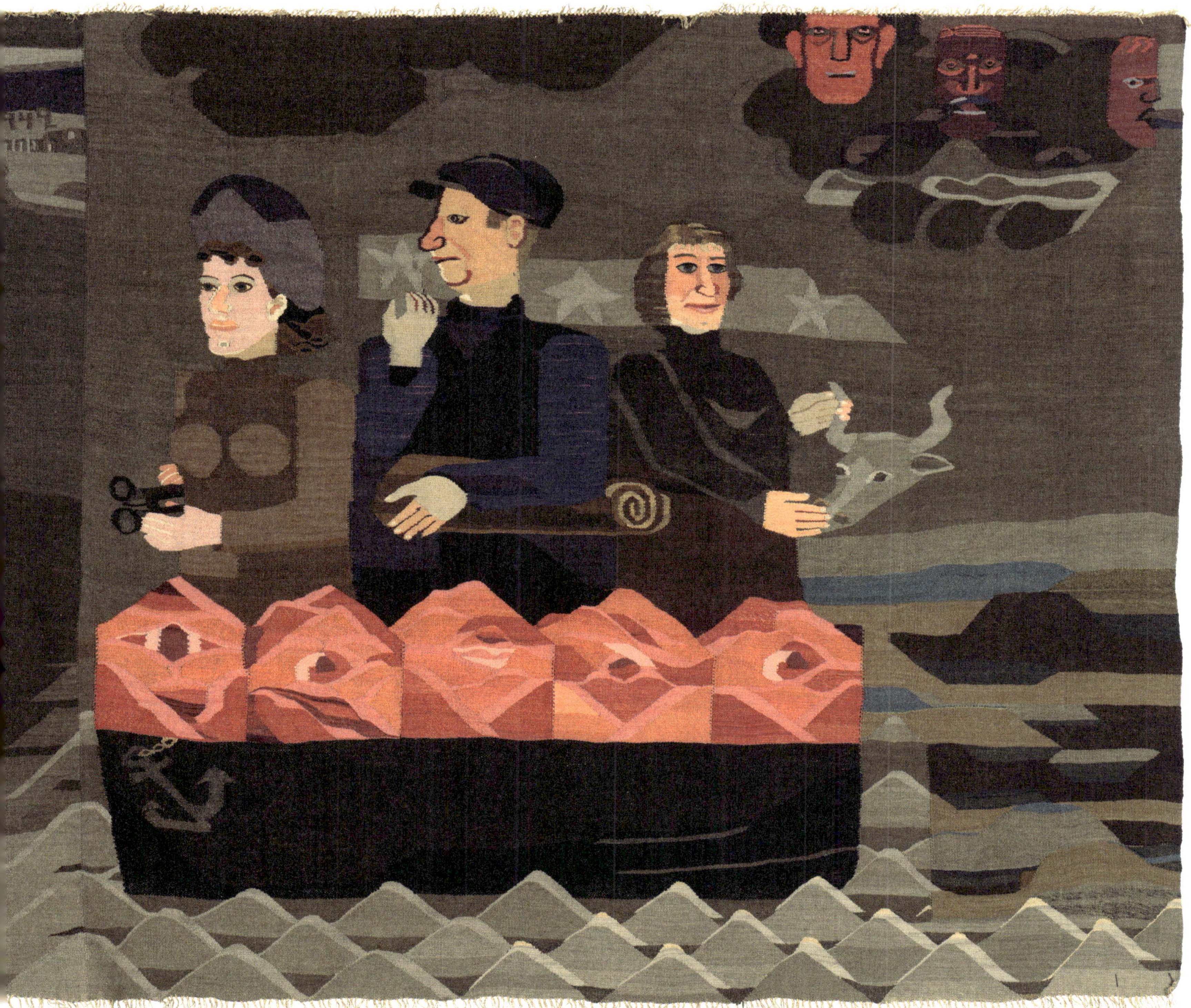

6. oktober 1942 (*6 October 1942*)
Detail

When Norway was occupied by the Nazis in April 1940, Ørlandet, the region where the Ryggens lived, was chosen as the location for a new airstrip and base. Large tracts of agricultural land were destroyed, while at the same time the local population increased dramatically due to both the military facilities and the large prison camps established there. The Ryggen family witnessed a great deal of suffering.

In *6 October 1942* we see how Hannah Ryggen is able to organize a variety of events, references, and inner images within a single composition. To the left, tragedy takes place as if on a stage. The actor, theater director, and resistance member Henry Gleditsch, in costume for the role of Doctor Relling in Ibsen's *Vildanden* (*The Wild Duck*), lies in his wife's arms after being shot. Gleditsch was among those singled out by Reich Commissioner Josef Terboven for execution as "propitiatory sacrifices," and his execution took place the day before the premiere of the play. Synnøve Gleditsch, also an actor in the play and depicted in costume, kneels by her husband's side. Their positions are evocative of a pietà, and the reference is intensified by the presence of a naked man bound to a post behind them. The man is not a Christ figure, however, but a Serbian prisoner of war whom Ryggen personally witnessed being tortured and executed at one of the concentration camps. Above them, Hitler, with a pistol in each hand, floats like an omnipresent devil. The shots he fires strike Gleditsch. Ryggen ridicules Hitler by depicting him with oak leaves issuing from his anus. She also denigrates the Norwegian writer Knut Hamsun, a Nazi sympathizer, and the Norwegian Prime Minister Vidkun Quisling, set up by the German occupiers, who are portrayed as pitiful black birds.

The scene to the right expresses the Ryggen family's desire to flee. They are sitting in a boat that is as black as death but surrounded by red roses. Three sinister crimson heads float above them. The face in the middle bears a strong likeness to Terboven's, and the one to the right resembles Jonas Lie, the Norwegian chief of police under Terboven who authorized death sentences against Norwegians during the war. The face to the left could be the SS officer Gerhard Flesch. This trio echoes that of Hitler, Göring, and Goebbels in ***Drømmedød*** (*Death of Dreams*, pp. 38/39).

The tapestry's mid-section was the last to be woven, as is noticeable from a purely compositional perspective. Ryggen felt that a measure of red was called for to balance the sections on the left and right. Thus, in the middle panel, a stalwart Winston Churchill stands guard over his country in an orange-red fortress tower.

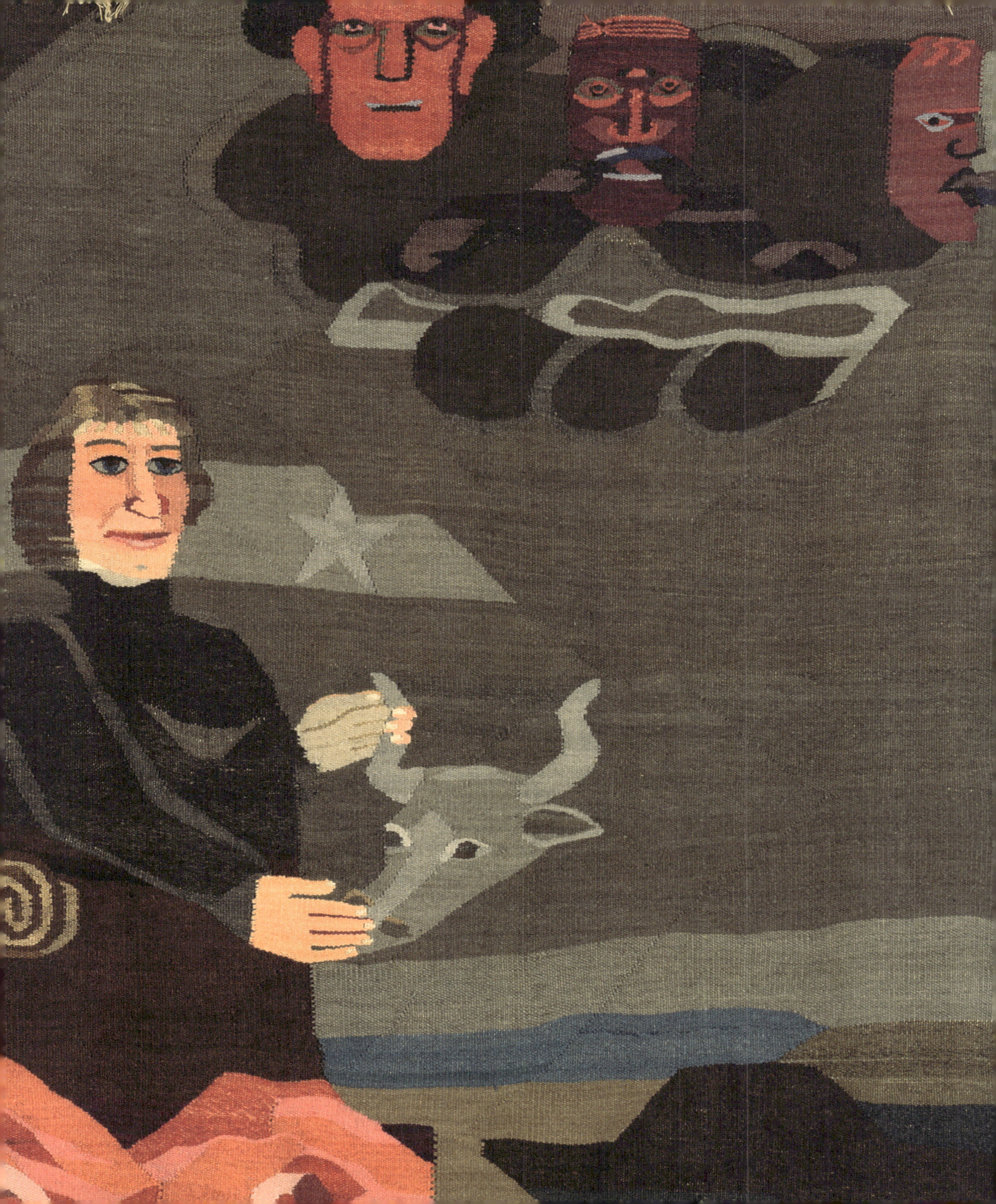

Grini, 1945
Tapestry woven in wool and linen,
191.5 × 168.5 cm

In May 1944 Hans Ryggen was seized by the Nazis, accused of having committed illegal acts including having helped prisoners escape from the labor camps in Ørlandet. He was first held at a prison camp just outside Trondheim, and later transferred to Grini, outside of Oslo—the largest camp in Norway. From having lived in Dresden, Hans spoke some German, and with his training, he was assigned to painting warning signs for minefields. Hannah was deeply worried about Hans, yet she was not able to leave Ørlandet. She was tied to the farm and all the chores she now had to do alone.

So in *Grini*, with the help of dreaming and imagination, Ryggen sends Mona on horseback to free him. Hans is in his numbered prison uniform, and in the background we see smoke rising up from the barracks, as well as terrified faces behind rows of barbed wire. The faces are a reminder of how quickly the situation could worsen for Hans and the others. From 1941 until peace came in May 1945, there were 19,788 prisoners registered at Grini, 3,402 of whom were sent to concentration camps in Germany and other occupied territories. The column with the gray faces along the right-hand edge depicts a number of Hans' fellow prisoners, many of whom were also artists.

Along with *Livet glir forbi* (*Life Slides By*), *Grini* is one of the works in Ryggen's oeuvre that draws most heavily on folk art motifs. The fiery red hues symbolize both intensity and danger. The nude woman on horseback sent with flowers to liberate the captive is like an image from a fairy tale, but the prisoner number and the skull and crossbones Hans is painting attest to the brutal reality.

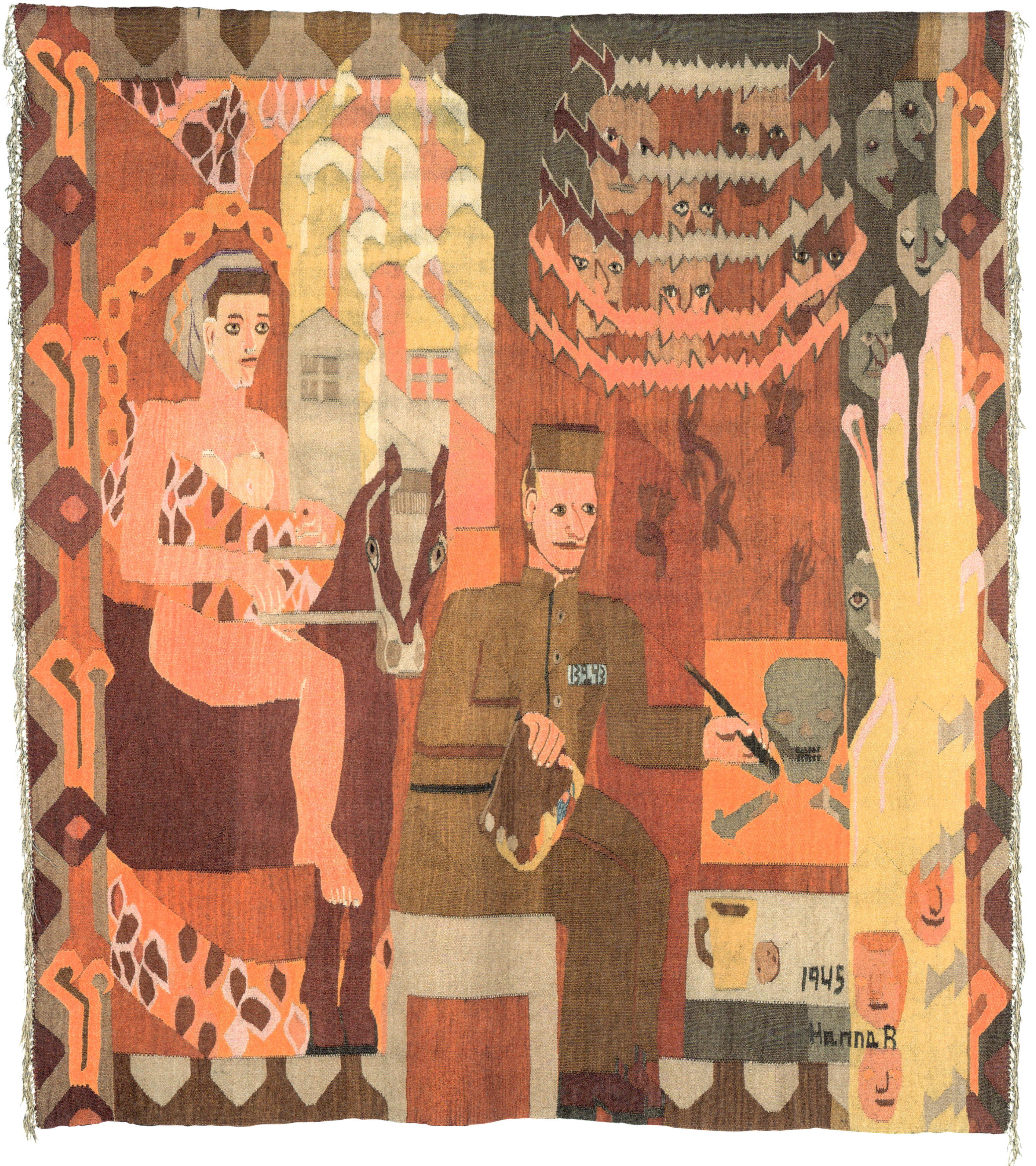
1945
Hanna B

Schweden (Sweden), 1946
Tapestry woven in wool and linen,
190×175 cm

Although Hannah Ryggen was born in Sweden, she emigrated to Norway in 1924 and lived there until her death in 1970. From her notes we know that *Sweden* was based on a photograph printed in the Norwegian newspaper *Dagbladet* on January 11, 1946. The picture depicted Anders Österling and Hjalmar Gullberg, members of the committee for the Nobel Prize for Literature, caught in a lighthearted moment with Sven Hedin, a famous Swedish explorer and Nazi sympathizer. This normalization of Nazism outraged Ryggen.

In *Sweden*, she places Hedin, dressed in brown, at a coffee table with a scruffy version of the Nazi eagle tucked under his arm. To his left is a woman wearing a crown and a regal dress in the country's national colors, yellow and blue: this is Mor Svea, the personification of Sweden. The tiny man sitting on her arm is Rütger Essén, a Nazi-friendly Swedish diplomat and a foreign affairs editor for the Swedish newspaper *Dagsposten*, which Ryggen described in a letter as the Nazi newspaper.

The 'other' Sweden, the good and altruistic Sweden, is represented by the vertical rectangular form to the right in the tapestry, with a pattern also in the country's national colors. The form creates a rostrum for Torgny Segerstedt, editor of the newspaper *Göteborgs Handels- och Sjöfartstidning* and an important, popular voice of opposition. Segerstedt's ruthless critique of Sweden's foreign policy provoked deep scorn in some Swedish circles but earned him a strong following in Norway, something which Ryggen alludes to by weaving in Norway's national colors, red, white, and blue, at the bottom of the heart that envelops Segerstedt. To Segerstedt's right is the opposition against him, symbolically represented in the figure of a single, anonymous person.

In Sweden's national coat of arms, Mor Svea has two lions. One of them, noticeably brown in color, is seated in the foreground, vomiting soup into a little girl's pail. Sweden's emergency relief to Norway was extremely significant during the war, and *svenskesuppe* (Swedish soup) rations for the most part given to Norwegian children, was important. Ryggen nevertheless could not forgive the fact that Sweden, which had the resources to protect and aid Norway, had remained so passive.

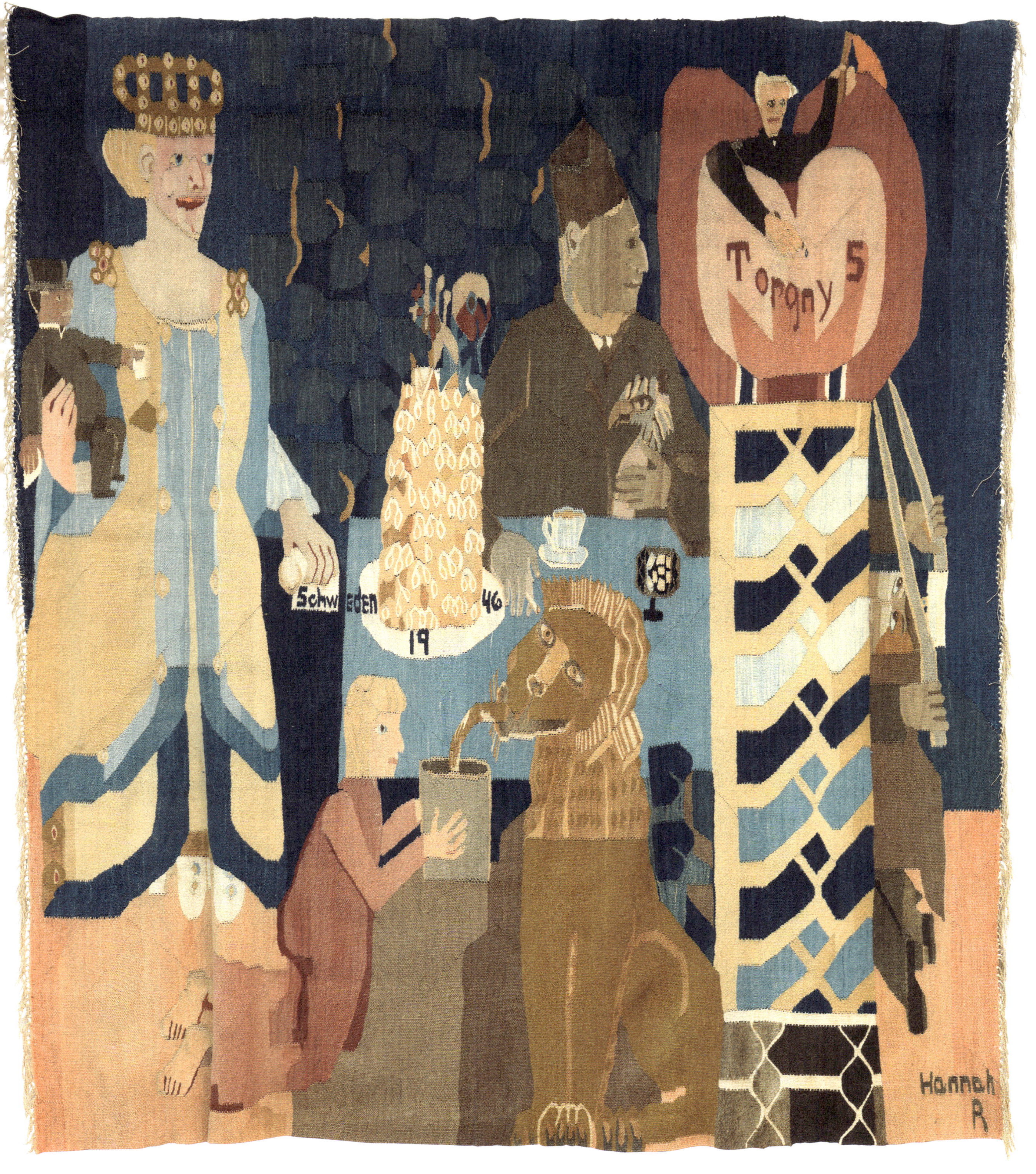
Torgny
5
Schweden
46
19
Hannah
R

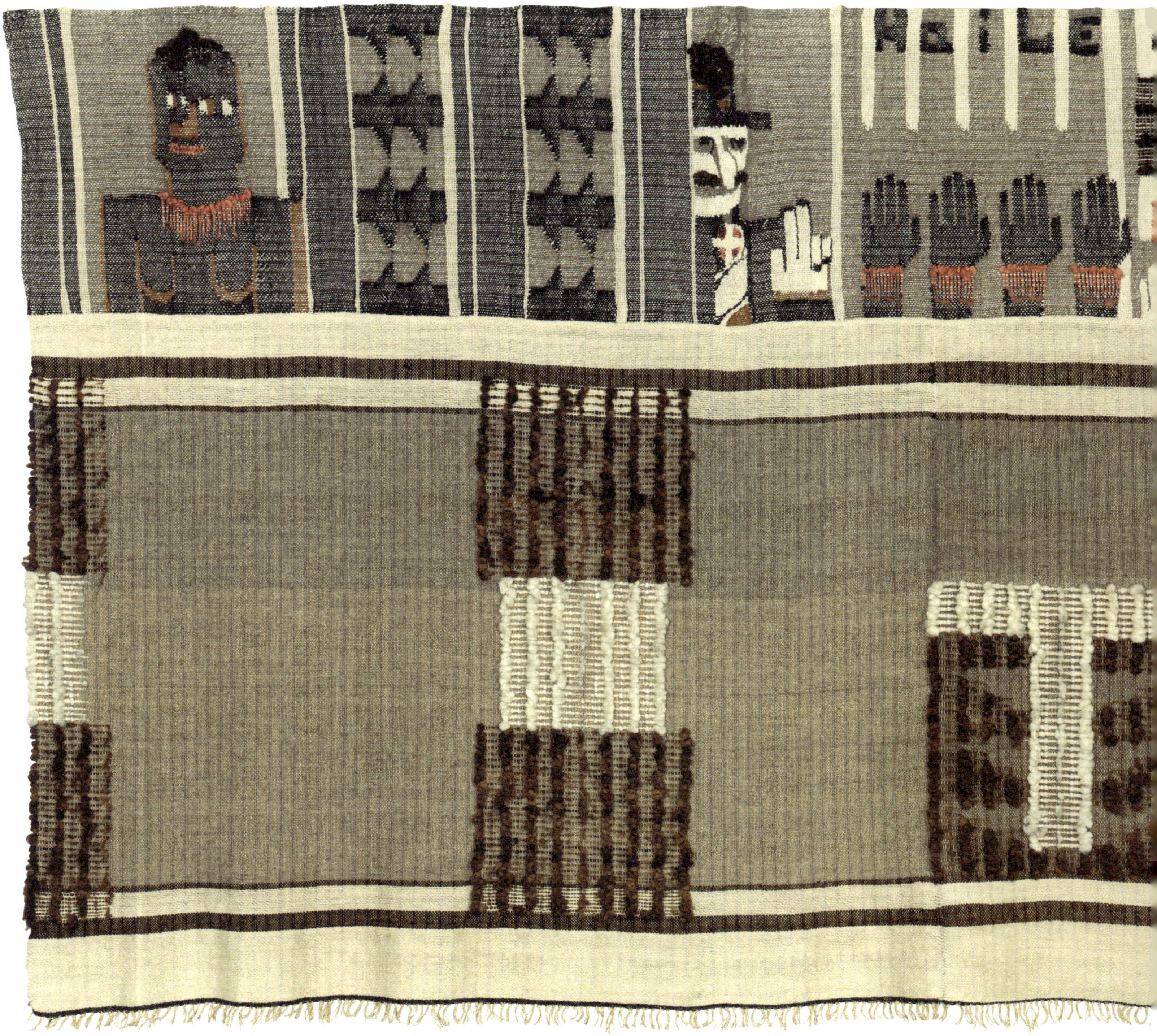

Etiopia (*Ethiopia*), 1935
Tapestry woven with pile in wool and linen, 160 × 380 cm

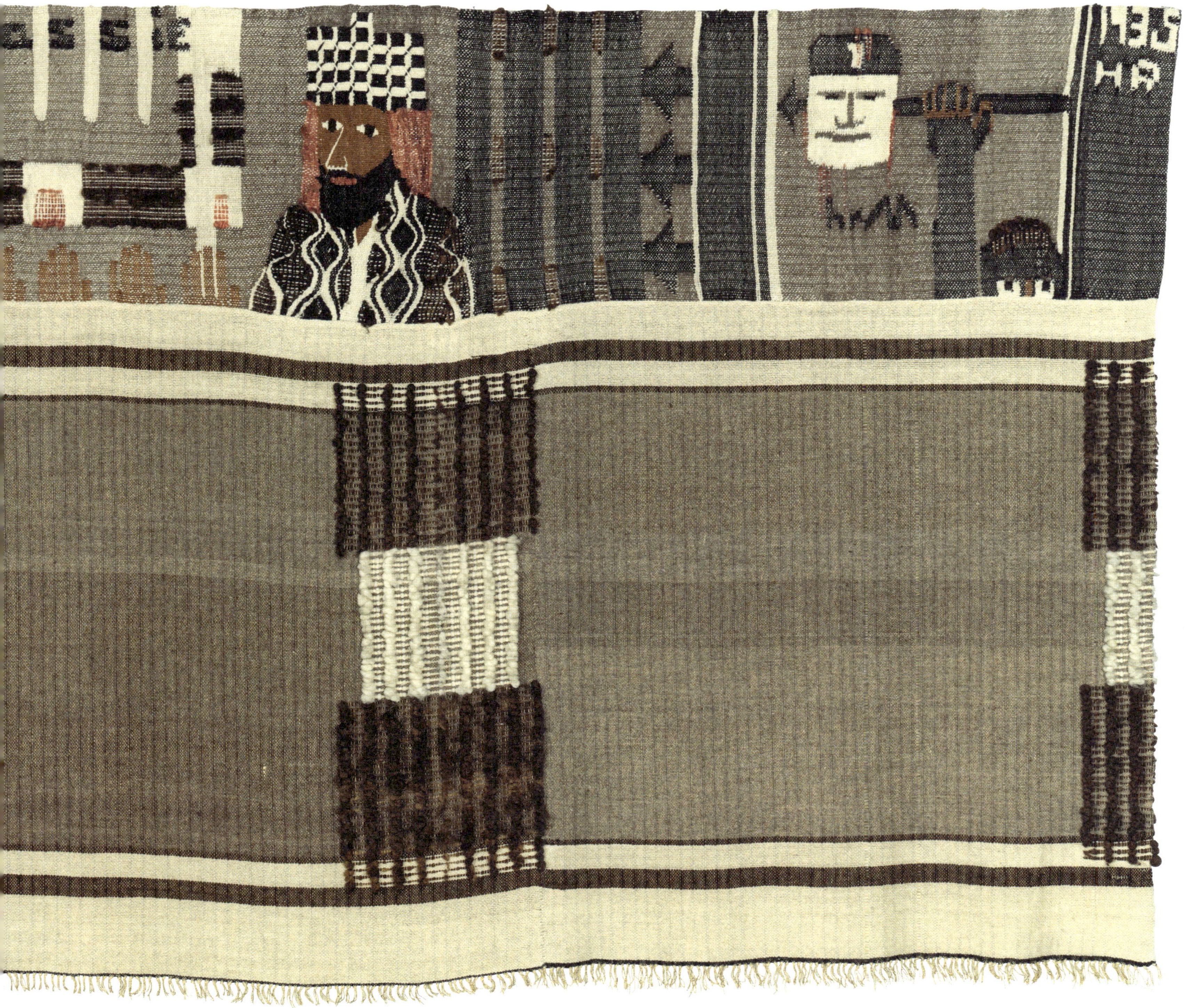

Etiopia (*Ethiopia*)
Detail

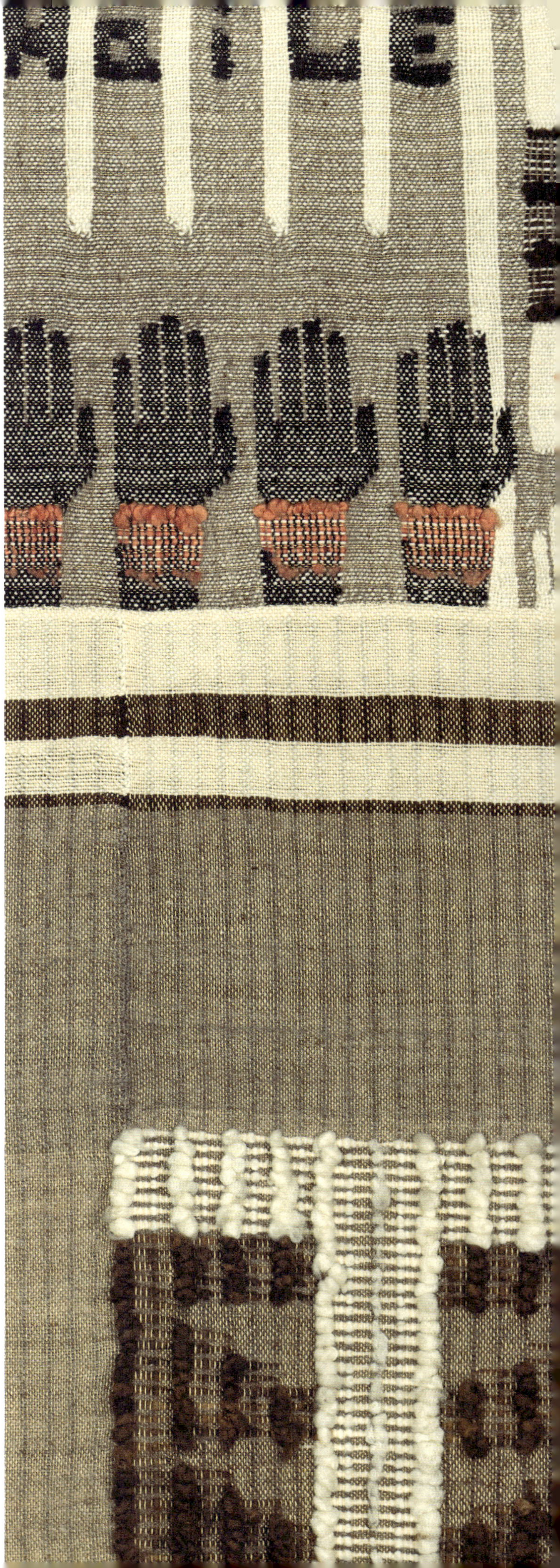

Hannah Ryggen was on the side of the communists at the beginning of the 1930s, but lost her faith in Russia when the country declared war on Finland in November 1939. However, she continued to believe in communism's basic tenets, such as the ideas of a classless society and fundamental equality, and she often described herself as a "red rebel." Even though she lived remotely in Ørlandet, she remained well-informed and had good access to newspapers and other channels of information. The news of Mussolini's invasion of Ethiopia reached her, therefore, with only a few days' delay.

Ethiopia is, to the greatest extent possible, an activist work. Ryggen's desire to express solidarity through art is fully realized here—by showing an Ethiopian driving a spear through Mussolini's head, as depicted in the right-hand corner.

Haile Selassie, Ethiopia's emperor, had requested economic and military aid from the League of Nations, but to no avail; the young nation was essentially left in the lurch. England and France wanted Mussolini on their side against Hitler and therefore submitted the proposal known as the Hoare-Laval Pact, which allowed Italy to annex Ethiopia. Ryggen fills the uppermost register with some of the central figures from these events. From left to right, we see an African woman, then most likely the French prime minister Pierre Laval, a series of hands in varying skin tones (representing the League of Nations), Haile Selassie, and lastly the Ethiopian warrior with the head of the fascist Mussolini.

The stage-like arrangement is interrupted by geometric patterns and constellations that correspond with the those of the lower register, which Ryggen wove separately. The two parts were then stitched together. This tapestry was exhibited at the Paris World's Fair, where it was censored. [See p. 28] Something similar occurred when she showed *Spania (La hora se approxima)* (*Spain (The Hour is Approaching)*, 1938), a work made in protest against General Franco's coup in Spain, at the Venice Biennale in 1964. She wrote to her Norwegian friend, Odd Hølaas: "The strange thing is that the arrow I lobbed in the Spain tapestry against Franco in 1938 has now hit its mark (the Spanish ambassador protested here at the foreign ministry over the insult at the Biennale). I fear for the tapestry, that they might do something to it." [1]

1 Letter to Odd Hølaas, 25.10.1964. Letter collection 902, National Library of Norway.

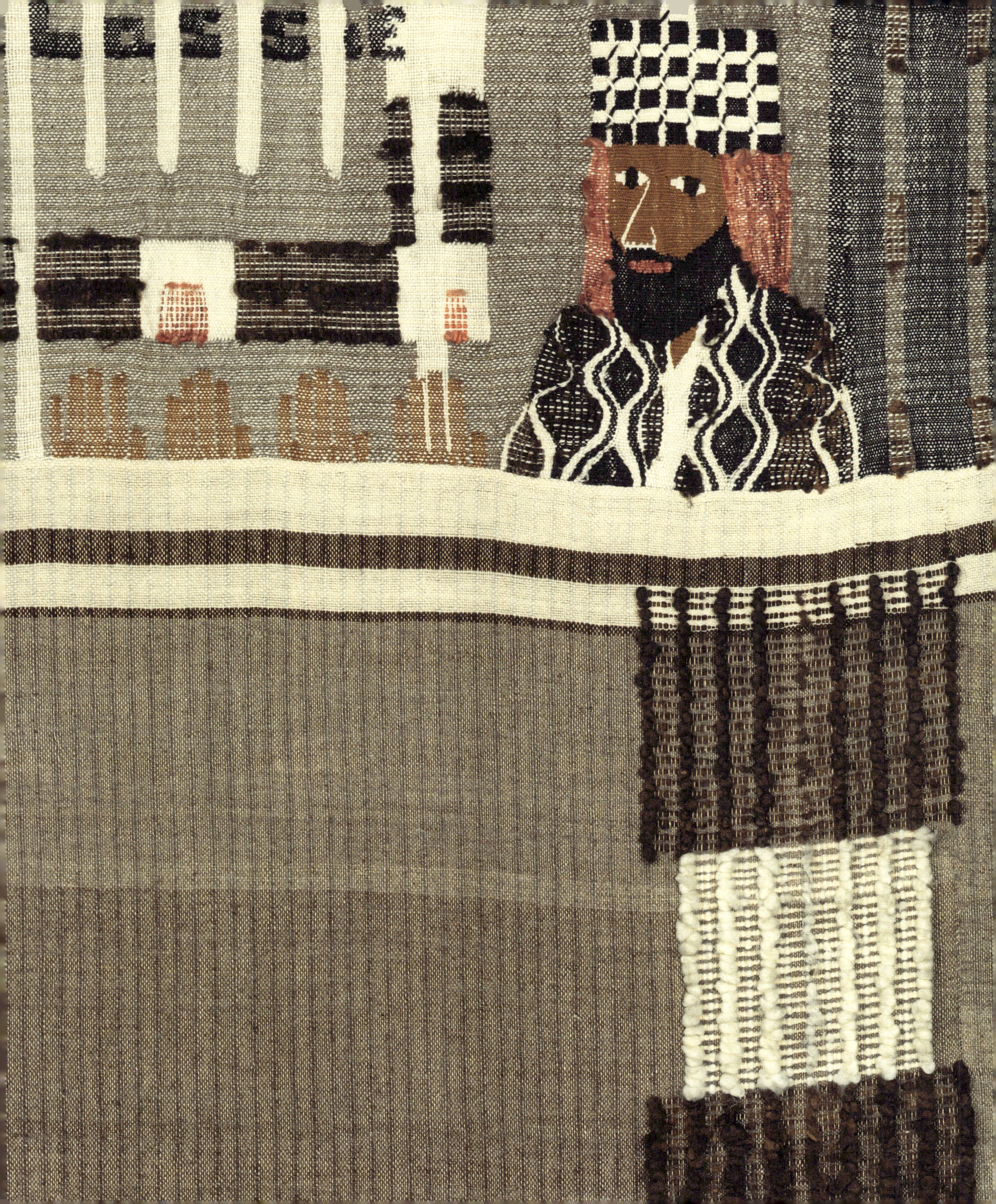
LASSIE

Sisyfos (*Sisyphus*), 1966
Tapestry woven in wool and linen with fringes, 96×66 cm

Sisyphus is a character from Greek mythology, a cunning figure who manages to fool death, not once but twice. The gods punish him severely for this: he is forced to roll a boulder up a steep hill, and each time he approaches the top, he loses his grip, and the rock rolls back down to the base of the hill. Sisyphus' destiny thus describes a state of perpetual labor, and the myth is frequently used in art and philosophy.

Ryggen's *Sisyphus* is a puzzling work, inasmuch as the traditional imagery of toiling with the rock is absent, and the portrait is that of an African (according to myth, Sisyphus was king of Corinth, in Greece). Nor is Ryggen's Sisyphus a worn-down or beaten man; rather, he gazes proudly at us while his hands grip two spiral-patterned rods (the spiral is a common symbol of eternity). Below the portrait are two forms that resemble empty hands, as well as a repetitive use of geometric patterns. The dominant colors in the tapestry are brown and blue, but there are also traces of light mauve, black, and white. Ryggen has inserted pile in several places, adding a sense of movement.

The figure in Sisyphus bears some resemblance to the Ghanaian socialist Kwame Nkrumah, who died in 1972. Nkrumah led the independence of the British colony, the Gold Coast, and was elected the first president of the new nation of Ghana. He was also a pioneer of pan-Africanism and an inspirational figure to both Malcolm X and Martin Luther King, Jr. In 1966 Nkrumah was deposed by a military coup and he lived the rest of his life in exile. The title *Sisyphus* may therefore refer to the eternal struggle for freedom and autonomy.

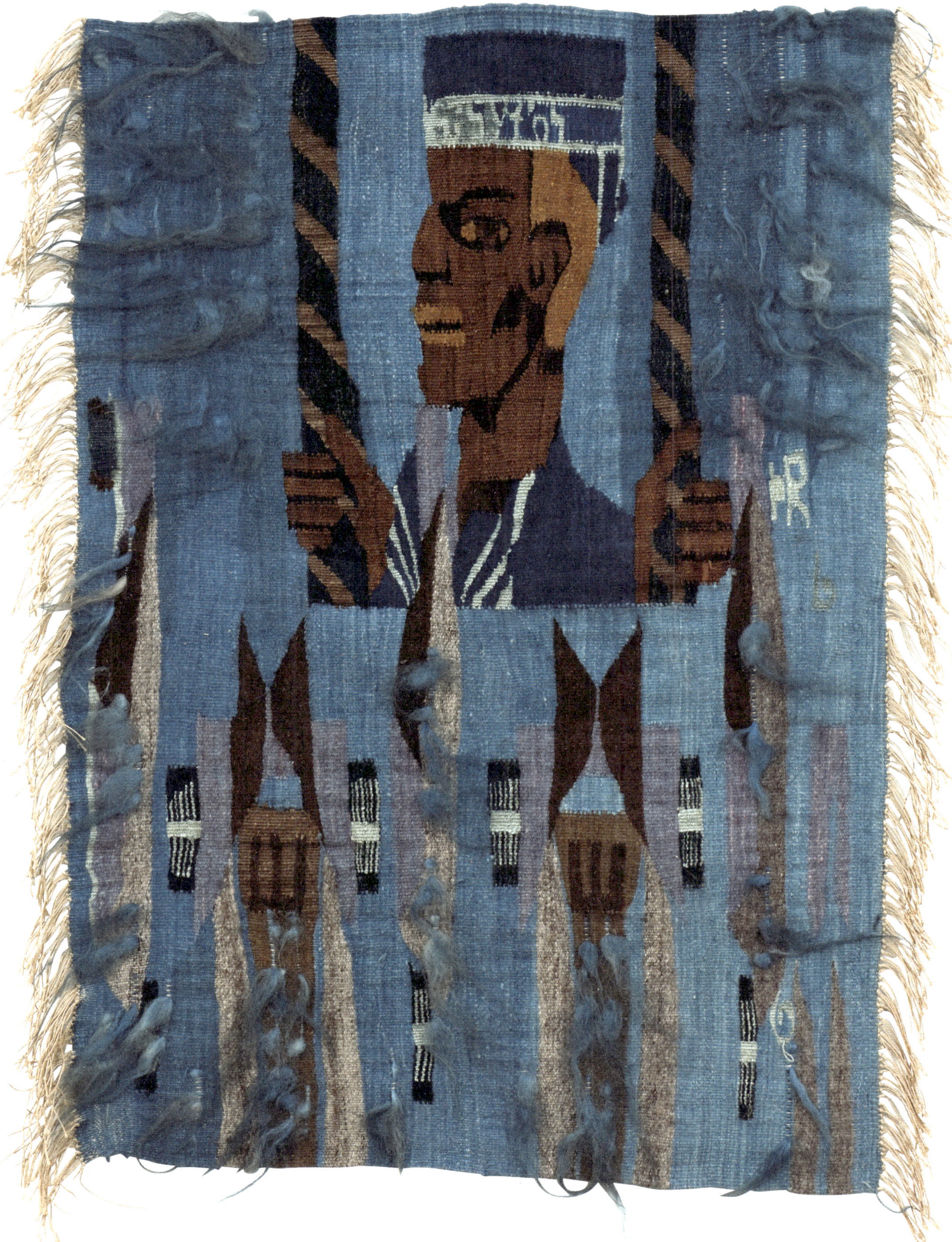

Jul Kvale, 1956
Tapestry woven in wool and linen,
200 × 190 cm

On Christmas Eve in 1955 the newspaper *Dagbladet* ran an interview with the civil servant and communist Jul Kvale. Kvale was openly opposed to arms production and was one of the first to declare his objection to NATO's armament plans. Ryggen read the interview and was moved by Kvale's solitary 'no' versus the majority's 'yes.' Weaving *Jul Kvale* became an act of solidarity that also made apparent her own opposition.

In this intense blue tapestry, the popular majority occupies the left side, creating three rows, with the middle one 'locked' in a column-like chain pattern, presumably meant to express consensus. The top of this column is crowned with the head of the German statesman Konrad Adenauer (1876–1967). Adenauer was also a vocal supporter of NATO and he believed that selected NATO countries (including Germany) ought to be "equipped in the event of an atomic war."

The alliance's military committee accepted this proposal in 1956.

To Adenauer's right is the Norwegian foreign minister Halvard Lange. Immediately after the war, Lange took an anti-military stance characterized by non-alignment, bridge-building and peaceful coexistence. But when the Cold War set in, he changed his position, and when Sweden declined to join a Scandinavian defence association during the period 1948/1949, he became a strong advocate for Norwegian membership in NATO.

In *Jul Kvale* Lange grips a sword, broken in several places, which bears the acronym "NATO." A pale yet confident Jul Kvale is depicted standing full-length on the right side of the work. He is holding the hand of a child who emerges from a varied blue background, while with his left hand he is unfolding a document out of the abstract pattern of the tapestry on which is written, "Jul Kvale. Nei Nei 1956 Hanna R" (*nei* is the Norwegian word for no).

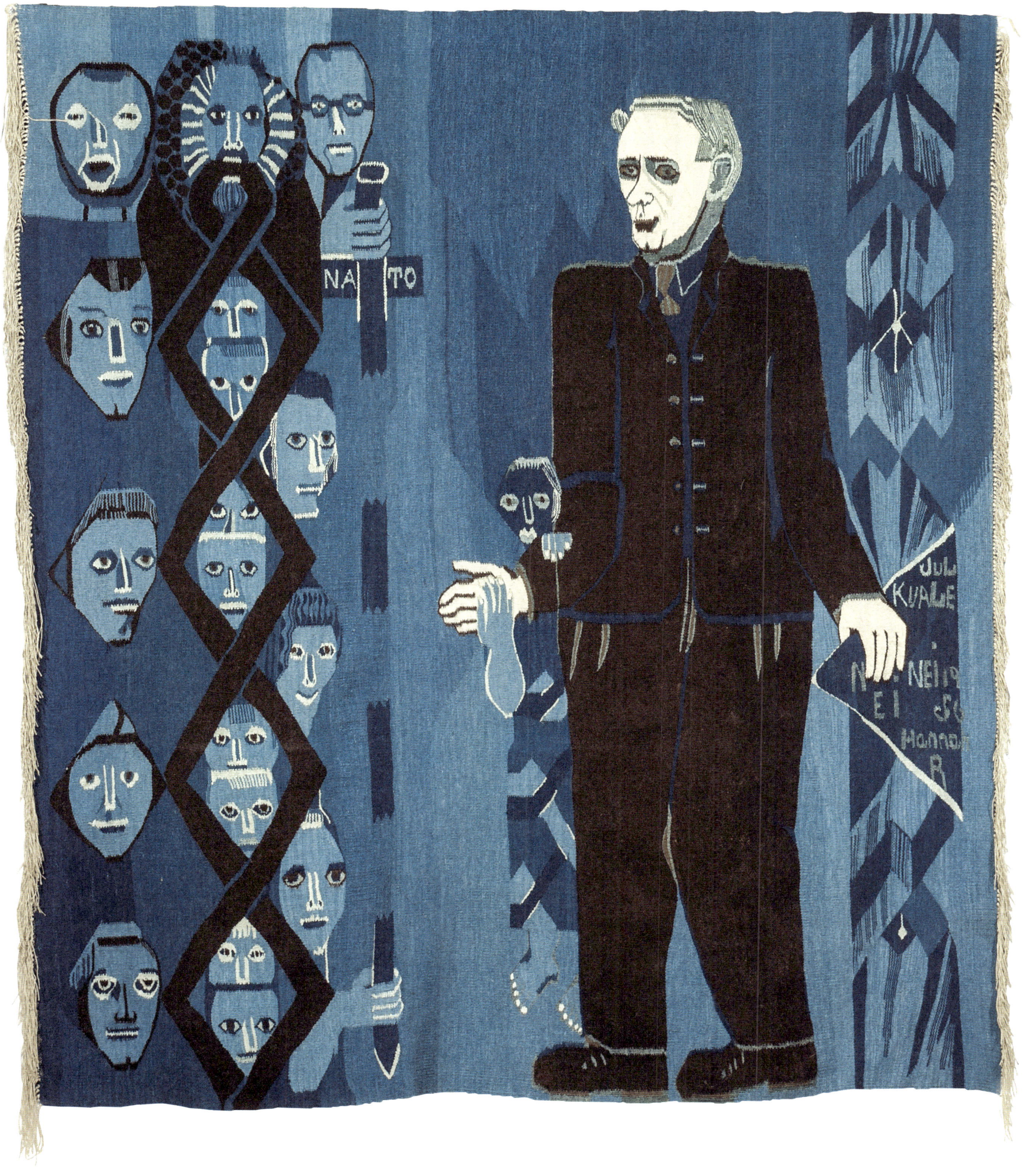
NA TO

Marie Luise Knott

In Life’s Shirt of Flame

"There was little I could do.
But without me the powerful
Sat more securely, or that was my hope."
Bertolt Brecht, *To those born after*, 1939

Hands, Truncheons, Spears

Art possesses a mysterious power, wrote Jacob Burckhardt in his lecture *Über erzählende Malerei* (On Narrative Painting): it can impart an eternal dimension to an event that the event itself does not possess, yet if it aligns itself too closely to everyday events, it can run the risk of becoming their servant.[1]

At the Paris World's Fair in 1937, Pablo Picasso's painting *Guernica* was on show in the pavilion of the Spanish Republic. A tapestry entitled *Etiopia* (*Ethiopia,* pp. 50–53) hung in the neighboring Norwegian pavilion. It was with this work, woven in protest against Mussolini's plans for a new Roman Empire, that the Swedish-Norwegian textile artist Hannah Ryggen from Ørlandet first came to the attention of an international audience—created as an intervention against the colonialism of fascist Italy, which barbarically attacked Ethiopia under the pretext of bringing it civilization.

Both Picasso's and Ryggen's works arose from protest, and addressed the questions of their time without subordinating their art to it. This freedom characterizes their oeuvre. But how did Ryggen—who lived in a small, remote settlement in the Norwegian district of Trondheim—come up in 1935 with the idea of creating a nearly four-meter-long tapestry in reaction to a war in distant Abyssinia? The deplorable war was covered in the newspapers at the time: the pride of the Ethiopian people, who had successfully defied all attempts at foreign domination in its nearly thousand-year-long history, the brutal tactics employed by Mussolini's troops, and the flight of the Ethiopian emperor Haile Selassie into exile in London, in his urgent search for global public support for resistance. Hannah Ryggen understood herself as part of this international public. Massacres, conquests, and gas warfare—this world was bleak. In response, Ryggen expressed herself in her own language: through the loom.

Ryggen took only a month to produce this large-format tapestry of 160 × 380 cm. The lower section is predominantly monochrome, and creates a beige-brown expanse with (in part plastically emphasized) vertical stripes that call to mind iron bars or columns. Above this expanse, in a friezelike section, are the protagonists of the conflict depicted with-out hierarchical differentiation: a proud Abyssinian woman, a white person taking an oath of allegiance to the war, Emperor Haile Selassie, and an Abyssinian anti-Mussolini-fighter. Unlike Picasso's *Guernica,* which focuses on the horror of aerial bombings, for example, or Francisco de Goya's *Desastres de la Guerra* (*Disasters of War*), Ryggen's *Ethiopia* does not depict the actual suffering of thousands of people, neither resistance fighters shot down, nor the victims of Mussolini's gas warfare. A static, nearly icon-like tranquility emanates from the work. Executed for the most part in bright, seemingly sun-bleached shades of brown, the composition's reds and whites stand out due to their sparing use. Both the lower expanse and the motifs woven into the middle of the upper frieze—hands, truncheons, spears—symbolize Ryggen's resolve. They graphically assert: "These things shall not pass." Our desire for a free world must prevail.

In a Europe with dramatically rising mass unemployment, economic crises, and growing fascism, such engagement was of paramount importance to those who would defend freedom. But weaving, due to its inherently

1 See Jacob Burckhardt, *Vorträge, 1844–1887,* commissioned by the Historical and Antiquarian Society of Basel, ed. Emil Dürr (Basel, 1918).

time-consuming nature, is not well suited as a reaction to daily news, nor for agitation or propaganda. The specific impact of Ryggen's art is how it bestows dignity on the oppressed. With *Ethiopia,* Ryggen began a whole series of large anti-fascist tapestries. *Drømmedød* (*Death of Dreams*) was created in 1936 in solidarity with Carl von Ossietzky, and *Spania (la hora se approxima)* (*Spain (The Hour is Approaching)*) in 1938 as a condemnation of Francisco Franco's civil war. One of her works, with the title *Schweden* (*Sweden,* 1946), addresses her home country's collaboration with the National Socialists, while another, entitled *Grini* (1945), deals with the detention of her husband, who was arrested by the National Socialists on the suspicion of being a communist in 1944. One of Ryggen's largest pieces, 175 × 420 cm, was created in 1943 and bears the title *6. oktober 1942* (*6 October 1942,* pp. 42–45). This date refers to one of the blackest days in Trondheim's history. After Norway was occupied, the city became a naval base of vital importance to the Nazis. A state of emergency was declared. Besides depicting Knut Hamsun and Vidkun Quisling's collaboration with the Nazi occupiers, the tapestry above all responds to the events of October 6, 1942 when, to spread terror among the civilians, the occupiers executed ten residents of Trondheim—in supposed "retaliation" for acts of sabotage in the region. Thus with her work, at this time of increasing radicalization and threat, Hannah Ryggen not only denounced tyranny and collaboration with the enemy: but her work's focus was a return to the responsibility and dignity of each individual in the fabric of the world.

On Letting Go—The Path of Freedom

Such artistic interventions were not something that came naturally to Ryggen. How did she develop her artistic independence? Born in Malmö in 1894, she was earning her living as an elementary school teacher when she began to study painting; but, when she had completed her fine arts studies, she gave up not only teaching, but painting as well. Perhaps she let go of painting in 1923, shortly after her trip to Dresden, because she had encountered the vanity of (mainly male-dominated) stylistic rivalries—impressive, expressive, abstract. Moreover, as is clear in biographies of women artists of the time, female painters had difficulties in attracting any notice at all. But perhaps Ryggen also let painting go because she sensed something missing in her own art. Thus, in the midst of modernism, where it seemed as if everything had already been discovered, she embarked on her own journey of discovery.

On the face of it, Ryggen's breaking free from painting was a departure into arts and crafts. In textile art at the time, artists (mostly male) usually provided designs on cardboard, which were then executed on the loom by women. Most tapestries conformed to specific stylistic conventions. But Ryggen was not looking to follow any artistic current or emulate the Old Masters and she was not part of a tapestry manufactory. Initially, she worked based on her own sketches, but she gradually left this division of labor; she did not want to design for others' hands nor did she want her hands to serve the designs in others' heads. She did not want to follow in anyone else's footsteps, be they renowned makers of medieval tapestries,

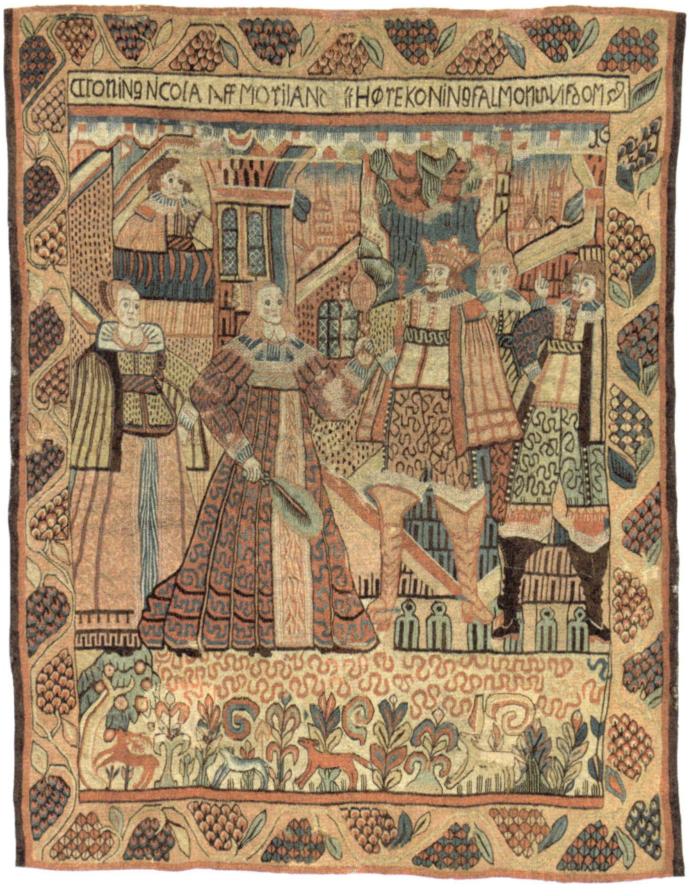

FIG. 1

Kong Salomo og dronningen av Saba (*King Salomo and the Queen of Saba*), approx. 1650–1750, Gobelin tapestry woven in wool and linen, 192×140 cm, The National Museum of Art, Architecture and Design, Oslo

FIG. 2

Frida Hansen, *Semper Vadentes*, 1905, tapestry, 288×360 cm, Stavanger kunstmuseum

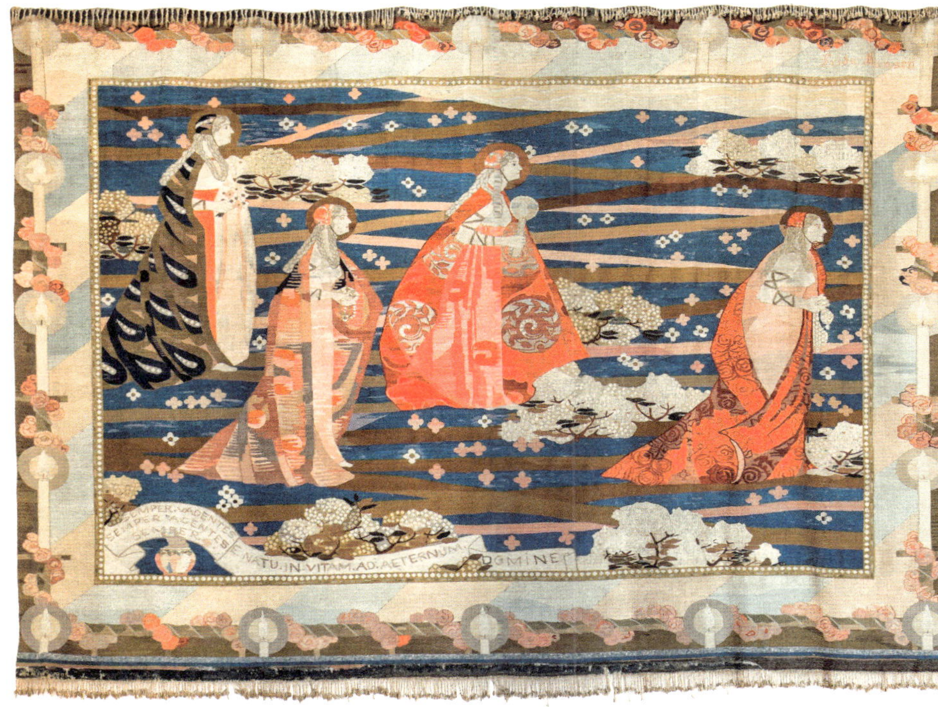

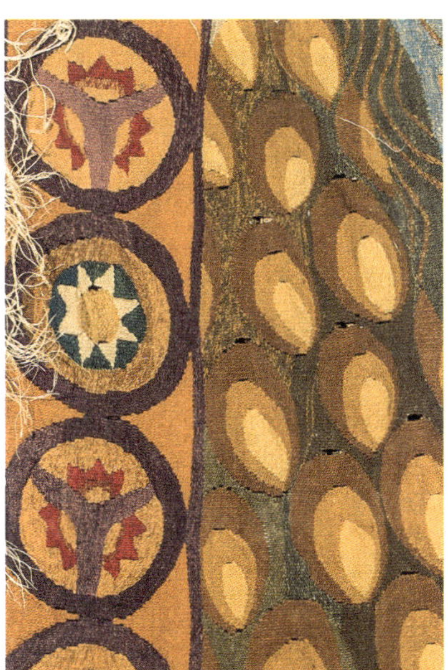

FIG. 3

Hannah Ryggen, *Synderinnen* (*The Sinner*), 1926, detail (see pp. 68/69)

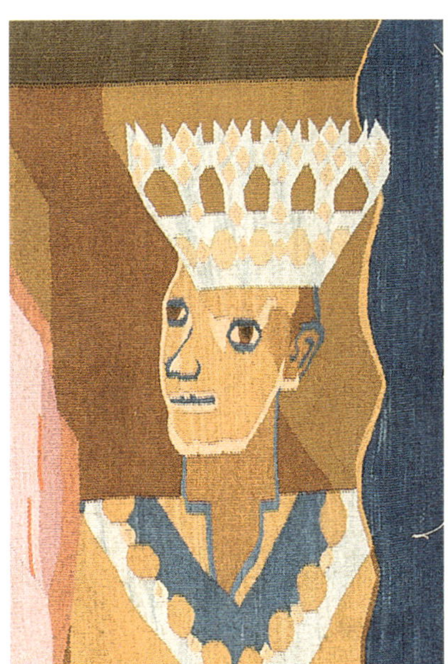

FIG. 4

Hannah Ryggen, *En fri* (*A Free One*), 1948, detail (p. 97)

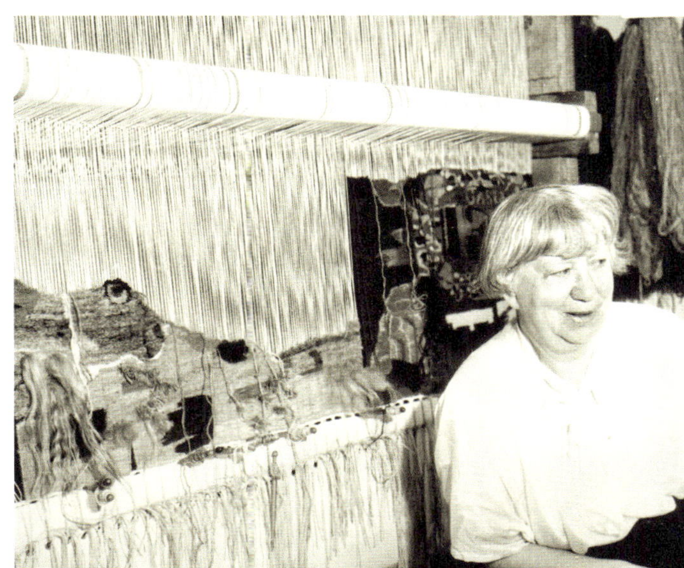

FIG. 5

Hannah Ryggen in front of the loom, undated

Norwegian artists such as Gerhard Munthe, whose textile works adhered to the traditional division of labor at the turn of the century, or Frida Hansen with her Art Nouveau tapestries. FIGS. 1, 2 Further, unlike the weavers of the Bauhaus such as Gunta Stölzl or Anni Albers, what interested Ryggen in tapestry was not design; she did not regard tapestries as an embodiment of theories about the relationship between art and life, nor, above all, as furnishings.

Ryggen was looking for something different, something of her own. To achieve this, she questioned the entire tradition of tapestry art, which looked like cottage-industry work in the industrial age (thus in an era of assembly lines, time clocks, photography, radio, and silent film, and the age of diverse aesthetic *isms*). Through her investigations, she found her way to an art that confronts the political questions of her time by means of both its content and its aesthetic. As her biographer Marit Paasche cites from one of Ryggen's letters, "I have red worker's blood in my veins."[2]

Hanna Jönsson (her maiden name) had immersed herself in the debates of contemporary art over many years during her studies in Sweden and Germany; but her tapestries do not reflect any of the artistic trends that were popular at the time. Her visual imagery was neither Symbolist, nor expressive, nor impressive; she combined figurative, ornamental, *and* abstract elements in her own distinctive way. FIGS. 3, 4 Warp and weft.

As we know, every artistic departure is a new beginning: to break new artistic ground, one works one's way through the history of art and simultaneously plunges into the unknown. Everything takes time: How do slit weaving, warp knitting, or color interlocking work? What techniques does one want to incorporate into one's own art in the first place?[3]

Studying tapestry from the Middle Ages heightens one's understanding of the importance of both artistic composition and visual imagery. In Ryggen's work, one senses the intensity of her examination, for instance, of the significance and effect of stylization in tapestries—with clavi, medallions, and vine ornaments.[4] She brought the riches of tapestry back into contemporary art and made it her visual medium *sui generis.*

Hannah Ryggen experimented and experimented. In this way, she developed the distinctiveness of her art. When one looks at the comprehensive list of her works,[5] one grasps the artist's long path to master this knowledge and then, after appropriating it, to free herself from it. Each step she took towards freedom and political expressiveness had to be undertaken; and she did.[6]

Especially in the realm of politically-engaged art, debates usually focus on content: on the "what" and less often on the "how." But in Ryggen's work, her political convictions are also reflected in her aesthetic choices, for example, her decision to exclusively use natural dyes. She collected plants and lichen and studied their particular properties; she explored traditional carpet-making techniques and adapted aspects that were relevant to her artwork. She extolled—as in medieval dye recipes—male urine as a mordant for intensifying colours. But not only that: She spun and dyed the yarn with her own hands. Ryggen's colors glowed. They glowed differently. From within. Her infinite range of blues are serene and haunting; the shades

2 Marit Paasche, *Hannah Ryggen: Threads of Defiance* (London: Thames & Hudson, 2019), p. 88.

3 Early on, historical, religious, or mythological motifs also frequently dominated: *Evas datter* (*Eve's Daughter,* 1922), *Nøkken* (*The Water Sprite,* 1923), *Dansen om gullkalven* (*The Dance around the Golden Calf,* 1930), *Synderinnen* (*The Sinner,* 1926), *Fortidsvepnet* (*Armed with the Past,* 1930), *Paris' dom* (*The Judgment of Paris,* 1933), etc.

4 See, for instance, the tapestry *Kunstens tre* (*Hierarchy of Art,* 1931, Paasche 2019, *Hannah Ryggen*) or *Mors hjerte* (*Mother's Heart,* 1947, pp. 80–83).

5 Paasche 2019, *Hannah Ryggen,* pp. 248–64.

6 As can be seen, for instance, in the development of *Fiske ved gjeldens hav* (*Fishing in the Sea of Debt,* pp. 34/35) from 1938 until *Vi lever på en stjerne* (*We Are Living on a Star,* pp. 110–113).

of red are dazzling and sharp, seductive to the eye. Further, her tapestries are like real life. No thread was the same as the other, no line like the next.

Each of Ryggen's tapestries was an act of protest: be it against the cataclysms of fascism, the fragmentation of life in modern times, or the thorough industrialization of all human relationships, which divided what had been understood as the integrity of the *individuum.* Through her choice of means, her works protested against the progressive disunity of the present—an act of resistance against division of labor, alienation, and exploitation.[7]

Tapestries have a concrete tactile presence, similar to physical events.[8] They endure. Even the most elaborate pieces bear the memory of nomadic life within them, of the fact that carpets and tapestries were first objects of everyday use, and as such, they might be considered anti-elitist.

Unlike in painting, with weaving nothing can be quickly painted over, nor simply removed. The surface is slowly built up, color field by color field. FIG. 5 From every failed attempt, and there must have been many at the beginning, Ryggen obtained new insights and new skills. It was an arduous path until she mastered the fundamentals of these techniques in such a way that her head and hands were no longer preoccupied with such questions.

As Ryggen developed professionally, and gave up working from designs or sketches, she was open to artistic inspiration while in the process of creating. Thus, she made the loom into a "brush," as she termed it.

Making Visible

The Latin word *textura,* meaning texture, is at the origin of the words textile and text. Ryggen made *textile* into text—her *own* text. On the loom, warp follows warp, woof follows woof—a row upon row of solidarity, which the artist further compacted with a comb after every weft. The warp, generally of linen, established the background, while the weft, generally of wool, provided the beauty: forms, colors, patterns, and compositions.

In work after work, Ryggen expanded her alphabet, her pictorial language—an iconography marked by its time. In her tapestries from the war period, dictators have crimson faces. The majority of the subordinated and the oppressed are increasingly represented by heads and hands—separated from the body of life. The individual, the *indivisible,* was threatened in such dark times.

When Hannah Ryggen moved to join her husband in Ørlandet in 1924, the couple owned very little: a few animals and some arable land. In reaction—also against her own hardships and constraints—she created the tapestry *Vi og våre dyr* (*Us and Our Animals*) in 1934, even prior to her anti-fascist work: a sweeping secular triptych of 187.5 × 491 cm (pp. 36/37). On the right is a man with the animals of the field: horses and birds; on the left is a woman with the animals of the household: geese, chickens, and cows; and in the center is the sacrificial animal: the roast. One immediately recognizes how the hands establish a rhythm across the work's expanse. In the center a women shields her view of the decapitated goose with one hand—the cruel reality that the picture nevertheless addresses. The work seems to ask: Do we raise animals only to slaughter them in the end?[9] And implicitly: Do we let others die? Indeed, do we murder them, so that we may live?

7 "Every man and woman, rich or poor, ought to be raised capable of two things: producing their own food and supporting themselves. ... no one should be above another. ... We are all flesh and blood, just the same." Paasche, *Hannah Ryggen,* p. 13.

8 The Bauhaus artist Otti Berger writes in her text "Stoffe im Raum" that understanding a cloth with the hands is as beautiful as sound is for the ear or color is for the eye, see e.g. Sabeth Buchmann and Rike Frank (eds.), *Textile Theorien der Moderne. Alois Riegl in der Kunstkritik* (Berlin: b-books, 2015), p. 159.

9 Paasche 2019, *Hannah Ryggen,* p. 65.

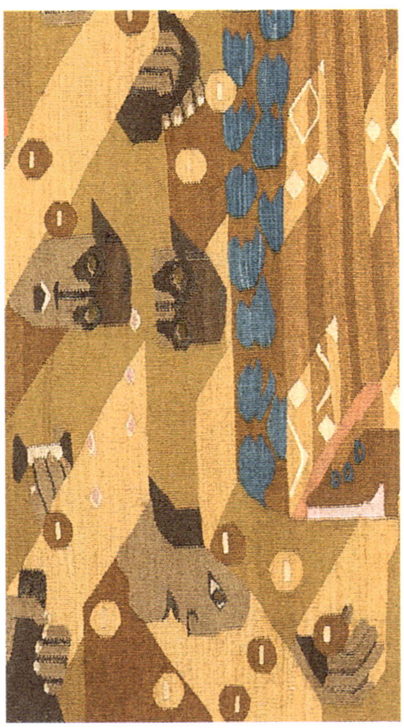

FIG. 6

Hannah Ryggen, *En fri* (*A Free One*), 1948, detail with view of the "gray ones" (see p. 97)

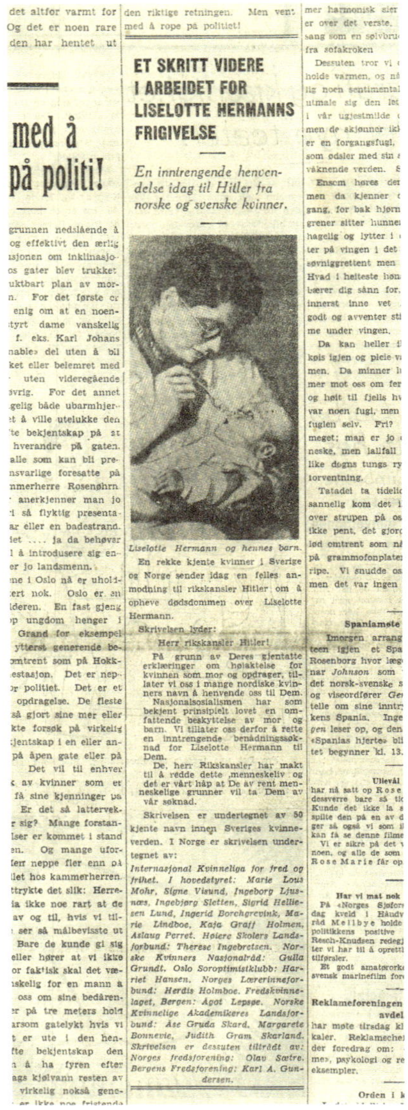

den riktige retningen. Men vent med å rope på politiet!

ET SKRITT VIDERE I ARBEIDET FOR LISELOTTE HERMANNS FRIGIVELSE

En inntrengende henvendelse idag til Hitler fra norske og svenske kvinner.

Liselotte Hermann og hennes barn.

En rekke kjente kvinner i Sverige og Norge sender idag en felles anmodning til rikskansler Hitler om å opheve dødsdommen over Liselotte Hermann.

Skrivelsen lyder:

Herr rikskansler Hitler!

På grunn av Deres gjentatte erklæringer om høiaktelse for kvinnen som mor og opdrager, tillater vi oss i mange nordiske kvinners navn å henvende oss til Dem.

Nasjonalsosialismen har som bekjent prinsipielt lovet en omfattende beskyttelse av mor og barn. Vi tillater oss derfor å rette en inntrengende benådningssøknad for Liselotte Hermann til Dem.

De, herr Rikskansler har makt til å redde dette menneskeliv og det er vårt håp at De av rent menneskelige grunner vil ta Dem av vår søknad.

Skrivelsen er undertegnet av 50 kjente navn innen Sveriges kvinneverden. I Norge er skrivelsen undertegnet av:

Internasjonal Kvinneliga for fred og frihet. I hovedstyret: Marie Lous Mohr, Signe Visund, Ingeborg Ljusnæs, Ingebjørg Sletten, Sigrid Helliesen Lund, Ingerid Borchgrevink, Marie Lindboe, Kaja Graff Holmen, Aslaug Perret. Høiere Skolers Landsforbund: Therese Ingebretsen. Norske Kvinners Nasjonalråd: Gulla Grundt. Oslo Soroptimistklubb: Harriet Hansen. Norges Lærerinneforbund: Herdis Holmboe. Fredskvinnelaget, Bergen: Agot Lepsøe. Norske Kvinnelige Akademikeres Landsforbund: Åse Gruda Skard, Margarete Bonnevie, Judith Gram Skarland. Skrivelsen er dessuten tiltrådt av: Norges fredsforening: Olav Sætre. Bergens Fredsforening: Karl A. Gundersen.

FIG. 7

Liselotte Herrmann with her son, front page of *Dagbladet*, March 5, 1938

FIG. 8

Hannah Ryggen, *Liselotte Herrmann halshuggen* (*Liselotte Herrmann Decapitated*), 1938

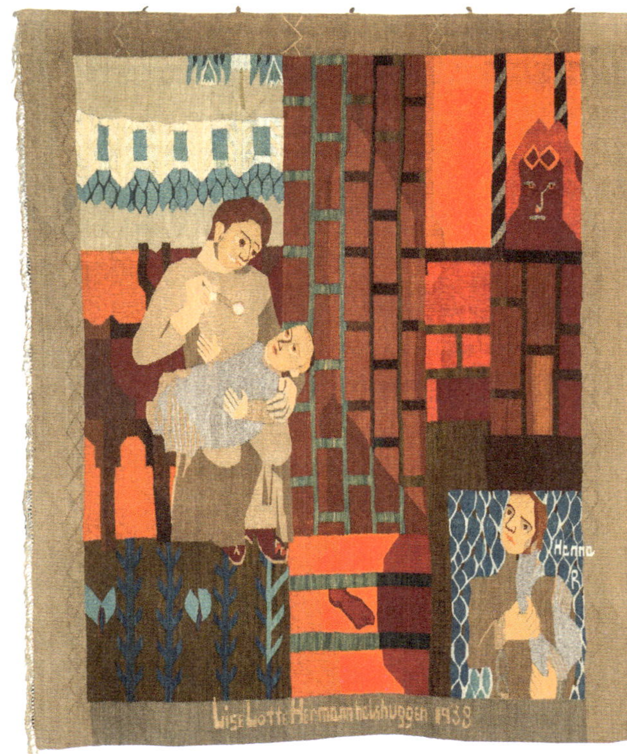

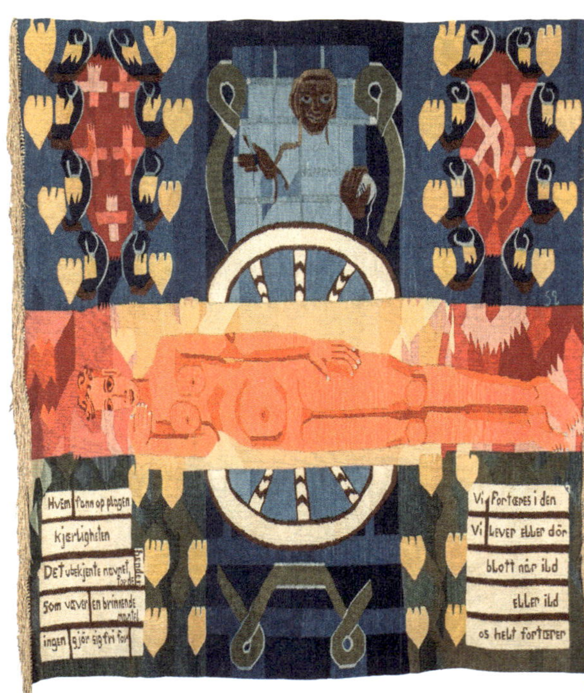

FIG. 9

Hannah Ryggen, *Dikt av T. S. Eliot* (*Poem by T. S. Eliot*), 1952

Ryggen takes up the motif of decapitation as a characteristic of tyranny in quite different ways in several tapestries.[10] This also appears in her 1948 social commentary from the postwar period, *En Fri* (*A Free One*)—whose title directly incorporates the question of individual freedom—where hands and heads are motifs that structure the picture.[11] They stand for the "gray ones," she said, who work "for us" day after day. FIG. 6 Next to them are those who cling to the blue pillars in their striving to ascend. But on the very right, beyond the bands, one recognizes a "gray one"—someone from below, "from the proletariat"—a free person. He could be seen as an artist who has broken free, Ryggen commented, only to add: "Though I don't believe so, for we are all bound in one way or another."[12]

Ryggen's art can be read as a grand undertaking to weave a picture of freedom. That said, despite how unequivocally she positioned herself politically, she did not align herself with any specific political movement or with any eschatological solutions; the works penetrate and transcend their time rather than, to once again recall Jacob Burckhardt, becoming its servant. This is what makes her art so important for us today. Her works raise the question: what is our truth, and how can art approach it and make visible something of the world's menacing New Order?

Liselotte Herrmann Decapitated

For her works, Ryggen repeatedly made use of images selected intuitively from newspapers, magazines, or well-known paintings. For remembrance. The pictures often reflect the visual vocabulary of her time: a black man holding a spear, Winston Churchill, an umbrella, Albert Einstein, a violin, and the Norwegian prime minister wearing a laurel wreath. In certain cases this simplification results in a caricatural quality, as with the case of the flying Hitler with oak leaves (an attribute of military orders) leaking from his rear in the tapestry *6 October 1942.*

Many of Ryggen's artworks also employ elements of traditional visual-pictorial languages and compositions, which, like the attributes, function as vehicles of remembrance. In one of her works, for example, one sees a picture of a young mother feeding her child. The words "Liselotte Herrmann halshuggen" are woven on a band at the bottom of the tapestry. This image was based on newspaper photos that had spread around the world as part of an international campaign of solidarity at the beginning of 1938. FIGS. 7, 8 Shortly after the scene captured in the photo, the young mother was imprisoned by the Gestapo in 1935 on spy allegations, interrogated, tortured, and finally sentenced to death in June 1937 in Stuttgart. Despite huge international protests, in which the women's organization of the Norwegian Labour party was also involved on a massive scale, Liselotte Herrmann was decapitated in Berlin Plötzensee on June 20, 1938.[13]

In terms of its composition, *Liselotte Herrmann halshuggen* (*Liselotte Hermann Decapitated,* 1938) is a classic tapestry: the earth-colored framing has an ornamental border on three sides and a band of text at the bottom. The subject's depiction recalls the portrayals of the lives of saints. Vibrant shades of red predominate; the wall is blood red, the jailer crimson, while the severed foot in the work's center symbolizes the subject's personal ordeal.

10 For example in *Morgengry* (*Dawn,* 1936), *Liselotte Herrmann halshuggen* (*Liselotte Herrmann Decapitated,* 1938), and *Freiheit* (*Freedom,* 1941).

11 The tapestry was woven from left to right. If one turns one's head in the direction in which it was woven, one recognizes the heads of the "gray ones" particularly well.

12 Paasche, *Hannah Ryggen,* p. 195.

13 Pictures of the courageous young communist with a bob, health service glasses, and a baby were circulated around the world—accompanied by copies of her journal entries about the steps in her son's development. Leaflets of solidarity were printed. In Norway, the women's wing of the Labours' party (50,000 members) collected signatures and also wrote a letter of protest. The justice department in Stuttgart must have received vast numbers of requests for amnesty from abroad at the time, since the Gestapo complained in a report to the Reich Minister of Justice on March 2, 1938: "The letters of protest have been piling up into mountains for months. Delegations pester authorities and party officials, to then publish mendacious reports after returning to their home country"; the processing of such letters required a "large number of personnel," they complained (see the information brochure *Lilo Herrmann – eine Stuttgarter Widerstandskämpferin,* published by the Hausgruppe des Linken Zentrums Lilo Herrmann, Stuttgart, 2012).

The communist woman is associated with life, with the blue of the sky and green of the earth. On the right, thrown over her shoulder as a symbol of her martyrdom, is the shirt of her child, which the Nazis—as reported in the international press after her decapitation—threw into her cell to try to break her in her final hours, and persuade her to betray her comrades.

Every community lives according to internally agreed upon rules—based on facts, on collective memory, as well as on courageous acts of individual action. In magazines and newspapers, photographs serve the dual purpose of evoking familiar subjects as well as presenting new, moving or shocking images of current events to the public. Magazines must stay in touch with the times and know how to address their audiences. They try to provoke empathy, outrage, sorrow, despair, pride or courageousness. By consciously working with well-known symbols, myths, and images from magazines, Ryggen not only integrated collective memory into her works, but played an active part in shaping it herself. Through such moments of remembrance and recognition, she created a community of artists and viewers.

Ryggen's works were not intended for living rooms. Even though she and her family were in need of money for many years, she did not want to sell her tapestries to private collectors. She wanted to have an impact on the public, her works were thus intended for the street, for schools, parks, museums, and public collections.[14] They were meant and created to instigate public debates.

"Consumed by Either Fire or Fire"

Ryggen understood the loom as a place where individuals, threatened by isolation could find their way back into the fabric of the world. To prevent the world from falling apart. It was necessary to use one's own head and hands again—to weave the world anew. Weft by weft.

In one of her most colorful tapestries, *Dikt av T. S. Eliot* (*Poem by T. S. Eliot*) from 1952, Ryggen introduced lines from Eliot's *Four Quartets;* they can be read as Ryggen's own artistic credo. FIG. 9 The tapestry itself is almost square, and the structure of the picture calls to mind traditional square compositions. At the work's top is the blue of the sky, at the bottom, the green and brown of the earth. Two women form the central axes: one of them, in fiery shades of orange and red, resembles a toppled sculpture; the second, framed by olive green, and light blue (vegetal) ornamentation, appears to spin yarn for the shirt of flame that appears in the poem's lines of the poem. On the left and right, stylized flames (half hand, half tongue) ascend into or descend from the sky. In the lower part, on either side of the tapestry, Ryggen cites lines from "Little Gidding," the last section of the *Four Quartets*—each of Eliot's quartets using one of the four natural elements as its warp. The fourth quartet is dedicated to the theme of fire, and also reflects Eliot's experience of the Blitz, the nights of bombing in London ("flames of incandescent terror"). It can be assumed that Ryggen translated the verses into Norwegian herself. The original passage is:

14 See the list of owners in the detailed compilation of works: Paasche 2019, *Hannah Ryggen*, pp. 248–64.

Who then devised the torment? Love.
Love is the unfamiliar name
Behind the hands that wove
The intolerable shirt of flame
Which human power cannot remove.
We only live, only suspire
Consumed by either fire or fire.[15]

Life's shirt of flames, woven by Love, consumes the living. Nevertheless one must travel the path of hope ("And all shall be well") again anew, as Eliot writes at the end of the same quartet. The ornamentation in Ryggen's tapestry is a visual transcription of some of the poet's images—the tongues of flame, a knot of fire, and the intertwining of fire and the rose. The "either" in the final cited line gives the stanza its inner stability—life is a commitment, a fire of hope that is constantly aware of the fire of death. We live and breathe, and cannot do otherwise, as both Eliot's lines and Ryggen's art affirm, dedicating ourselves to the flames of our time for life's sake—and transcending them through art.

The significance of Hannah Ryggen's work, now better understood with hindsight, is not limited to her protests against Mussolini's barbaric war, the Nazi murders in Trondheim, or the decapitation of Liselotte Herrmann. It is true that, thanks to Ryggen's artistic interventions, these events will be remembered somewhat longer, as Jacob Burkhardt did put it. But today it is clear that the factors previously discussed—Ryggens immersion in the history of textile art, her icon-like penetration of reality, and her elaboration of a completely independent (political) aesthetic—combine here to create an immensely powerful artistic vision. In today's darkening times, we need the inner freedom and "mysterious ability" (Burckhardt) found in Ryggen's art.

15 T. S. Eliot, *The Poems of T. S. Eliot,* vol. 1, *Collected and Uncollected Poems,* ed. Christopher Ricks and Jim McCue (London: Faber & Faber, 2015), p. 207.

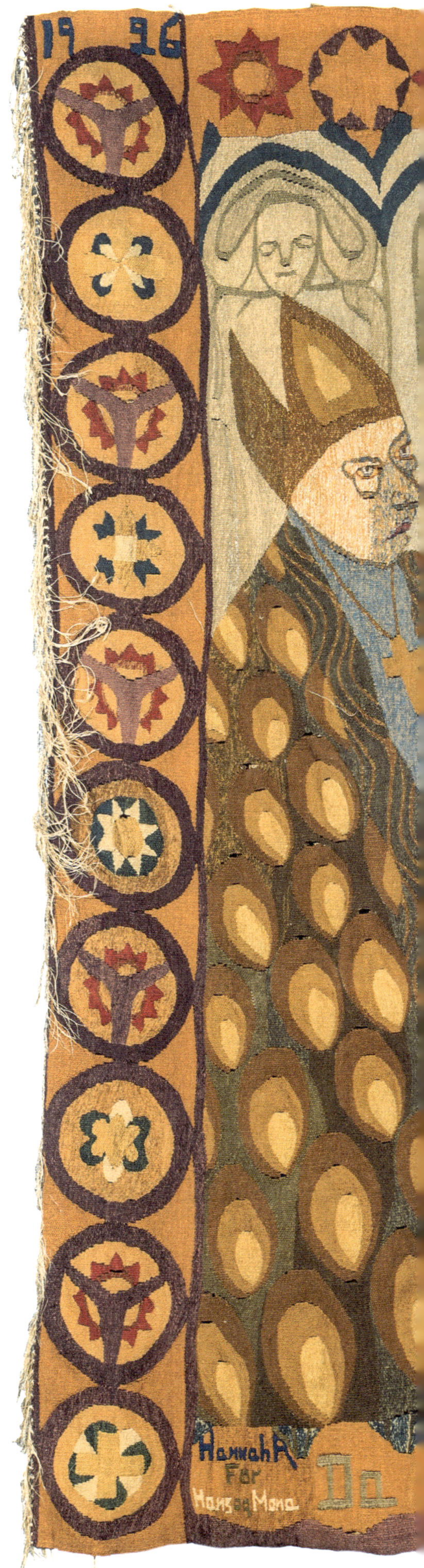

Synderinnen (*The Sinner*), 1926
Tapestry woven in wool and linen,
190 × 222 cm

The Sinner was Hannah Ryggen's first monumental tapestry. It is based on a passage in the Gospel of John (7:53–8:11), as is evident from the inscription woven along the bottom edge: *Da førte fariseerne og de skriftlerde til Ham en kvinde* (*Thus the scribes and the Pharisees brought to Him a woman*). Ryggen wove this tapestry using the Gobelin technique, which was utilized in Europe for large tapestries made from the 1500s onwards. The technique affords a nearly 1:1 transfer of a painted motif. The zig-zag technique utilized in folk art tapestries, on the other hand, does not lend itself so easily to creating a sense of three dimensions. Transitions between hues appear choppy, with visible edges, and it is more difficult to replicate the brushwork effects and modeling of the Gobelin technique. If we compare *The Sinner* with *Fiske ved gjeldens hav* (*Fishing in the Sea of Debt*, pp. 34/35), we can see how the different techniques result in different styles.

Hannah Ryggen exhibited *The Sinner* in Lund in 1926. This was her first exhibition of tapestries in Sweden, and it was not well received. She was criticized for both her choice of subject matter and technical execution. On September 18, 1926, the newspaper *Sydsvenska Dagbladet* wrote: "Mrs. Hannah Ryggen's textile art does not yet appear to have risen above the dilettante stage," and one week later, on September 25, the newspaper *Arbetet* printed the following: "Her sense of color is hardly cultivated and her attempts at naturalistic drawing and composition could scarcely be less successful. Even purely in terms of craftsmanship, she sins unabashedly against the most elementary requirements for pleasing textiles." Ryggen refused to cater to the expectation that women should make decorative, beautiful utilitarian objects. She continued with socially critical subject matter but never used the Gobelin technique again.

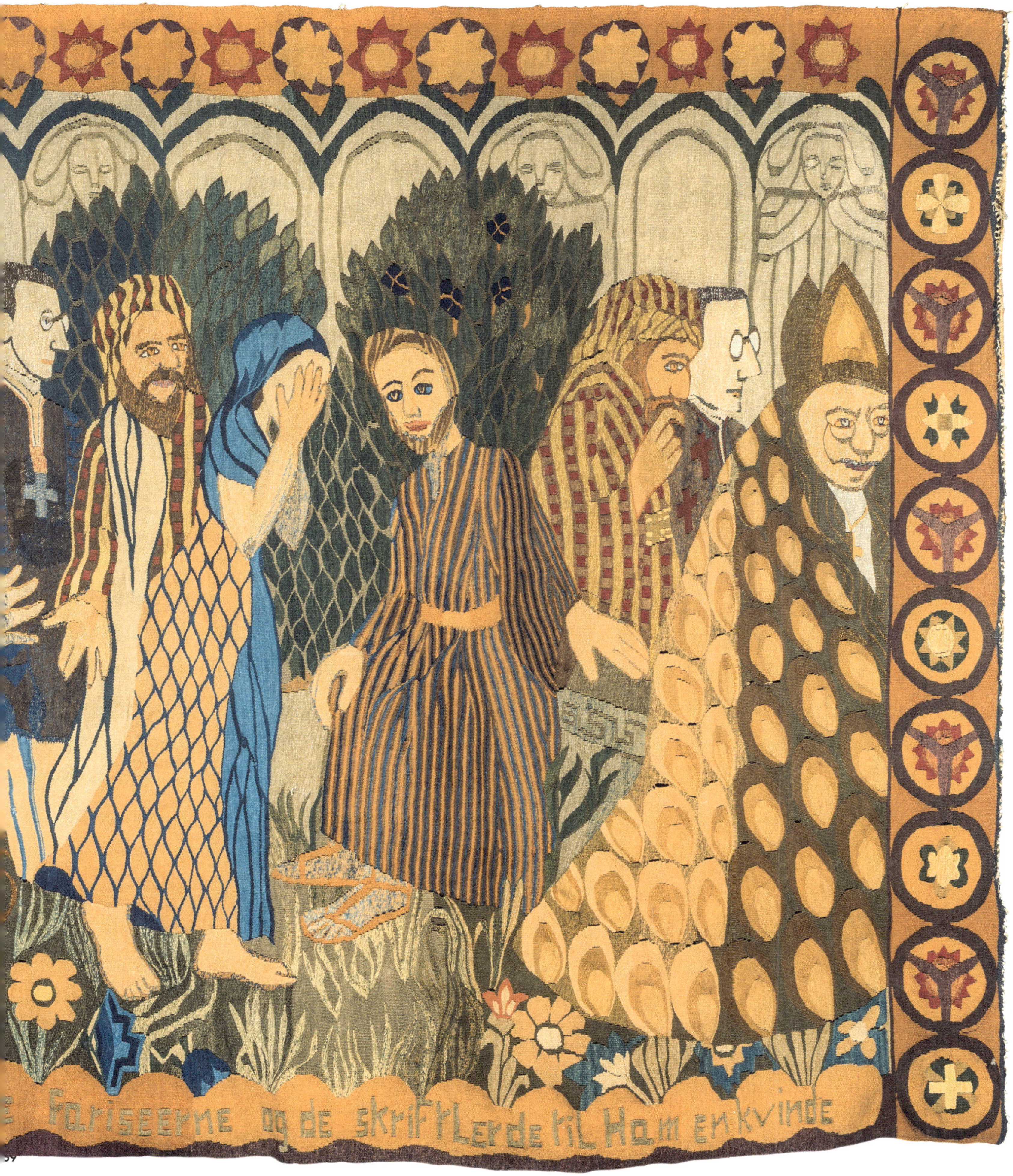
Fariseerne og de skriftlerde til Ham en kvinde

Gullammet Iselin (*The Golden Lamb Iselin*), 1935
Tapestry woven in wool and linen, 184×140 cm

The central figure in this tapestry is indisputably the woman standing in the middle of the space. She is a striking blonde in an elegant black gown, with high heels and red lipstick. She holds a cigarette in one hand, and the other hand is placed prominently on her hip so that the ring on her finger cannot go unnoticed. Behind her, to the left, sits a rumpled, somewhat older man, smoking, dressed in what appear to be pyjamas. He holds more cigarettes in his right hand. To the woman's right is a footstool on which she has tossed her jacket. In the area under the footstool, Ryggen has woven the title *Gullammet Iselin*. The setting is astonishingly theatrical. The space is framed by two drapes that are drawn back almost like a stage curtain, and there is no doubt that the woman is the one with the leading role. The floor is devised in a beautiful ornamental pattern (here Ryggen relied on her experience with applied arts), and the approach to color is serene compared to many of her other works.

The couple portrayed in this tapestry were people Ryggen had actually met. The man was an affluent shipping magnate from Oslo, and the woman a doctor's daughter from Trondheim. The pair met in 1934, when she was just nineteen and he was forty-seven, and married in 1935. That same year *The Golden Lamb Iselin* was exhibited at Kunstnerforbundet in Oslo, where it was purchased by the magnate—without Ryggen's knowledge. In 1939 Iselin committed suicide.

Precisely what Ryggen intended with this portrait is difficult to ascertain; there is very little information about it in her notes. The title, however, contains a double entendre: golden lambs were admired and often worshiped for their beauty. Beauty confers power. Yet lambs are also vulnerable, and the lamb has a long tradition as a sacrificial animal.

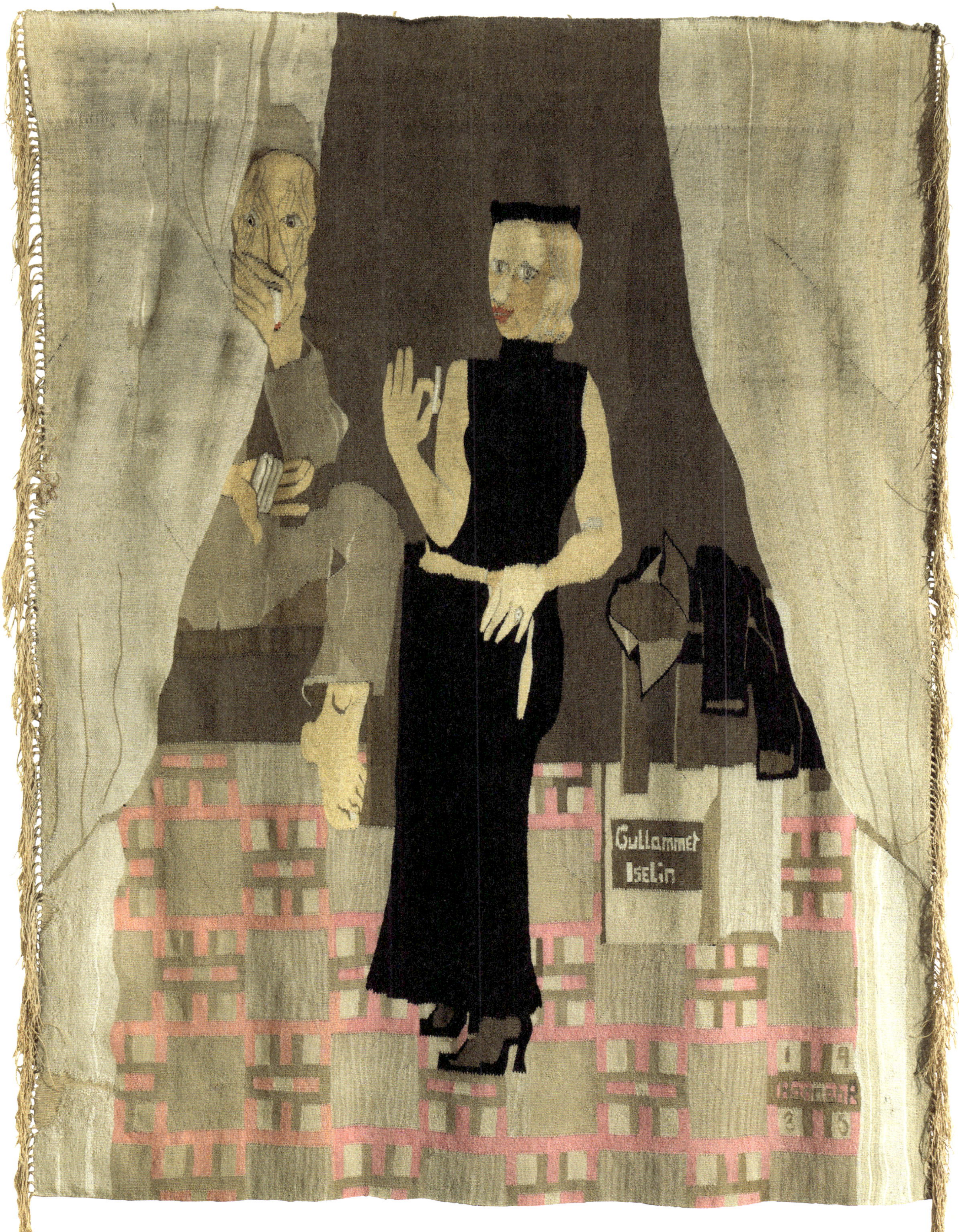
Gullammet
Iselin

Ugift mor (Unwed Mother), 1937
Tapestry woven in wool and linen, 190 × 375 cm

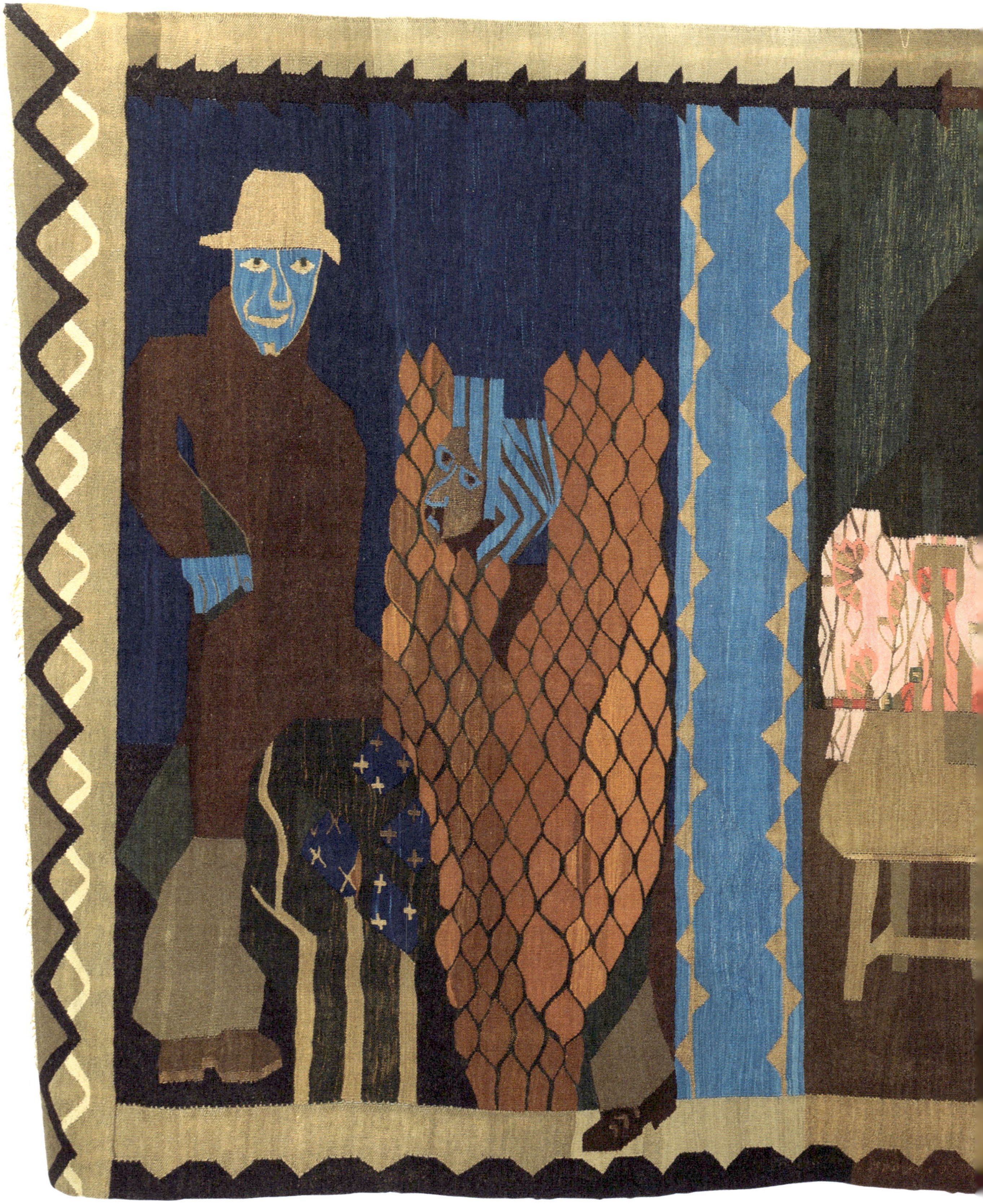

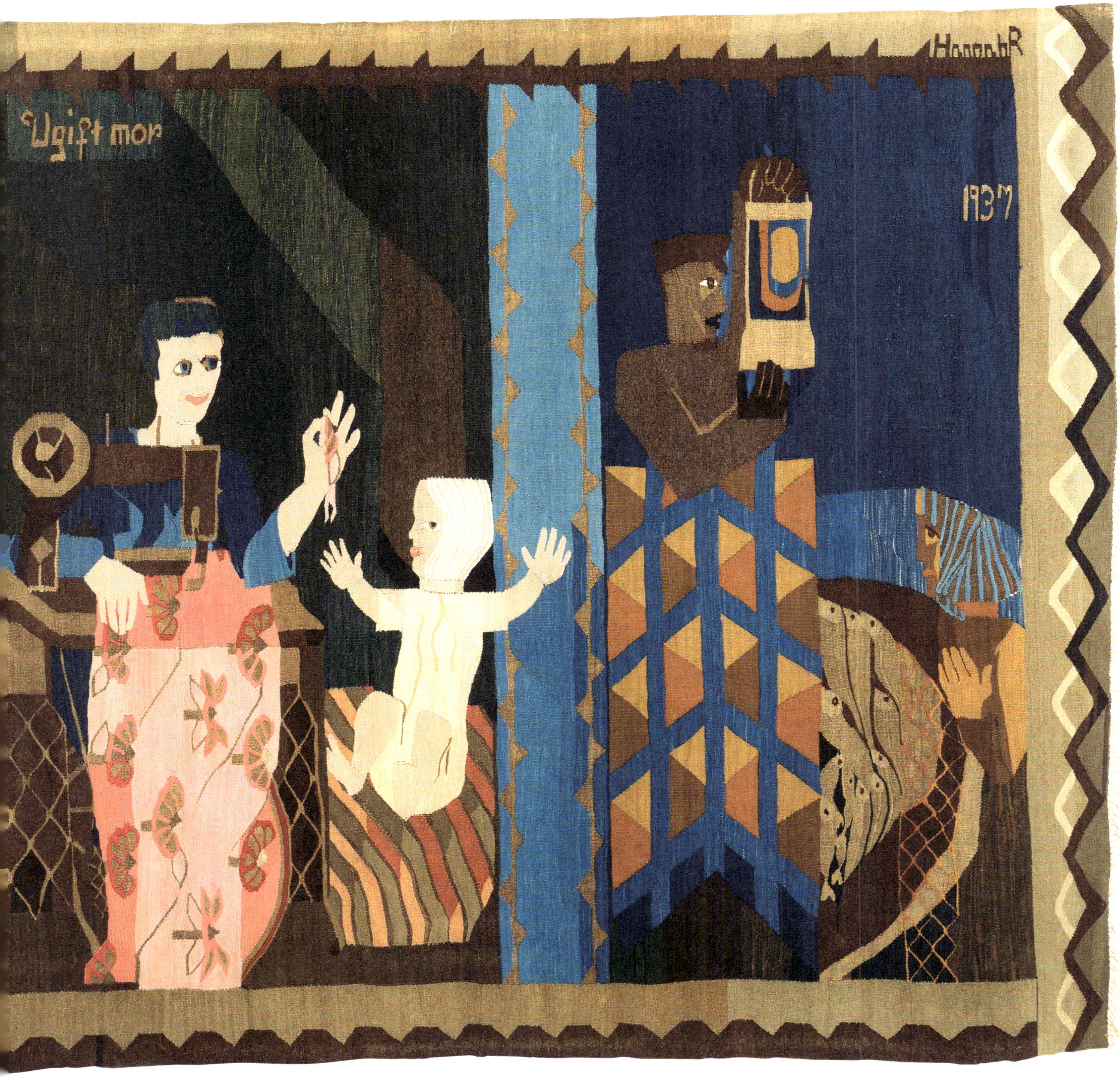
Ugift mor
1937

Ugift mor (*Unwed Mother*)
Detail

The subject of *Unwed Mother* is the status of women in society and the double standards that are applied to them: a theme that had previously been explored in Nordic naturalistic painting (see pp. 22–24). Ryggen depicts the motif in a three-part structure, not unlike a triptych. The same three-part construction recurs in *Us and Our Animals* (pp. 36/37) and *6 October 1942* (pp. 42–45), works whose dimensions were also larger than usual in her oeuvre. Motherhood fascinated Hannah Ryggen. As late as January 1954 she wrote in her journal: "A woman, good citizens—just think, so many creatures within such a being, one inside the other to infinity."[1]

A detailed description of this work can be found on p. 29.

1 Hannah Ryggen, journal entry, January 1954, NTNU University Library, Trondheim

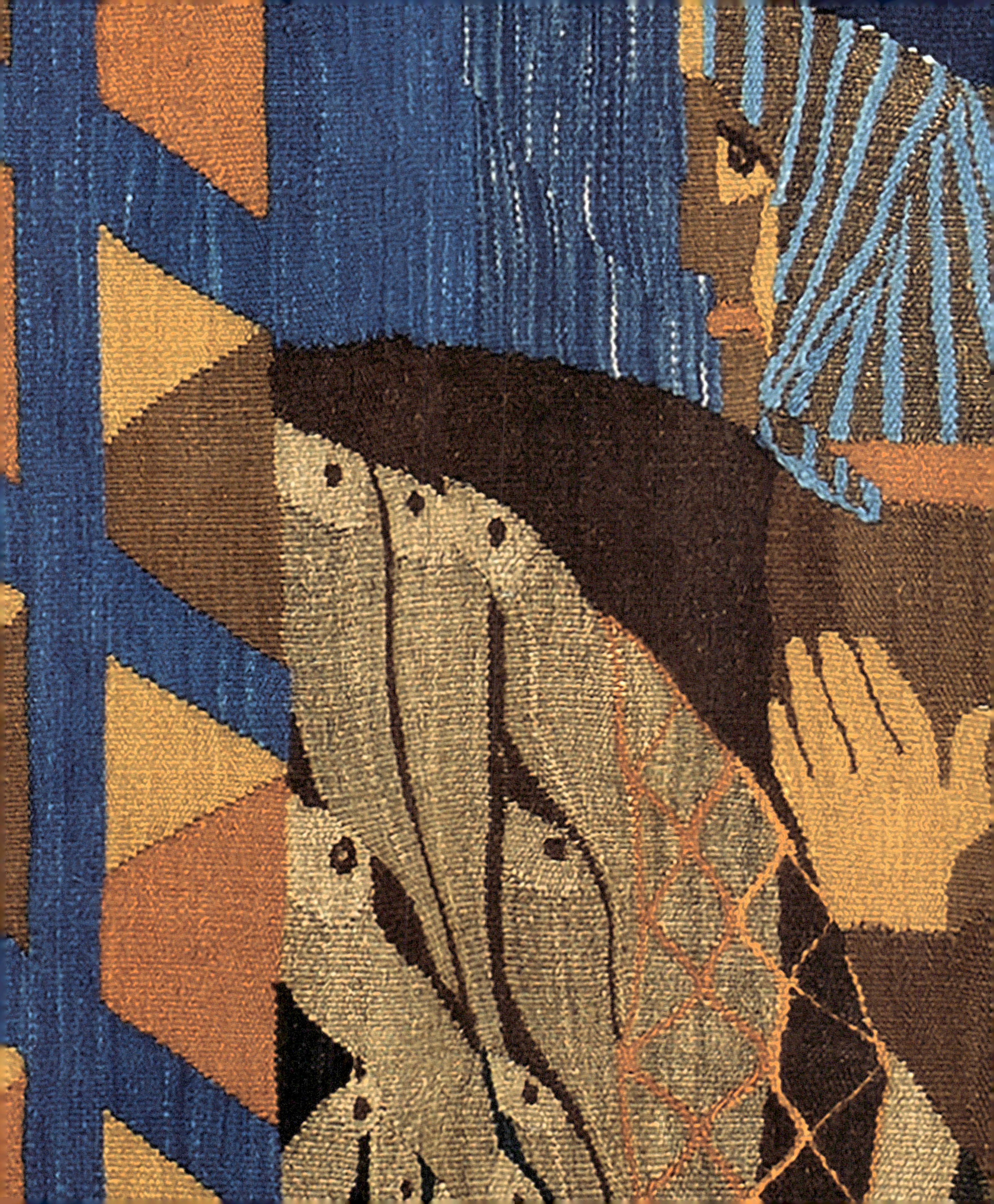

Henders bruk (*The Use of Hands*), 1949
Tapestry woven in wool and linen,
192.5 × 208.5 cm

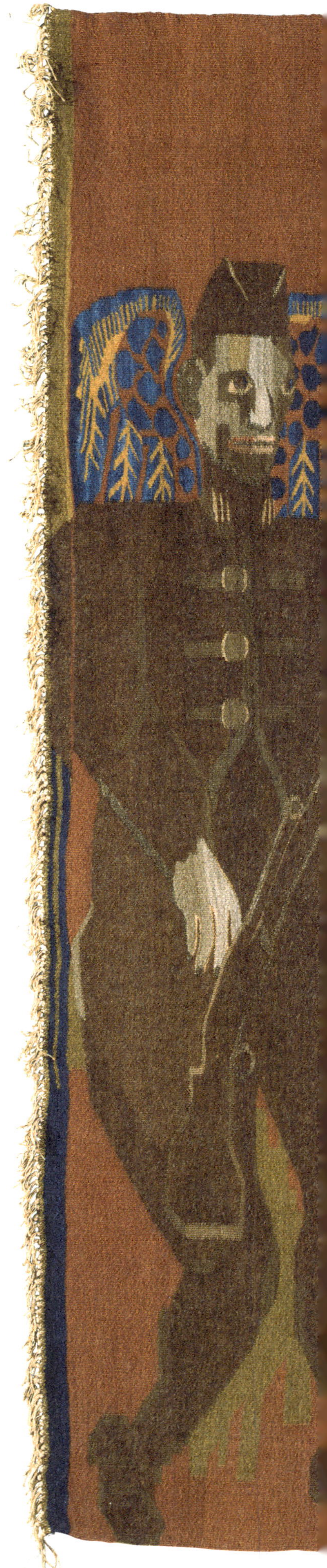

Both *The Use of Hands* and *Mors hjerte* (*Mother's Heart*, pp.80–83) are works that Hannah Ryggen began to conceive of while in Paris in 1946/47. In a journal entry from that time, she mused about the power that lies in hands—a central motif in her art—and their ability to leave their own legacy. This provides a glimpse of preliminary thoughts for *The Use of Hands*, but the idea did not surface in a work before a political issue arose: whether or not Norway should become a signatory to the North Atlantic Treaty. As a member country, Norway would be obliged to participate in the establishment of the military organization NATO, and Ryggen was greatly opposed to this. She finished *The Use of Hands* in March 1949 as a protest against NATO membership. It was in vain, however. Norway signed the treaty on April 4 that same year.

The Use of Hands thus refers to a particular event, but it is also an expression of visual lyricism, focusing on the power that lies in the hands. The tapestry's three main brown hues are complemented by three blues. These pairs, blue and brown, play on each other, and the dominant figure is the blue woman. She personifies the subconscious or the imagination, and, as in *Grini*, she is accompanied by horses. She is leading a soldier back home to the one he loves, while all around faces and rifle muzzles emerge from the brown (earthly) surfaces. In the lower right corner, under the reunited couple, we see a dying prisoner of war crossing himself in blood. The hands' potential lies in love, not war.

Ryggen's works were acknowledged as fine art, not handicraft, by her artist-peers and critics alike. Nevertheless, her work was mainly purchased by applied arts museums. It was not until 1953, in connection with a major solo exhibition she had at Kunstnernes Hus in Oslo, that the Nationalgalleriet (Norwegian National Gallery) purchased *The Use of Hands*. Ryggen viewed this purchase as institutional confirmation that she had arrived as an artist.

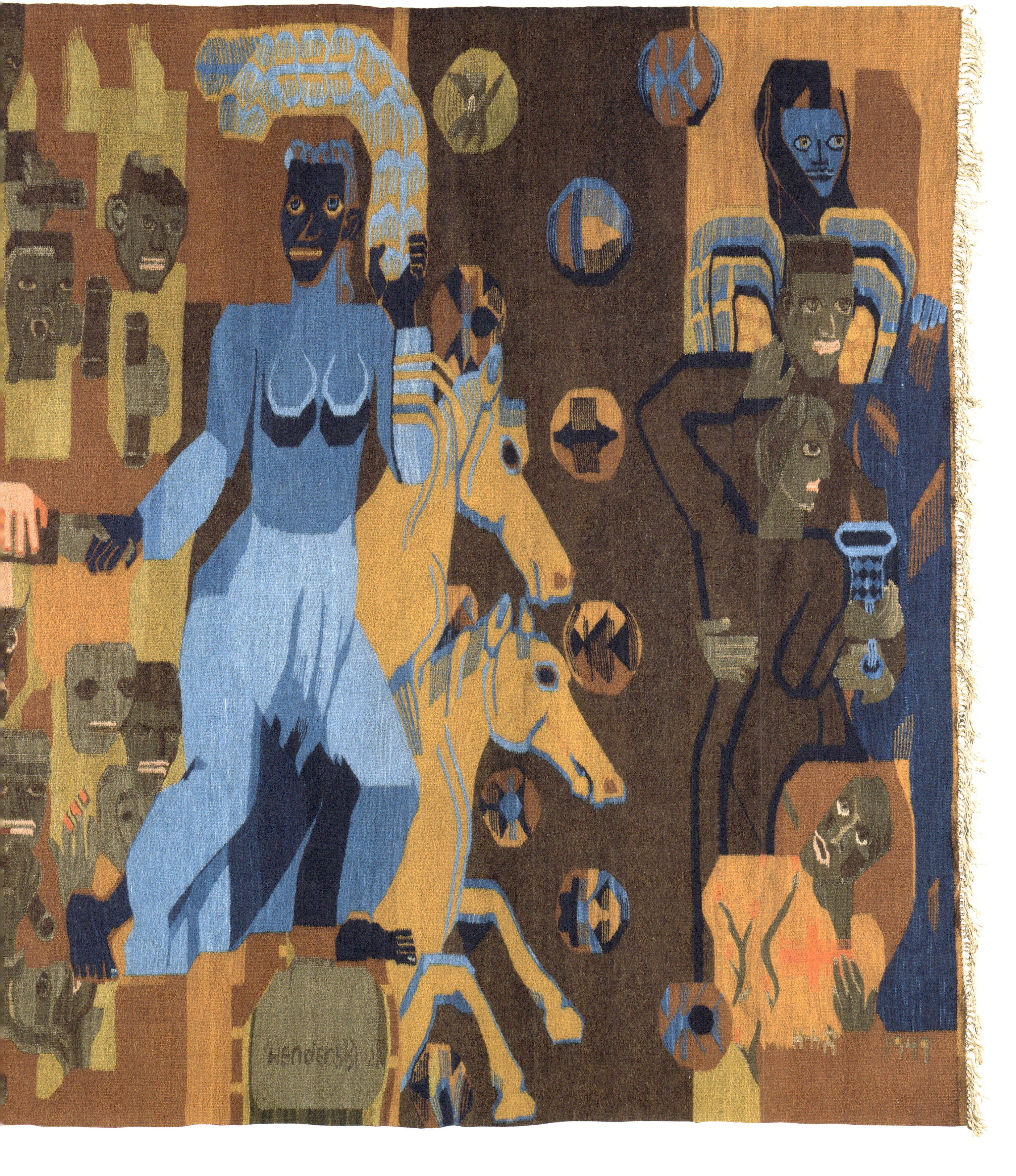

Atomsen (*Mr. Atom*), 1951
Tapestry woven in wool and linen,
170 × 190 cm

When the United States dropped the first atomic bombs over Hiroshima on August 6 and Nagasaki on August 9, 1945, the horrifying consequences were immediately apparent. The bombs decimated vast areas and killed hundreds of thousands of people. Many of those who survived suffered long-term injuries and serious after-effects. Hannah Ryggen was shocked to her core. The earth needed protection, not more destruction.

In *Mr. Atom* she personifies nuclear arms as a young and reckless man. He feeds a pig with his left hand, and around his head, like a halo, circulate particles or atoms. He is a ruler, with death and destruction waiting at his feet. The man and the woman on either side of him are as white as corpses, and the woman is holding a dead person's hand.

The entire area surrounding Mr. Atom and the deathly white couple is given a kind of grid-like structure, while the area below them is rendered through more organic forms. It is almost as though Ryggen believed that the realm of the dead was in the process of descending over the world. During the Cold War frequent nuclear weapons tests were carried out, and Ryggen experienced the threat as a genuine one.

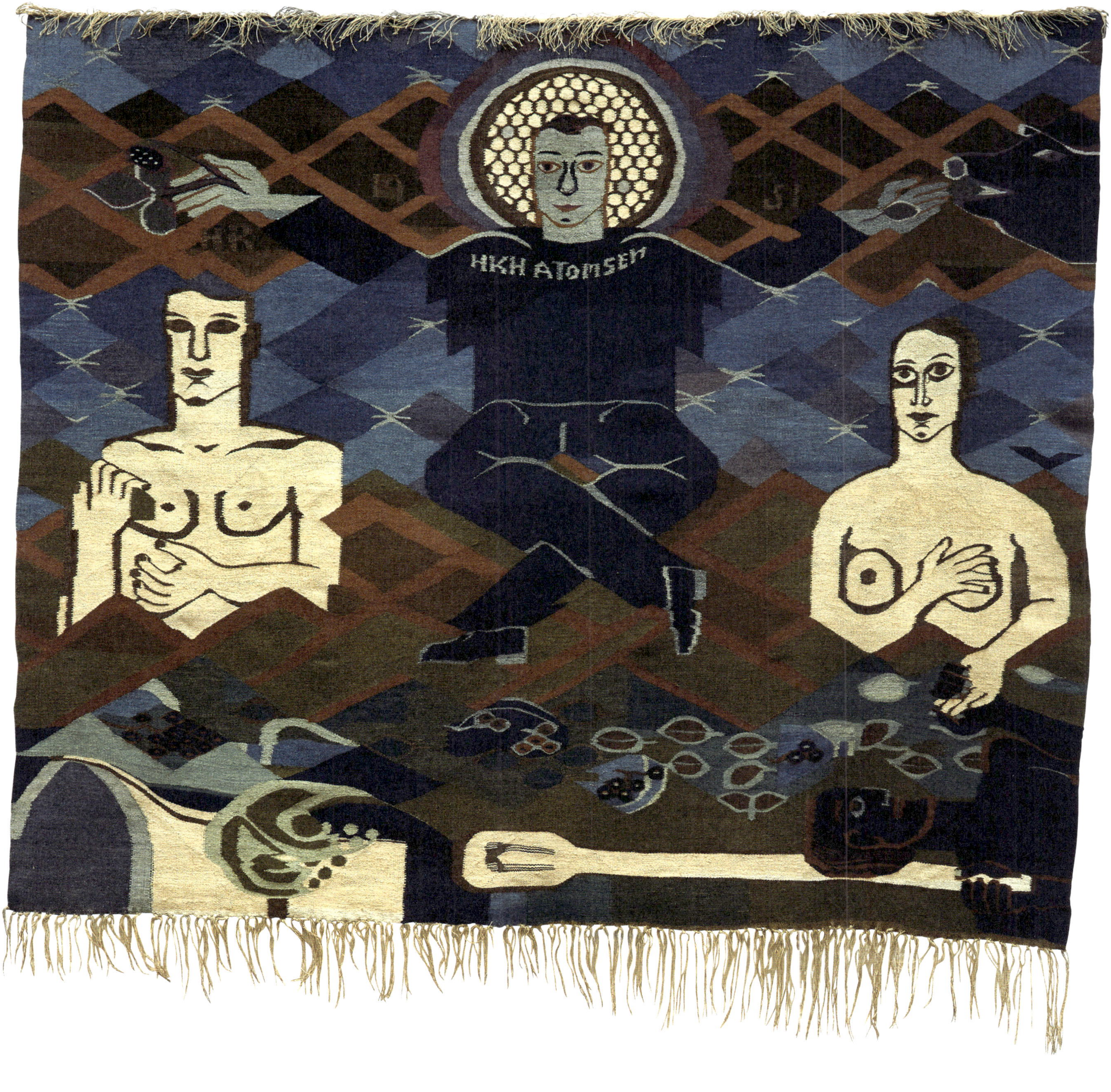
HKH ATOMSEN

Mors hjerte (*Mother's Heart*), 1947
Tapestry woven in wool and linen,
190×186 cm

Hannah Ryggen's relationship with her daughter, Mona, was a complicated one. Their communication was strained, and Mona generally preferred her father's company to her mother's. In early adolescence Mona experienced her first epileptic seizure. At that time, the Norwegian medical community's understanding of the condition was limited, and Mona was not adequately treated for many years. Hannah Ryggen wrote the following about this tapestry for an exhibition at Liljevalchs konsthall in 1948: "The mother's heart becomes so large. She herself disappears, the child comes first. Lightning strikes. The heart breaks. The mother is deeply down. Alone. Everyone is alone. The mother pulls herself together. She bears what she has to bear."[1]

The theme of the mother-daughter relationship had preoccupied Ryggen for some time. Her own mother died in 1930, and the relationship between them had not been simple, either, but it is possible Ryggen gained a more nuanced appreciation of the maternal role when she became a mother herself. *Mother's Heart* is one of the most powerful mother-child representations in the history of European art, and it is a pioneering work, made as early as 1947, long before feminism urged the inclusion of such subjects and themes in art. Ryggen lets the drama unfold, unconstrained, in every imaginable nuance of pink to red, and depicts how the tremendous love between mother and child can harbor both the deepest sorrow and the most profound joy.

1 From an article entitled "Kvinnokonst i Liljevalchs" (Women's Art at Liljevalchs) by Emmy Melin, published in the Swedish magazine *Vecko-Journalen*, October 23, 1948. The clipping was in Ryggen's possession, and was presumably sent to her by Swedish relatives. (The Nordic exhibition at Liljevalchs in 1948 where Hannah Ryggen showed eleven works had a separate exhibition room.) Ryggen herself wrote short texts for each work, and Melin quotes from Ryggen's own text for *Mother's Heart*.

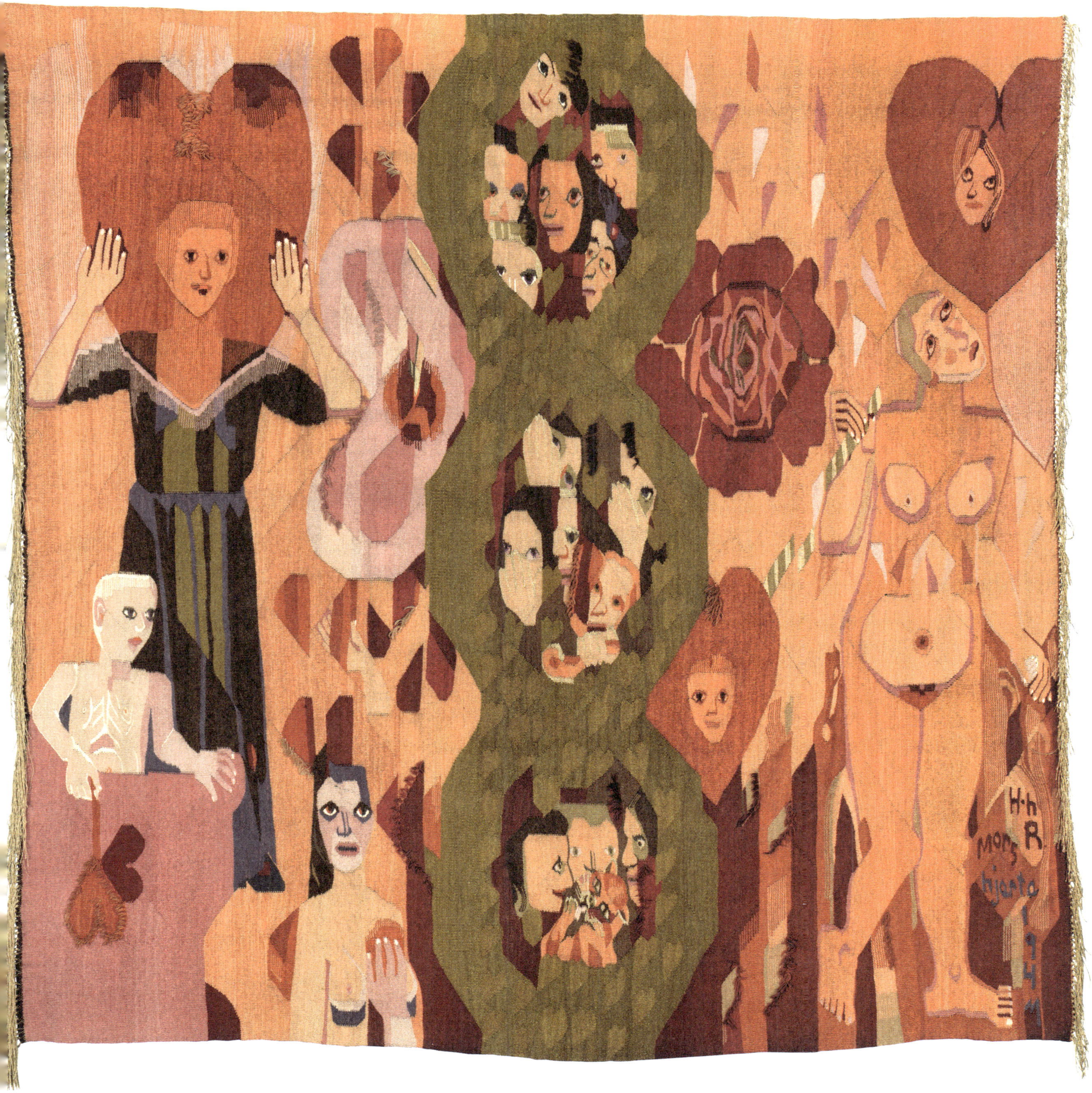
H·h
R
Mors
hjarta
1
9
4

Mors hjerte (*Mother's Heart*)
Detail

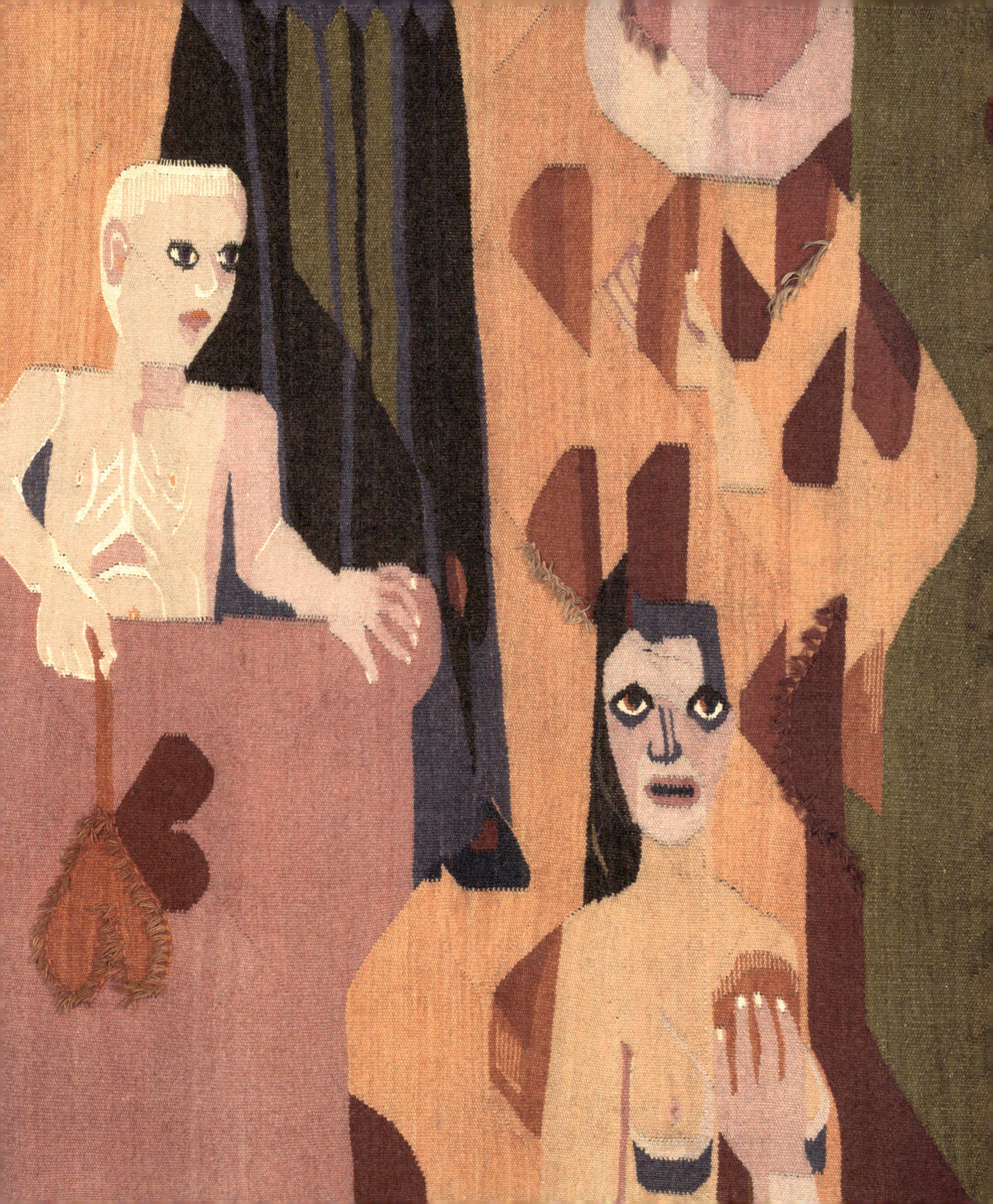

Hjemlige guder (*Homely Gods*), 1951
Tapestry woven in wool and linen,
94×192 cm

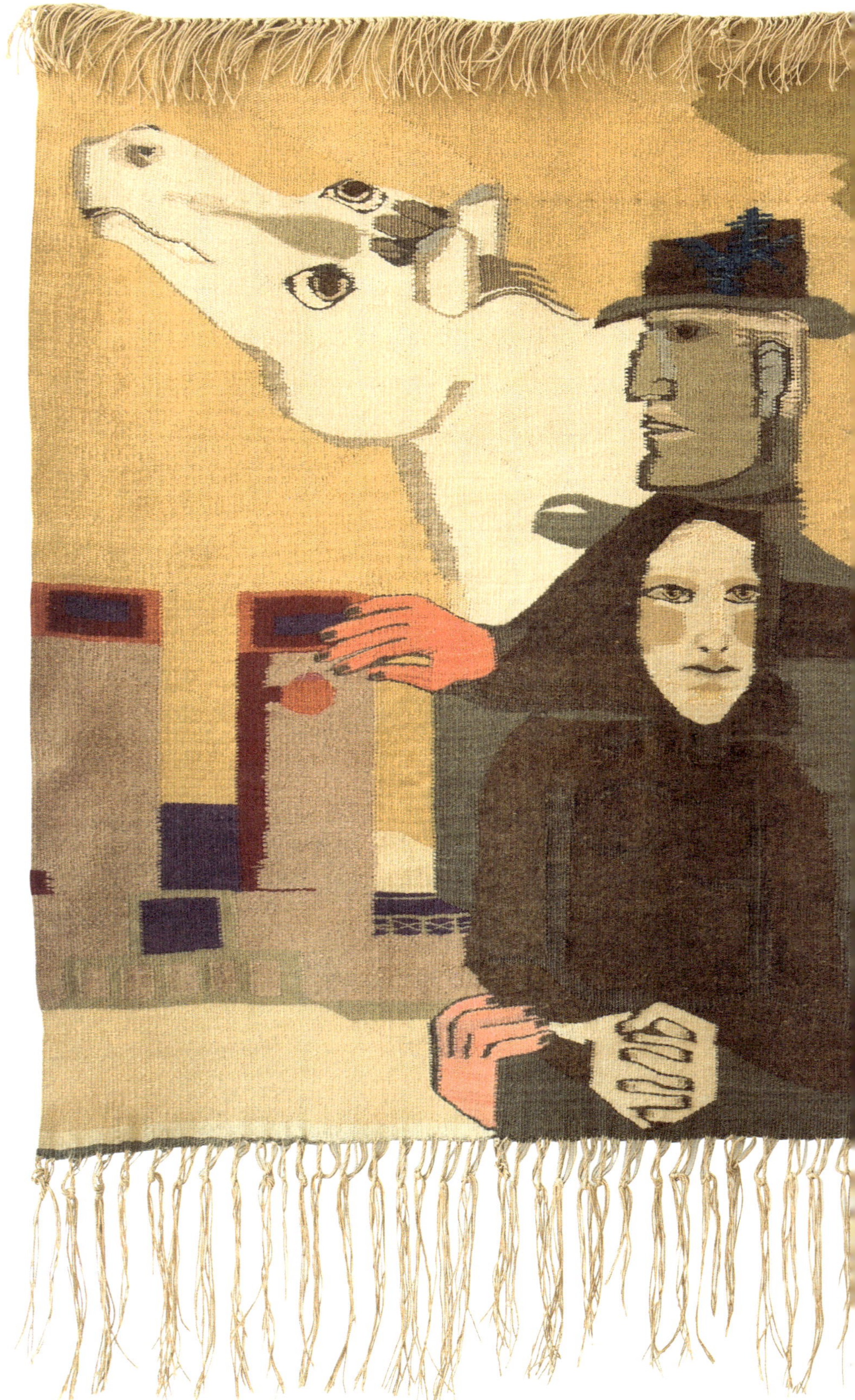

Homely Gods is a satirical comment on the power structures in the Norwegian art scene. It was made as a reaction (albeit many years later) to the rejection of *Us and Our Animals* for the decoration of the Oslo City Hall. On the left we see the prominent painter Henrik Sørensen, who rests one hand on Oslo City Hall and has his favourite model by his side, and on the right is Edvard Munch, floating in the sky. Ryggen also includes the Norse god Thor, bearing his hammer and riding in his chariot pulled by the goats Tanngrisner and Tanngjotne. This Thor, however, bears a striking resemblance to Rolf Stenersen, a wealthy Norwegian collector, especially of Munch's works.

A detailed description of this work can be found on p. 32.

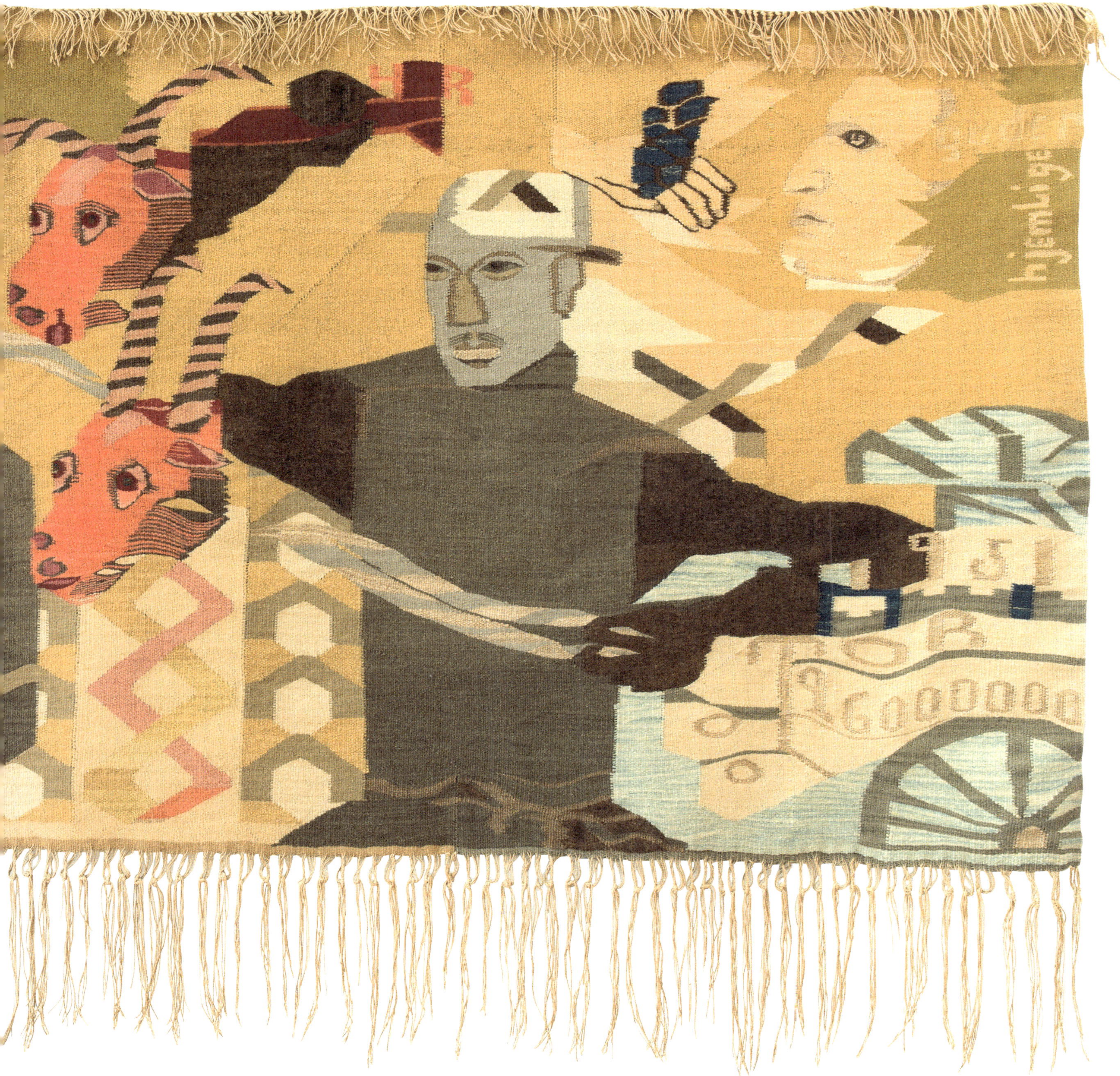

An Accidental Modernist
Ingar Dragset in Conversation with Esther Schlicht

ESTHER SCHLICHT When you think of Hannah Ryggen, what is the first image that comes to your mind?

INGAR DRAGSET It's the haunting, complex image of her incredible tapestry *Drømmedød* (*Death of Dreams*) from 1936. The Nobel Peace Prize laureate Carl von Ossietzky, who at that time was incarcerated in Berlin-Spandau and tortured and mistreated in the worst possible manner, is pictured behind bars in the upper left part of the work, along with other political prisoners. In the middle we see three Nazis strangling a defenceless, barefoot man. To the right, a man who looks like Einstein pokes his head through the prison bars, his hand clutching a violin. He might symbolize the inherent power of science and art to vanquish evil.

The bottom part of *Death of Dreams* is made up of gray ornaments on a brown background. It's shocking when you realize that the ornaments are actually deconstructed swastika symbols that are made to look like bricks in a prison wall. As early as the 1930s, Ryggen was using expressive devices that didn't become common in visual art until much later. She appropriates an existing symbolic language, a language of power, and by taking ownership of it and tweaking it, she exposes its weaknesses, and shows how evil can also exist in the decorative. I think *Death of Dreams* has such a strong impact on us because it is so striking in its composition and aesthetic virtuosity, but at the same time it speaks of human horror and evil.

ES If you could choose three words to describe Ryggen's art, which would these be?

ID Bold, emphatic, impassioned.

ES You were born and grew up in Trondheim, Norway, where most of Ryggen's tapestries are located, not very far from the place where she lived and worked for most of her life. Can you say something about your first encounter with and your personal relation to Hannah Ryggen and her work?

ID Some of the first original works of art I saw as a child were Hannah Ryggen's tapestries in the Nordenfjeldske Kunstindustrimuseum, which is the local museum for decorative art and design. I was deeply fascinated. The tapestries seemed simple, almost comic-like in their style, but very dramatic too. I tried to copy them on a small hobby loom at home. I think my fascination with Ryggen also came through the reverent way people talked about her, both in town and on Ørlandet, the stormy peninsula where she lived most of her life. I was born in 1969 and she died in 1970, so I couldn't have met her, but well into adulthood, I believed I had actually seen her in my childhood. This might be due to one particular story my mum told me once, when we were in town buying fish in Ravnkloa, the local harbor. According to legend, Ryggen had made friends with the drunkards who used to hang out there. They used to save their urine for her in bottles, which she in turn used to dye yarn with. Apparently their pee contained unnaturally high levels of ammonia, which provided brighter colors for the dyeing process. One might doubt her methods today, but my mum told me this to demonstrate Ryggen's kindness and compassion, and it certainly had an effect on me. I never went as far as trying to dye my own yarn though.

ES There is kind of a tale of origin related to how you and Michael Elmgreen started working together in the mid-1990s. It says that you were quite skilled in knitting and helped Michael to knit some pets, which was the starting point for your first performance. It seems you have a special relation to textile and handicrafts?

ID Yes, handicrafts were really important to me both as a child and as a teenager. I made patterns and knitted my own sweaters. I also did drawings, but somehow the knitting had more of a social dimension to it—it was more integral to developing an identity and also led to great friendships: people rarely sit and draw together, but crafts can be done in company. My collaboration with Michael actually started because he was planning a solo project at an artist's studio in Stockholm. At that time we were boyfriends, but I was still acting in a theater group. Michael wanted to include some abstract pink pets that people could interact with in his show, but he didn't know how to produce them. I offered to knit them for him. When I came up to Stockholm for the opening, it turned out that nobody understood this was an interactive piece, or maybe the audience was just Nordic, stiff and shy. Anyway, Michael and I sat down each in our corner, and cuddled our little soft pink monsters. This became our first—unofficial—performance piece.

ES A few other works in which the act of knitting played a crucial role came after that but then you turned to other, very different materials.

ID The next knitting piece was also a performance, in which I sit and knit at the end of a hundred-meter-long white cloth, as Michael sits at the other end and unravels it. Creation and destruction within one piece, so to speak. Had the piece gone on for longer, he would of course have caught up with me. At one point, though, we found that the soft materials were aligning too well with a certain perception of female and queer art at the time, and we wanted to explore other options, to subvert materials that were perceived as more masculine, such as wood, bronze, and stainless steel. It is important to have tried out handicrafts, though, since there's a certain intimacy with the material that one can keep in mind when working with other materials. There is also a satisfying directness in creating with yarn, and also a limitation and a slowness, which is maybe closer to how life really is. As the world seems to gain in velocity, maybe it is time for us to switch back to fabrics and handicrafts again...

ES Ryggen began her career quite traditionally with painting and then suddenly, in the early 1920s, she decided to quit painting and to start weaving instead. Do you have an assumption or a theory on why she made this shift?

ID I think weaving gave her greater freedom. She seems to have been interested in many things, like tradition, history, politics, form, color, and story-telling. In her tapestries, she could combine these interests in a different way than in painting, freed from the expectations of a painting, which often demands a different kind of clarity, one message. And we shouldn't forget that her husband Hans was a painter. She was obviously the better artist. Can you imagine that she left him to paint, so she wouldn't encroach upon his pride?

ES We touched on materiality and technique, but are there other aspects of Ryggen's work that seem crucial to you with reference to your own work, when you look at it today? I am thinking, for example, of the theatrical and narrative quality of her tapestries but also of a certain idea of public art that Ryggen stands for. Also, the way she connects the personal with the political could, in a certain way, be related to your and Elmgreen's interests and approach.

ID Obviously our art is so different from Ryggen's aesthetically, but yes, her way of seeing the world as an intricate net of personal experience, social movements and political affairs definitely resonates with us. Like her, we are constantly trying to understand processes and changes that are going on around us in the world and how these are affecting us, by dealing with them artistically. She must also have believed that she could reach people with a different language than what politicians, policy makers and news outlets could, somewhere at an intersection between the cerebral, the emotional, and the subconscious. The narrative aspect is also recurring in our art, as you say, but as with Ryggen, we try not to conclude the story. There should always be blanks, or an open end, to be filled out by (or co-authored by) the audience. There's a core belief in the potential for change, in the ability of people to engage.

ES Another quality you share with Hannah Ryggen is a specific, even though certainly very different, sense of humor.

ID As I mentioned earlier, the comic-like side to her figuration spoke very strongly to me as a child. I think the simplicity in her representation of people and actions is very much a part of why her work is so appealing, also to an audience outside of the arts—and to the arts-and-craft world. More than humor, there is a certain playfulness to Ryggen's work, like surprising placements, combinations, and unusual uses of colors. The work almost feels a bit mischievous at times.
Humor and a cleverly applied naiveté can be a tool to communicate difficult subject matter, when used in the right way. In her brilliant biography on Hannah Ryggen, Marit Paasche quotes from Ryggen's correspondence, which is sometimes also hilariously self-deprecating and funny—which goes to prove she was definitely someone who might be conscious about using humor in her work, too. As we know, humor can be a way of dealing with life, getting by, getting through it.

ES It seems there has been a renewed interest in Ryggen's work within the last few years and that it is slowly starting to get more attention outside of Scandinavia. What is it that makes it appear so relevant to us today?

ID Ryggen's work resonates well with a time that, at least to some extent, tries to rectify the wrongs done by (art-)history writers until recently, where both women's art and craft, like art forms such as tapestries, weren't respected, or worse, were simply ignored. Also, she was living far away from any art metropolis, but this doesn't matter anymore today. With Ryggen, we have an artist who was politically engaged, outspoken, talented, knowledgeable, different, tradition-bound and experimental, all at the same time. She could maybe be called an accidental modernist, but even this puts her in an interesting light today. She didn't try to live up to anybody else's expectations; she did what she believed in, all powered by her own urge and will and beliefs.

ES The freedom and independence you mention as essential elements of her position are also related to the fact that she worked in a quite self-sufficient way. On the one hand, technically, doing everything herself, from feeding the sheep, spinning the wool and dyeing it, to creating the image directly on the loom. On the other hand, economically, as she tried to stay independent from private buyers and wanted her work to be seen publicly. This is pretty amazing considering the very poor and simple conditions she lived in.

ID Yes, this is definitely admirable. She must have had this overwhelming urge to create and to express herself. There wasn't much in her immediate rural surroundings to keep her at it.

ES Ryggen's major tapestry *We Are Living on a Star* has been installed in the Highrise in the Government Quarter in Oslo ever since its creation in 1958 but it was damaged in the terrorist bombing by Anders Behring Breivik in 2011. The work has been repaired but the damage is still visible. How do you read this scar or wound?

ID Of course Ryggen would have been absolutely appalled by the views of Breivik, as we all are. But she was also someone who didn't seem to brush away uncomfortable truths lightly. The scars in *We Are Living on a Star* will never heal, just as the scars that Breivik has inflicted upon the world won't heal, and they shouldn't. We need to remember what is able to hurt us, what lies dormant in our midst.

ES Ryggen visited Dresden in 1922, at a crucial moment in her life, just before she gave up painting. Later her work became strongly related to German history. You have been living in Germany—namely Berlin—for many years now. What is your "German" view or perspective on her politically inspired work?

ID Ryggen studied in Germany, but moved to Trøndelag where she lived for most of her life. I studied in Trøndelag, but moved to Germany, where I have lived for most of my life. When she made her *Death of Dreams* tapestry—literally talking about dreams being strangled by the National Socialists—she must have been so disappointed in Germany, and so pessimistic about the future. After Norway was occupied by the Nazis, some of her friends were arrested, and various public figures were killed; she dealt with these events in her work. I wish she were alive to see that her dreams did not die, though: that art, humanity, and reason actually did win in the end. I live in a Berlin that was not only liberated long ago but is also incredibly liberal socially, where the freedom of art and minority groups really matters. I can't imagine a better place to live. But when you think about *Death of Dreams,* it's easy to remember that things can always change quickly. Even in Berlin the right-wing party AfD received 12 percent of the vote in the last Bundestag elections. Populist forces are on the rise in many places in Europe and also the rest of the world. Again, presidents want to build walls on the borders with other countries, rather than seek alliances and cooperation. One can only wonder what Hannah Ryggen would have woven today, but for sure she wouldn't have rested content with the status quo.

ES How do you see Ryggen's role and standing in Norway today? And would you say that she is an important figure for contemporary artists?

ID Of course people in Norway know her work but I feel she doesn't quite have the standing that she should have. It might have something to do with her having lived so remotely, far away from Oslo, and that her output was not the same as many of the big painters. This again means that she was never part of an art market, which probably also plays a role. The National Museum in Oslo owns some of her work, of course. They have an Edvard Munch room—they should make a Hannah Ryggen room as well.

Verhau (*The Squall*), 1928
Tapestry woven in wool and linen,
160 × 153 cm

The coastline along central Norway is extremely beautiful but also tremendously exposed, with frequent and dramatic fluctuations in weather conditions. This tapestry's title is a word in the dialect of the region for severe weather. The various visual elements are positioned close together and vibrate with energy, in an effective impression of a mounting storm just before it breaks loose. As the only large abstract tapestry Ryggen ever made, this work occupies a unique position in her oeuvre.
The Squall was made in 1928, a time when the relation between figure, abstraction, and ornament was still unsettled, and there is little doubt that Ryggen was inspired by modernism's styles here. *The Squall* falls somewhere between Gunta Stölz (1897–1983), Nordic folk art tapestry, and French primitivism.

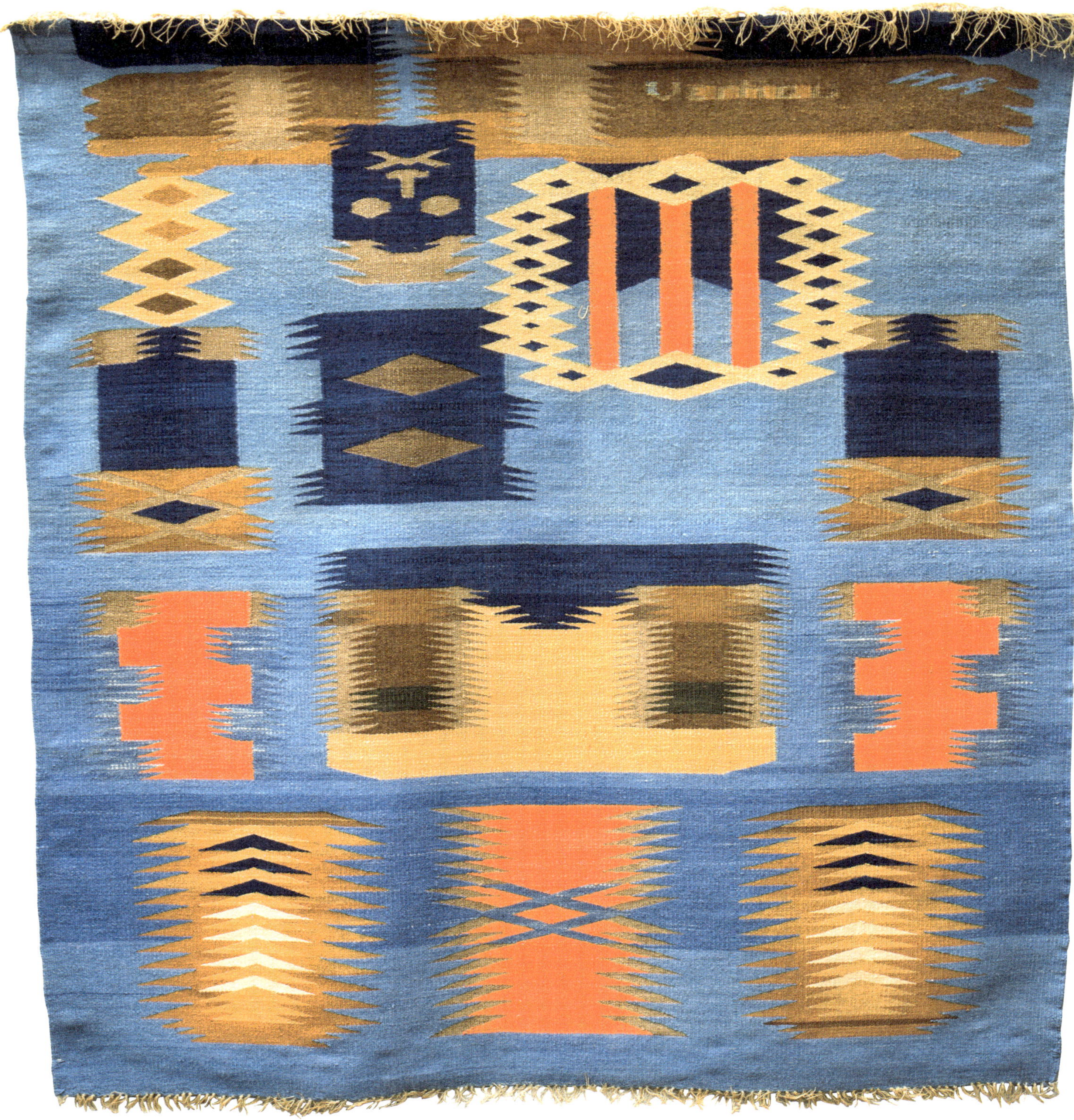

Livet glir forbi (*Life Slides By*), 1939
Tapestry woven in wool and linen,
190 × 185 cm

In 1939 Hannah Ryggen received a copy of Paul Gauguin's travelogue *Noa Noa* in which he documented his first visit to Tahiti in 1891. After having read it, Ryggen wove *Life Slides By* as a tribute to Gauguin. That the book made such a strong impression on her is perhaps not surprising; Gauguin's embrace of Tahitian culture, and his intense and original experimentation with woodcut as a medium, was like an echo of her own journey from Malmö to Ørlandet, and her shift from painting to weaving.

In this tapestry we see Tehura, the woman with whom Gauguin lived on Tahiti. She is offering a platter of fruit to Gauguin, who is floating in the water. The scene is based on an episode in *Noa Noa* in which Gauguin describes taking a foolhardy swim. In the tapestry, the surface of the water around him is choppy and in movement. Gauguin is looking up at Tehura, the personification of his new life, holding the platter of fruit—thus representing everything lush and sweet that the world now has to offer. The naked figure of Tehura evokes Eve in Paradise, standing on the back of a fantastic creature and holding out an apple from the tree that grows behind her. In the upper area of *Life Slides By* there are four gray human heads. Ryggen regarded Gauguin as someone who had seized the opportunity and broken free from the monotony of routine. Daily life was full of toil, and Ryggen was constantly struggling for 'space' in which to create. In connection with her participation in the 1964 Venice Biennale, she delivered this short, poetic description of *Life Slides By:* "Paul Gauguin's story / is arresting. He throws / himself into life's embrace. / He loses his own / but wins big / life touches / his brush."[1] Ryggen thus puts into words the idea of having to relinquish or sacrifice what is nearest and dearest—a spouse or child, for example—in favor of art. This is an idea primarily associated with major, male artists: in order to create masterworks, one must devote oneself to art, and art alone.

In this work Ryggen allows herself to toy with the idea of abandoning everything; and 'leaving' was to become an artistic theme in the ensuing years.

1 Else Christie Kielland, "Hannah Ryggen på Venezia-biennalen" (Hannah Ryggen at the Venice Biennale), *Kunst og kultur,* vol. 47, 1964, p. 67.

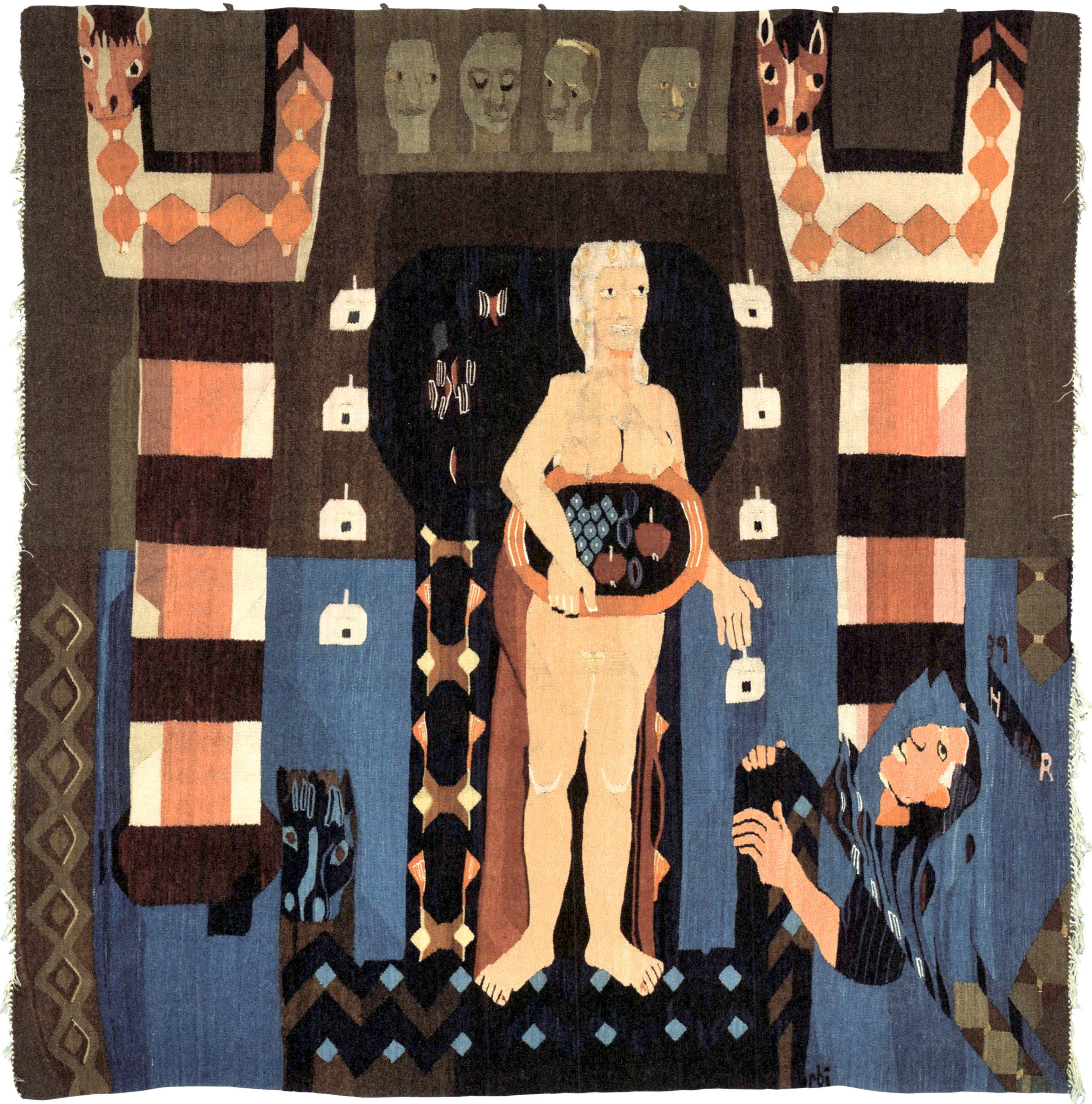

En fri (*A Free One*), 1948
Tapestry woven in wool and linen,
190.2×188 cm

Hannah Ryggen herself wrote about this work: "*A Free One* is a tapestry that made me happy. It includes the whole of society, everyone who works for us, when we are sleeping, shoveling, doing work in the street. I wanted to weave all these slaves, the gray ones, without heads, with their hands as tools. Then there are the blue pillars in the tapestry. In them are the ones who want to climb up, and the ones who have never worked, and the ones who are born to be up there. There is also a man, one of the gray ones who comes from down below, from the proletarians. He may be a poet who managed to free himself. Although I don't believe so, for we are all bound in one way or another."[1]

A detailed description of this work can be found on p. 27.

1 Katja Waldén, "Väverskans frihet" (The Weaver's Freedom), in the Swedish magazine *VI*, no. 11, March 16, 1963.

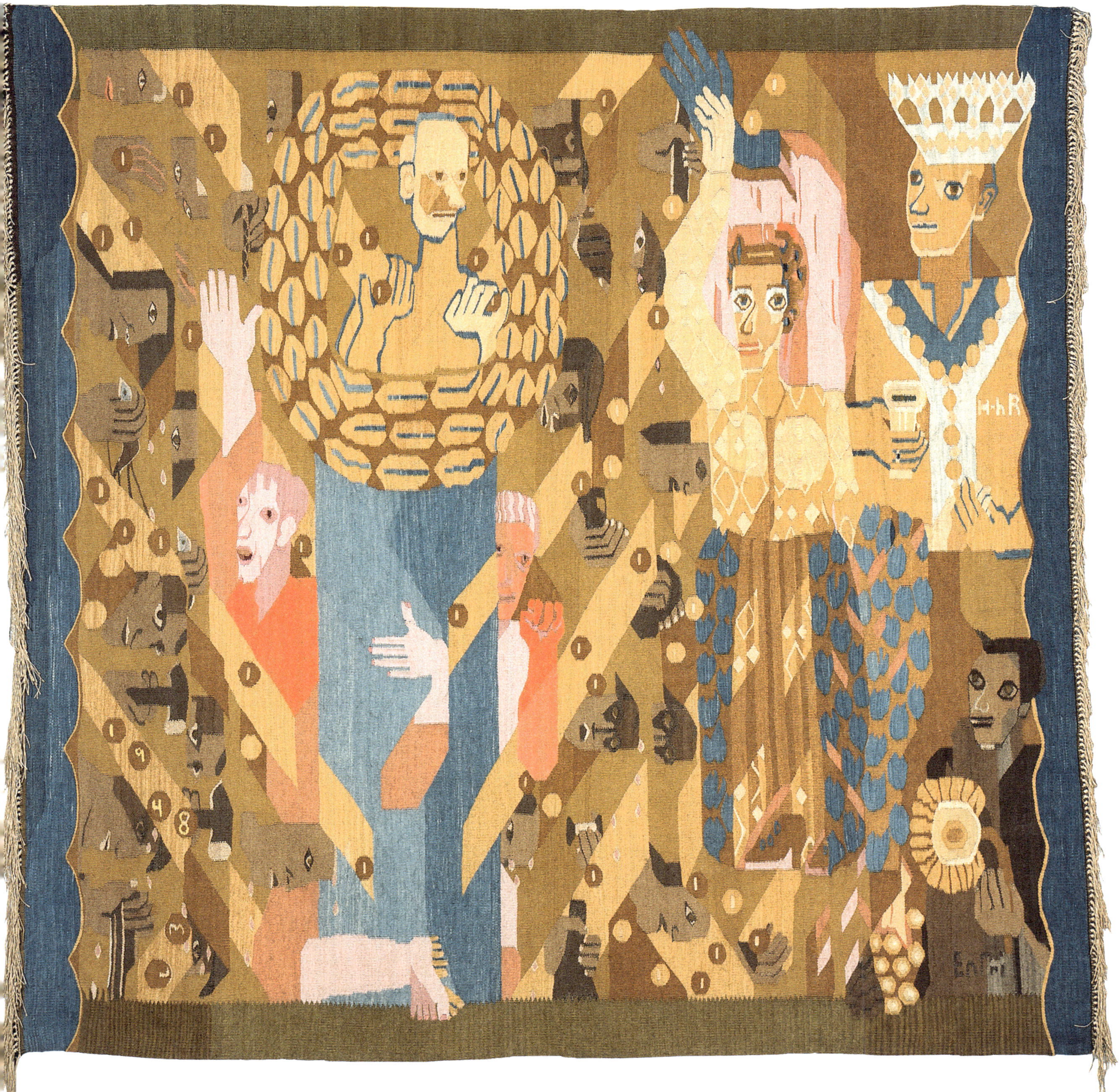

Picassoteppet (*Picasso Tapestry*)
Detail

When Hannah Ryggen decided to include present-day events in her subject matter, it was a move that both revitalized the medium and gave tapestry a new role. But this alone is not what makes her art so special; she also had an entirely unique way of combining reality, fiction, and myth, and she manipulated different pictorial traditions and effects with a rare ease.

After the Second World War, and a stay in Paris in 1946/47, however, there was a period when Ryggen became fascinated with antiquity and Greek mythology. In Paris she experienced the triumph of modernism in visual art, with Picasso as its standard-bearer. But it was not Picasso who irked her; rather, it was all the other artists who simply copied him. In 1949 Ryggen wove *Trojan Horse* as a commentary on contemporary art. In *The Odyssey,* Homer tells the story of how Odysseus conquered Troy with the help of an ingenious device: the Trojan horse. In her tapestry, Ryggen casts Picasso in the role of Odysseus and has him smuggle modernism into the kingdom of tradition with the help of a wooden horse. Some years later she wove the *Picasso Tapestry,* in which Picasso is depicted as a fiendish demigod who persuades other artists to do as he commands.

It is natural to read the whole composition as a visual tale of the development of art, in which Picasso's hegemonic position is established at the expense of classical art and representation. The span of time represented in the motif demonstrates weaving's central position as a means of communicating ideas in the European intellectual realm, from antiquity up to modernism.

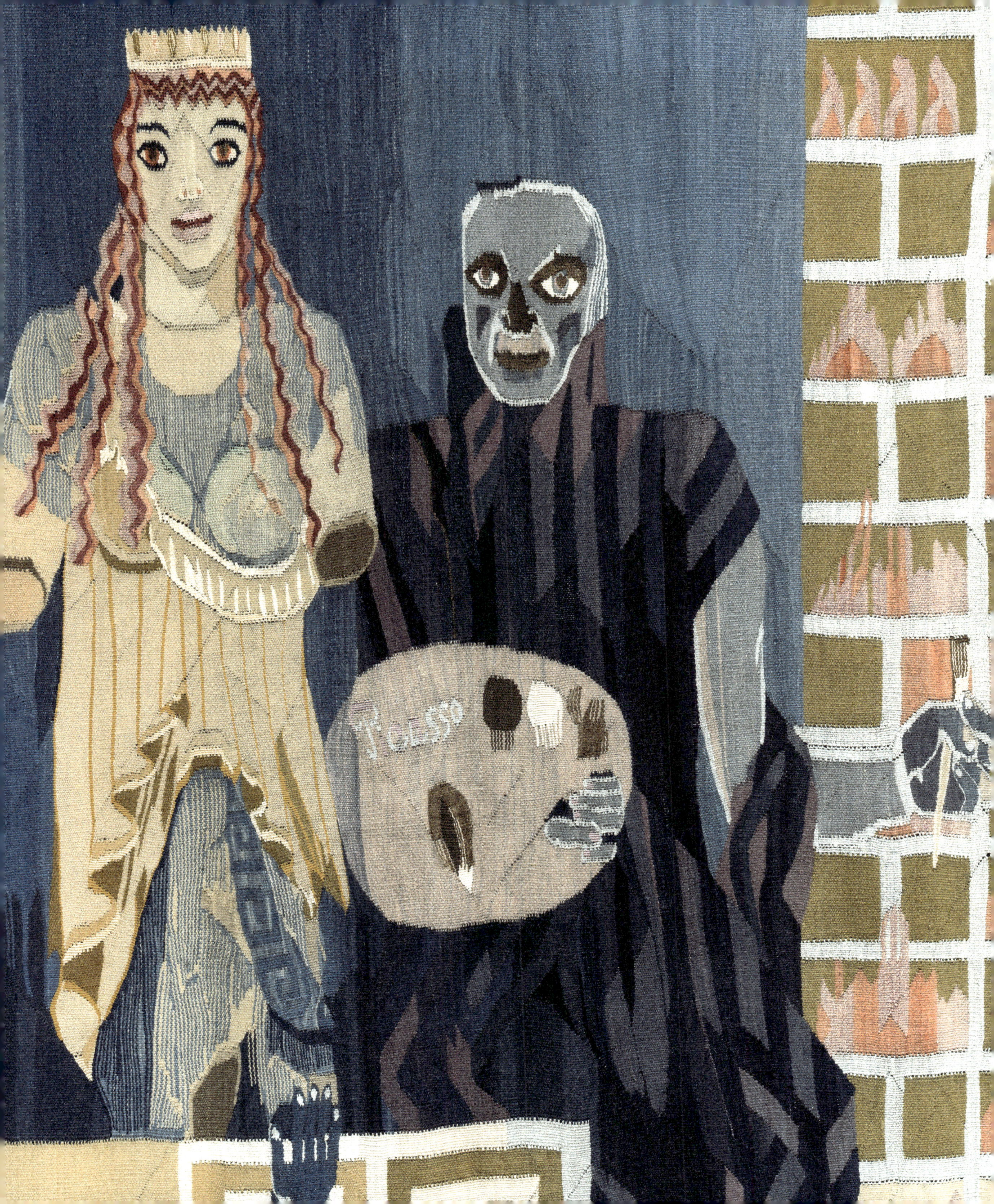

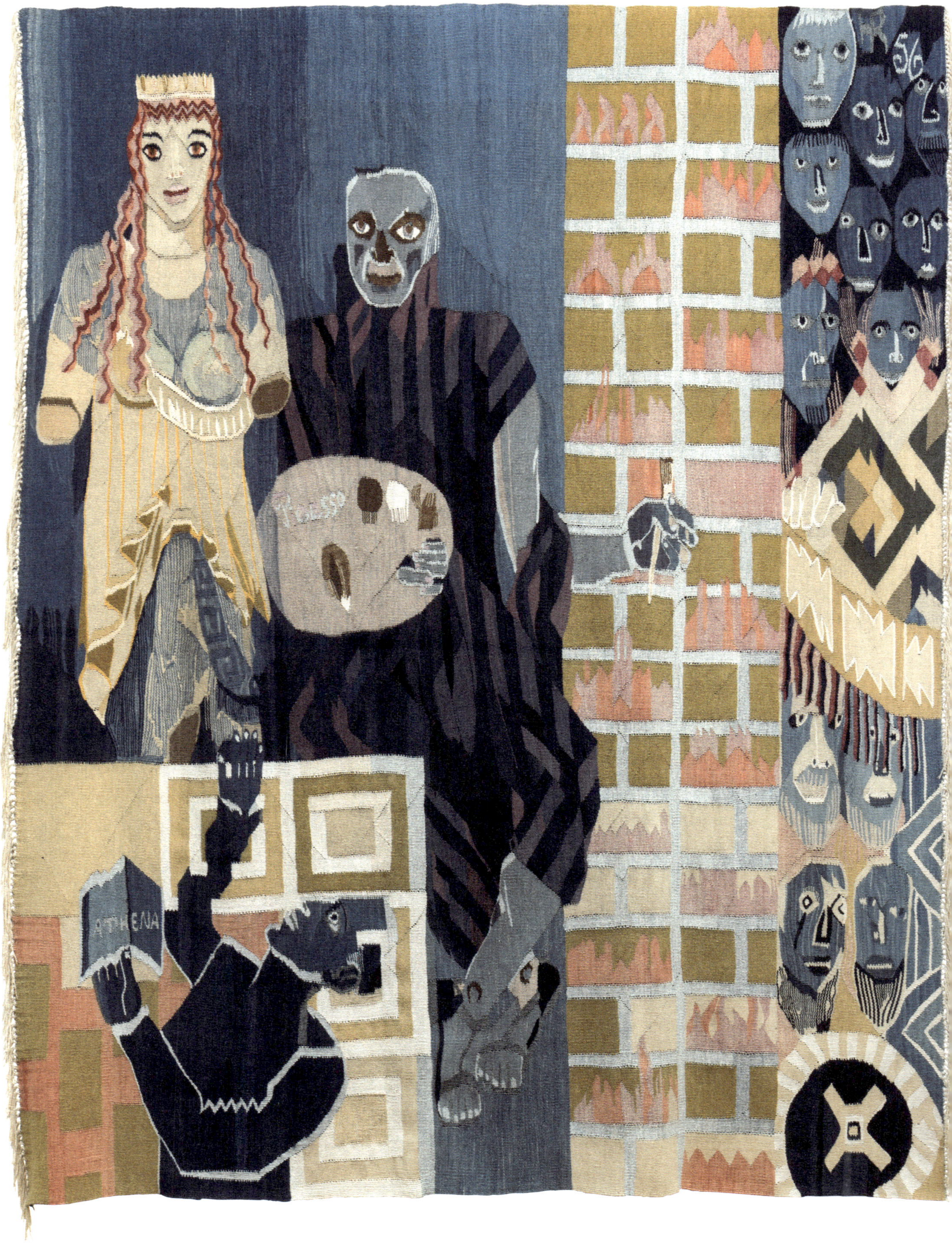

Trojansk hest / Picasso-teppet (*Trojan Horse / Picasso Tapestry*), 1949–1956
Two tapestries woven in wool and linen, 190 × 320 cm (overall dimensions)

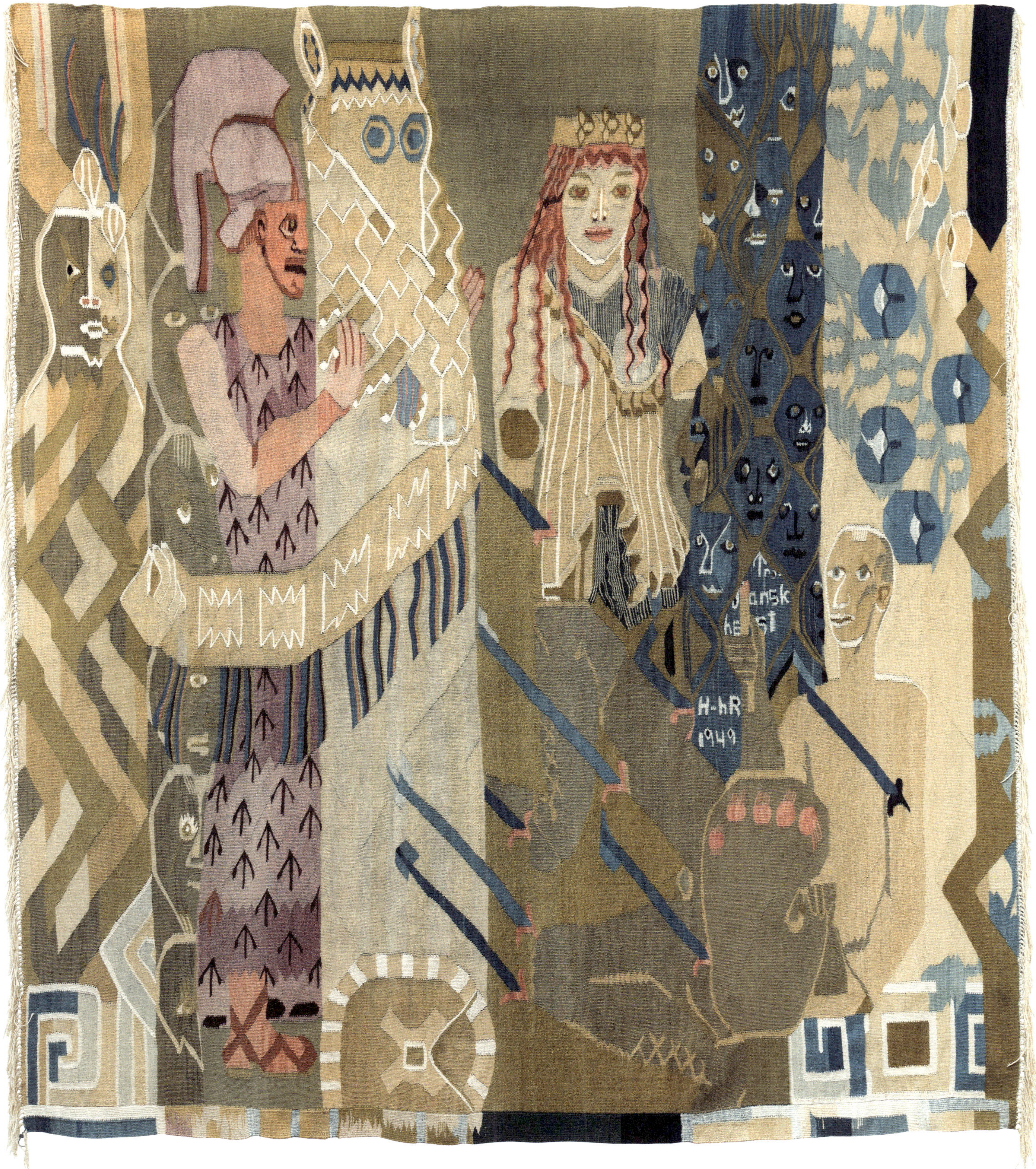
H-hR
1949

Trojansk hest (*Trojan Horse*)
Detail

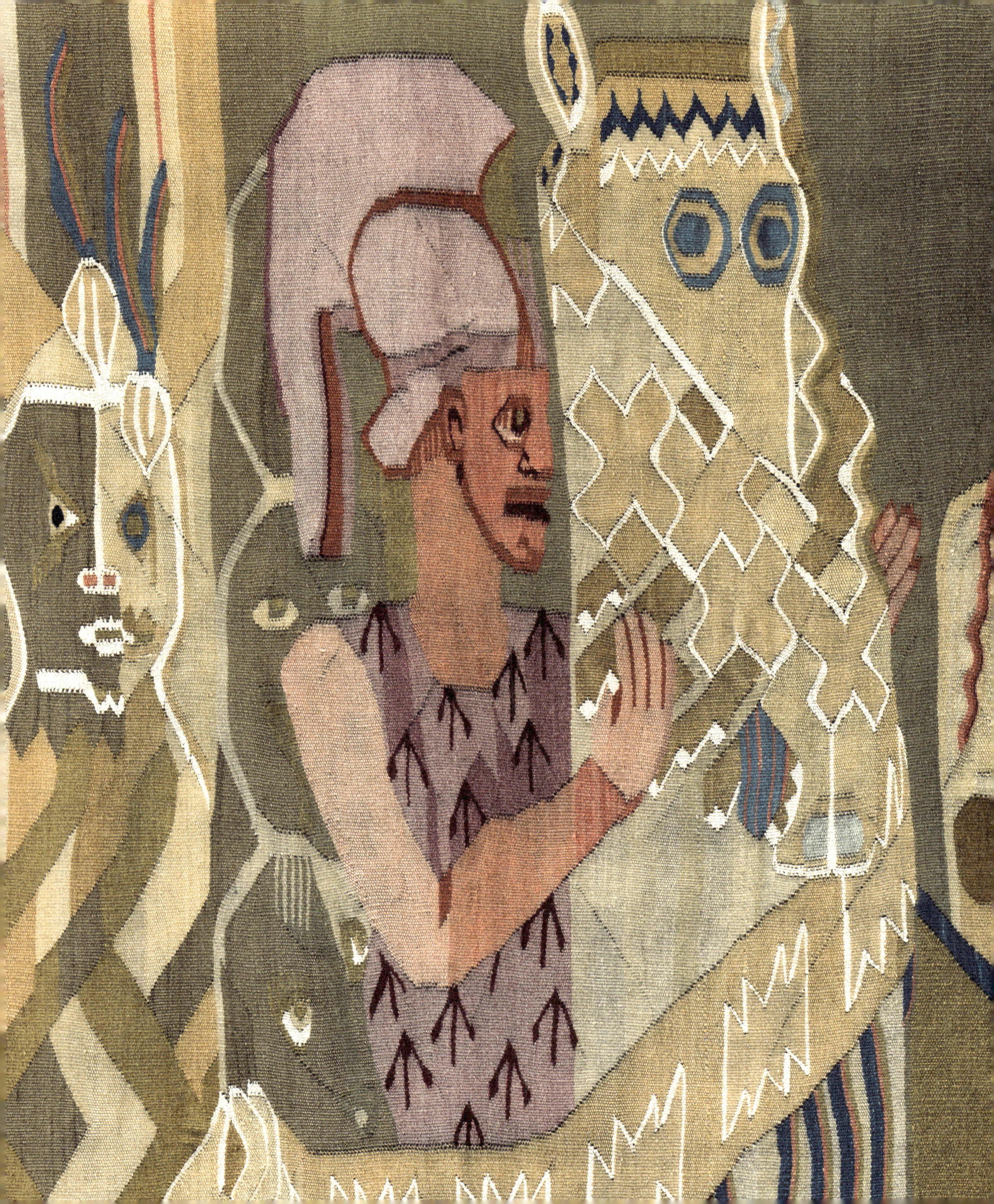

Bærestolen (*The Sedan Chair*), 1959
Tapestry woven in wool and linen,
167×195 cm

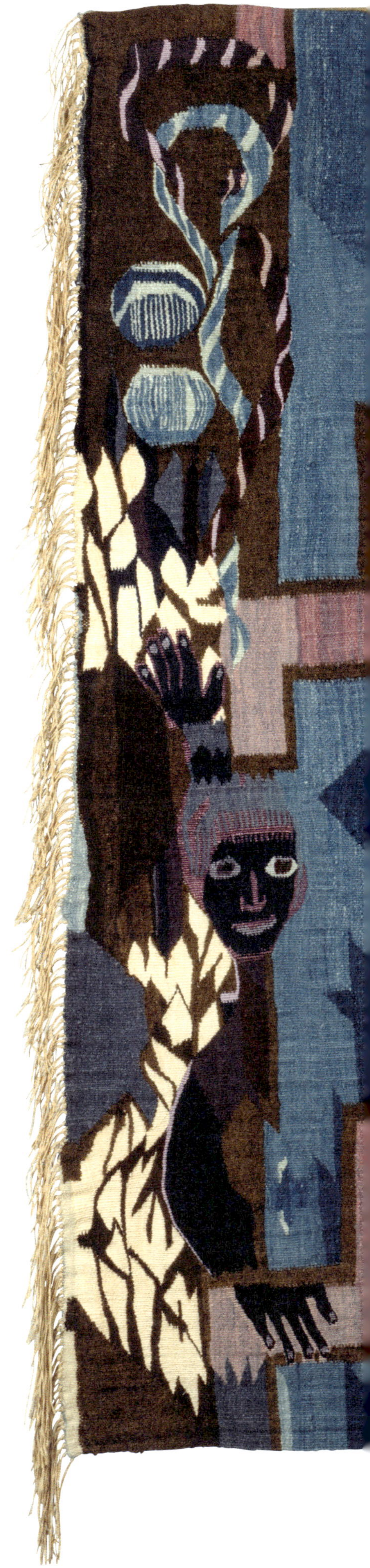

This is Hannah Ryggen's personal tribute to her husband. In the work, Hannah and her daughter Mona are carrying Hans to rest. The place they have chosen is full of flowers, especially lilies of the valley, the fragrance of spring. Hans is holding his palette, and beside him, on the right, Hannah has placed a red rose, the symbol of love. The lattice of lines, flowers, and figures runs together in an expression that keeps the memory alive.
In an undated journal entry after her husband's death, Ryggen wrote: "Is it any wonder that I am now once again sitting and weeping with longing for Hans who has left me [...]. When I have it worst and the emptiness and longing are overwhelming Hans wraps me in his arms and I hear his voice 'not you Hannah not you, be brave you have something to say to them: Weave. Weave!'"[1]

1 Hannah Ryggen's journals (notebook 4), NTNU University Library, Trondheim.

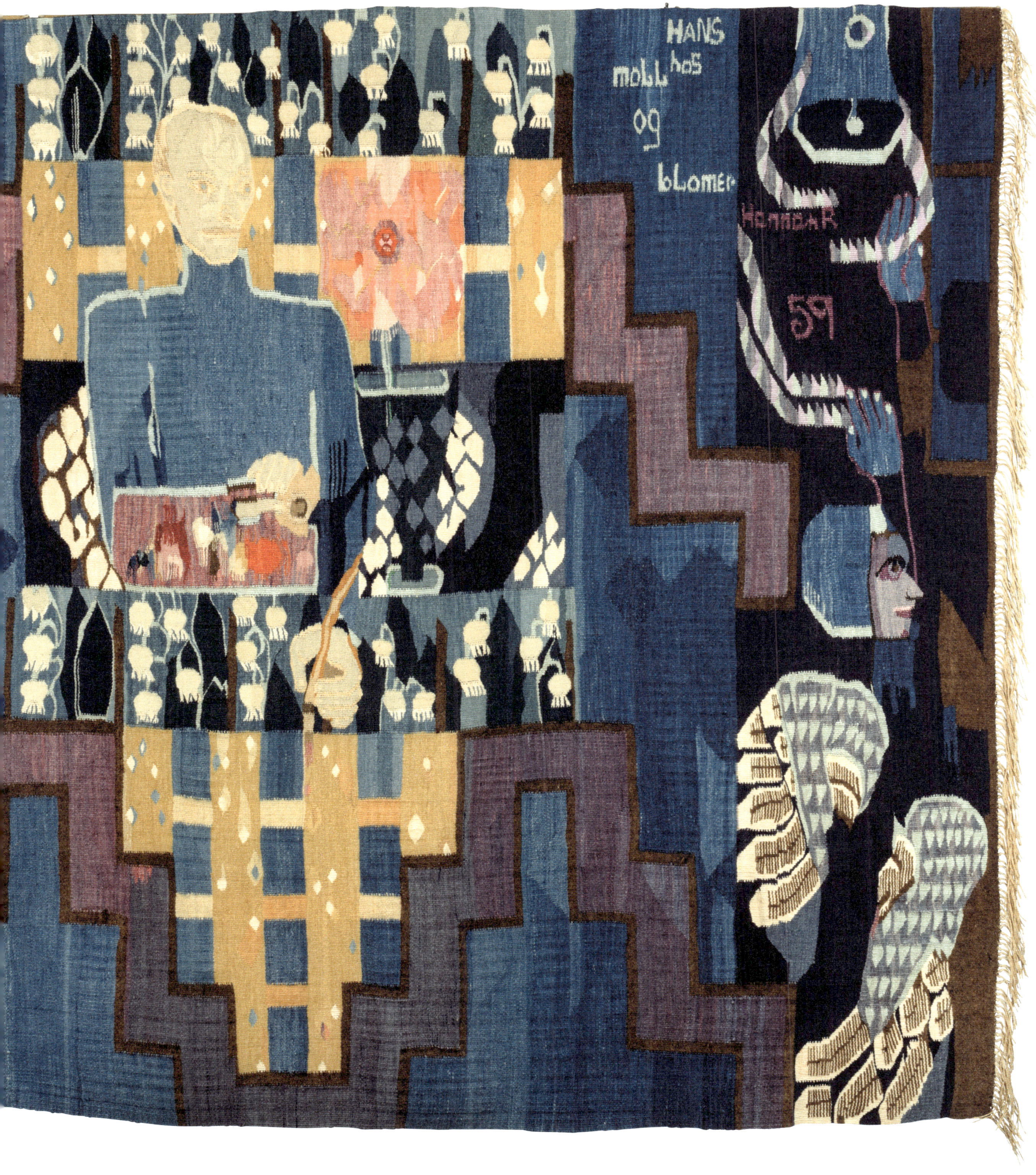
HANS
hos
moll
og
blomer
59

Bærestolen (*The Sedan Chair*)
Detail

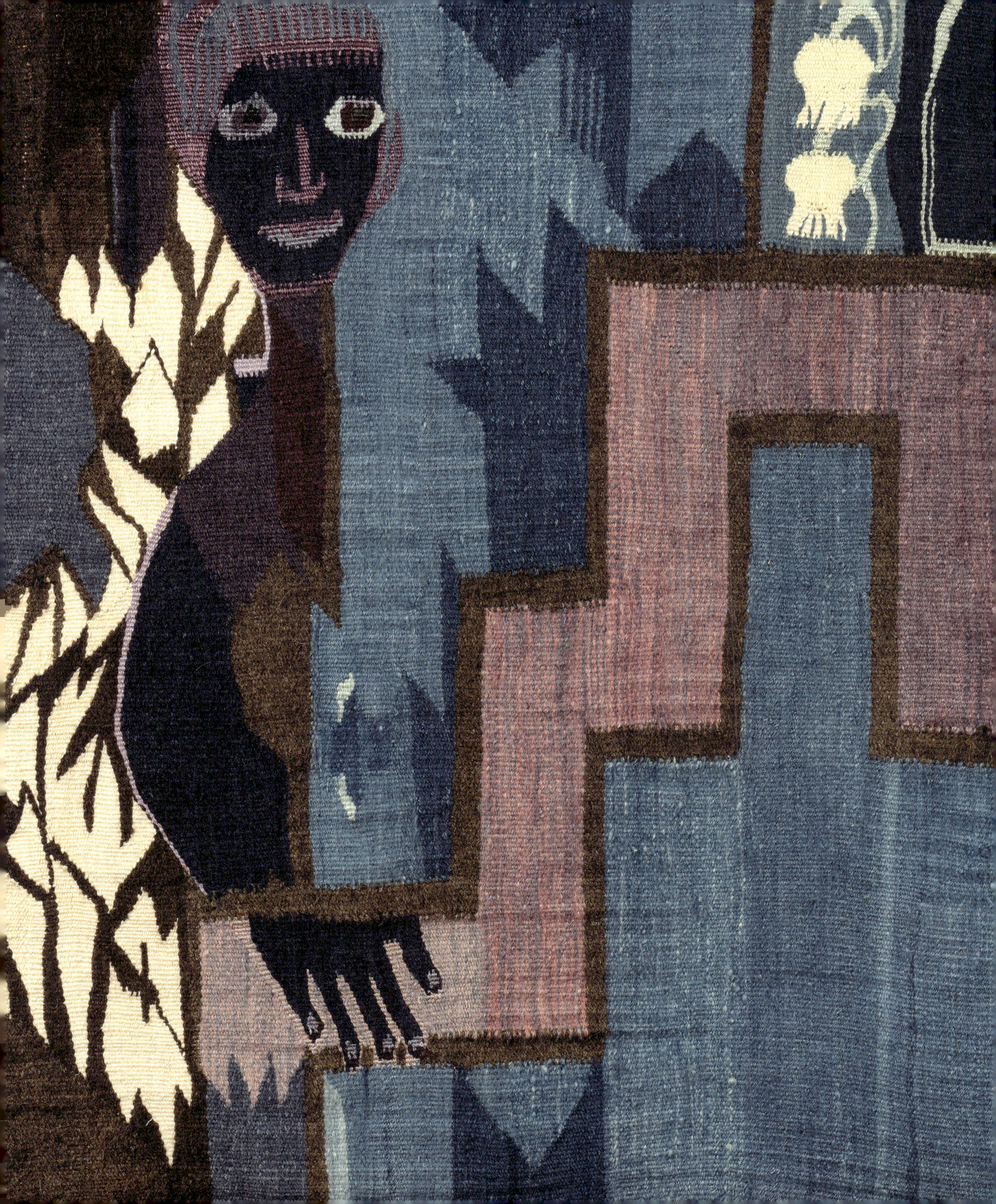

Dikt av T. S. Eliot (*Poem by T. S. Eliot*), 1952
Tapestry woven in wool and linen, 194×165 cm

Ryggen based this work on a verse from T. S. Eliot's famous 1942 poem "Little Gidding," which is the last of four poems in his *Four Quartets*.
In *Poem by T. S. Eliot,* she introduces an exploration of the power of love, both in the physical and political sense: a theme she continued to explore in *Svan* (1954), *Vi lever på en stjerne* (*We Are Living on a Star,* 1958), and *Bærestolen* (*The Sedan Chair,* 1959). Although she had touched on the theme of love earlier, in *Poem by T. S. Eliot* and the three subsequent works it is addressed explicitly.
Two female figures are woven in: one is lying down consumed by flames, while the other sits by a spinning wheel, with a shuttle in one hand and yarn in the other. The spinning wheel encircles the recumbent woman. The similarity between Ryggen and the woman holding the shuttle is obvious: the one who weaves is also the one who creates and observes the struggles of others. At the base of the tapestry Ryggen has woven in a Norwegian translation of these lines from Eliot's poem: "Who then devised the torment? Love. / Love is the unfamiliar Name / Behind the hands that wove / The intolerable shirt of flame / Which human power cannot remove. / We only live, only suspire / Consumed by either fire or fire."[1]

1 *The Poems of T. S. Eliot,* vol. 1, *Collected and Uncollected Poems,* ed. Christopher Ricks and Jim McCue (London: Faber & Faber, 2015), p. 207.

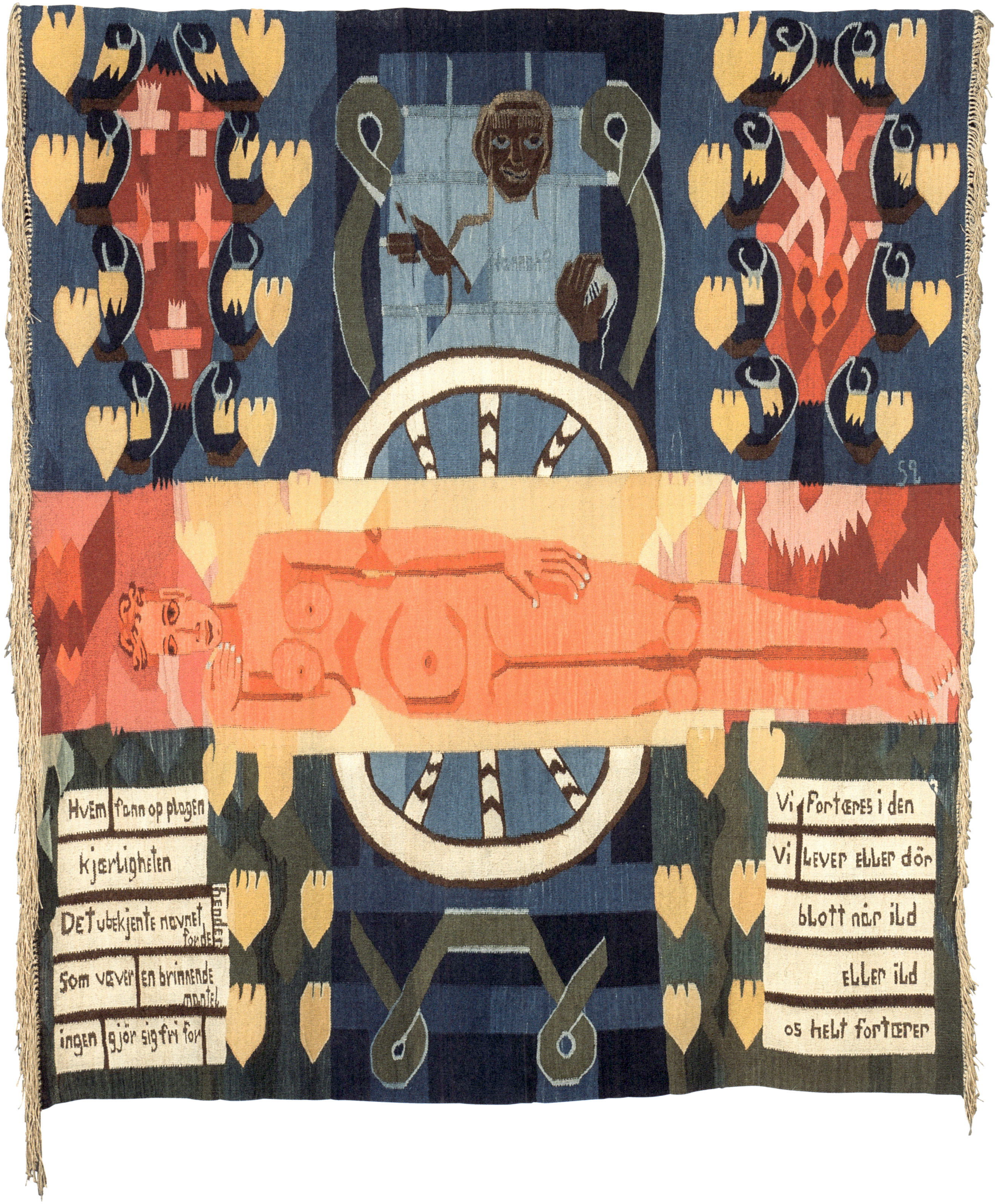

Hvem fann op plagen
kjærligheten
Det ubekjente navnet for den
hender
Som væver en brinnende mantel
ingen gjör sig fri for
Vi fortæres i den
Vi lever eller dör
blott når ild
eller ild
os helt fortærer

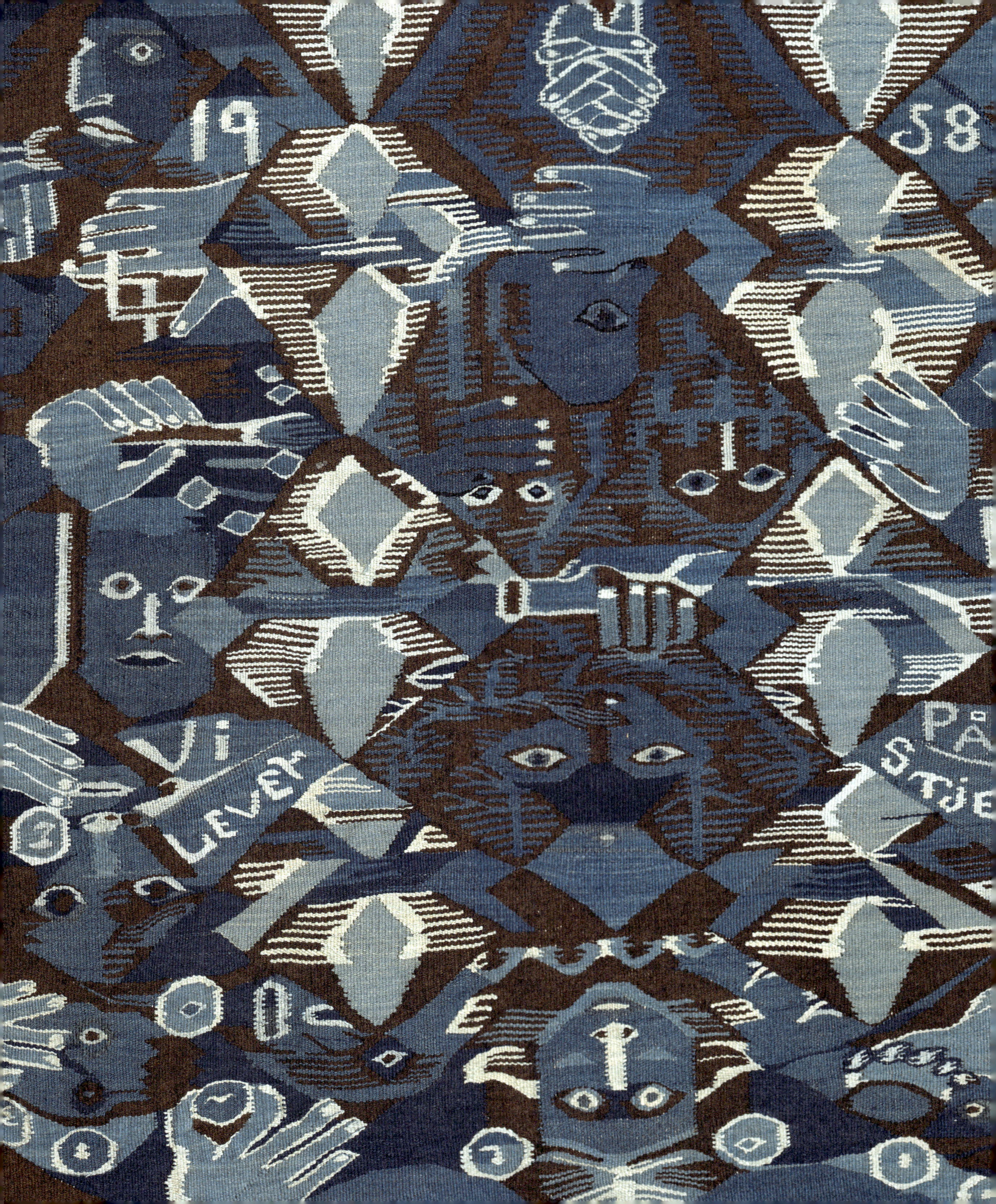
19
58
Vi
Lever
På
Stje

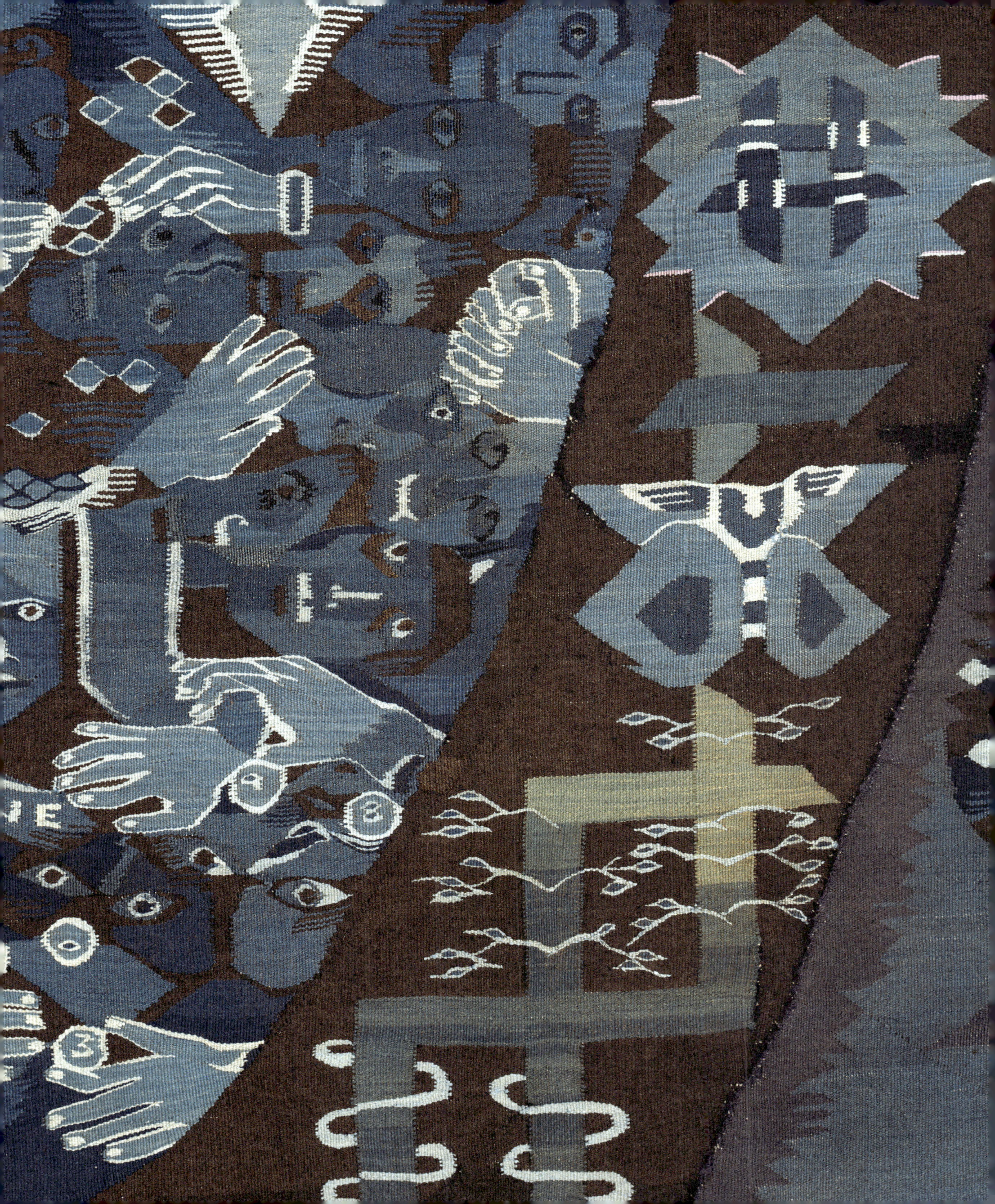

Vi lever på en stjerne (*We Are Living on a Star*), 1958
Tapestry woven in wool and linen,
400 × 300 cm

A brass plaque was mounted on the wall beside *We Are Living on a Star* when it hung in the lobby of the High-rise in Oslo's Government Quarter. In addition to the usual information—artist, title, year, etc.—it included an uncommonly poetic inscription:
"We Are Living on a Star."
1958, 400 × 300.
Property of the Norwegian State.
The Government Building.
The mysteries of the universe and love's essential place in our world.

A detailed description of this work can be found on pp. 31–33.

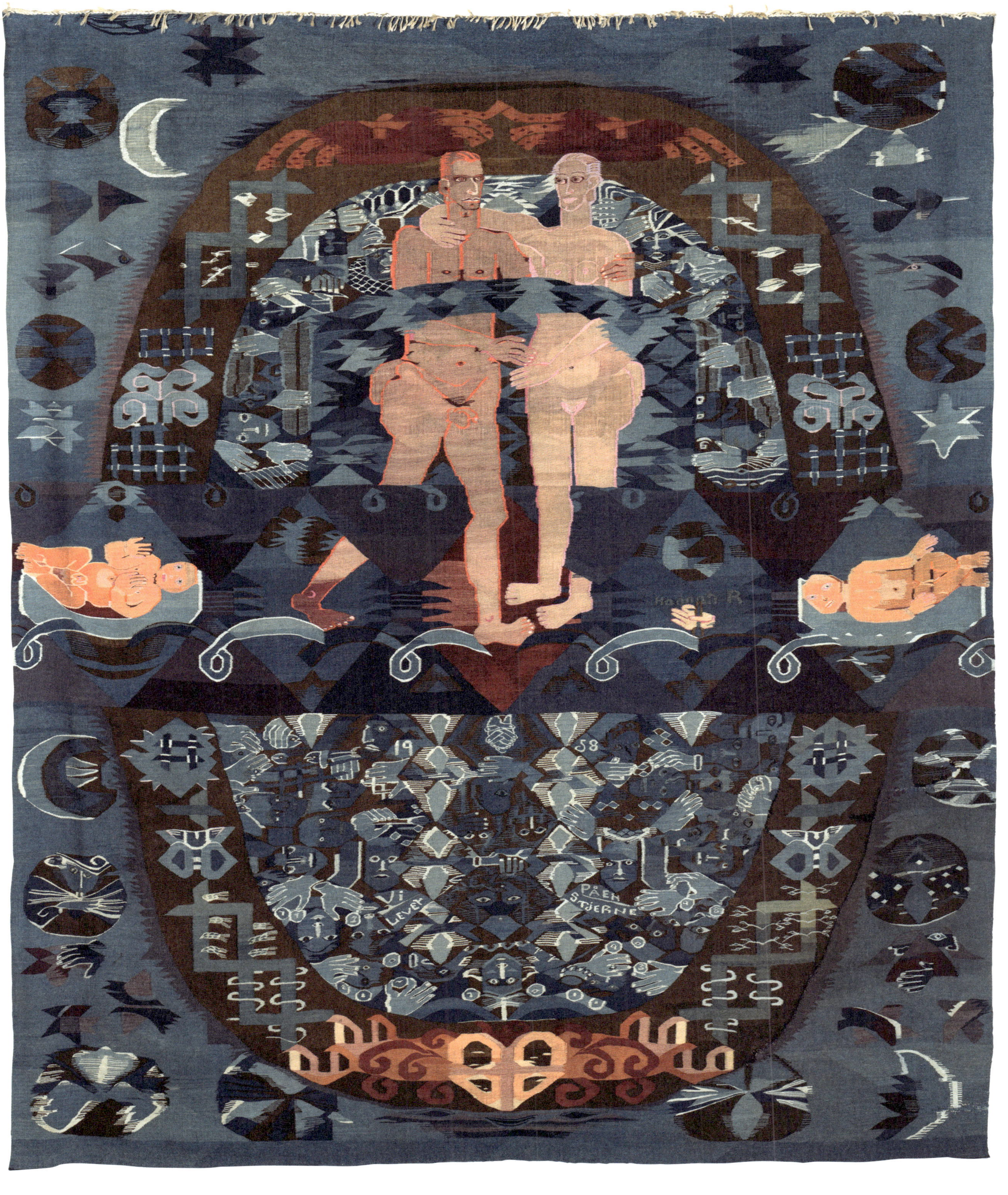
19
58
Vi LEVER
PÅ EN STJERNE

Johanna Laub
Biography and Chronology

1894

When Hanna Josefina Maria Jönsson was born in Malmö on March 21, 1894, her home country of Sweden was undergoing incredible changes: new technologies were revolutionizing the world of work and industrial production, a railway network connected important hubs, and better hygiene and medical care had reduced the mortality rate and made it possible for the population to double within one century. Yet the shift from an agrarian to an industrial society, which most countries in Europe experienced at nearly the same time, also brought with it severe supply problems and social conflict: in the late nineteenth century, around 2.5 million Swedes and Norwegians emigrated, primarily to the United States of America.

Hanna Jönsson's family remained in Sweden. Her mother, Karna Jönsson, neé Gall (1853–1930), worked as a domestic servant and her father, Gustav Jönsson (1864–1938), as a seaman and factory worker—a typical working-class family, as Hanna wrote later in an undated note: "My mother started to go out to work when she was eleven years old; my father started at Kockum's shipyard when he was fifteen years old. Work took up all their lives." Her parents made it possible for their children to obtain training for professions with a higher level of skills: Hannah—who added an "h" to the end of her name when she was a young woman—became a teacher, as did her sister, and her brother became a bank employee. She began working as an elementary school teacher in Gryt in the province of Östergötland at the age of nineteen, moving back to Malmö two years later. She was, however, somewhat at odds with her profession and in August 1916 she began taking evening classes with the painter Fredrik Krebs (1845–1925) in Lund. She studied the fundamentals of academic painting there for six years.

1914

Shortly after Hannah Jönsson left Malmö for her first teaching position, the First World War broke out on mainland Europe: when the heir presumptive to the throne of the Austro-Hungarian Empire was shot in Sarajevo in June 1914, the complex system of alliances entangled one country after the other in the conflict. While the population in many countries applauded their

+++ Ermordung des Thronfolgers Erzherzogs Franz Ferdinand und seiner Gemahlin Herzogin von Hohenberg. Eine Nachricht ist heute aus Sarajevo eingetroffen, welche die ganze Monarchie auf das tiefste erschüttern wird +++ **Neue Freie Presse, June 28, 1914**

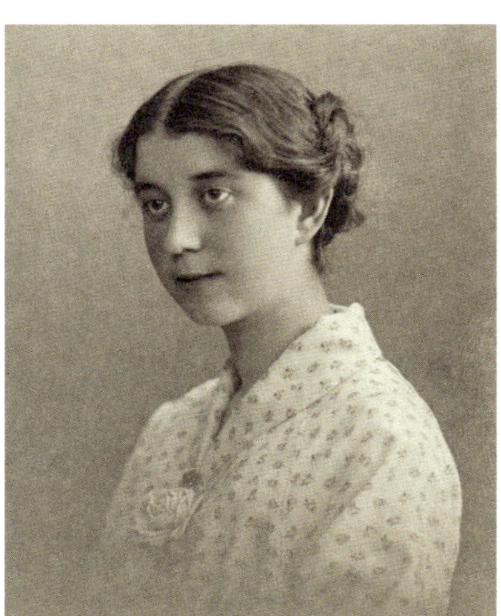

Hannah Jönsson, 1910s

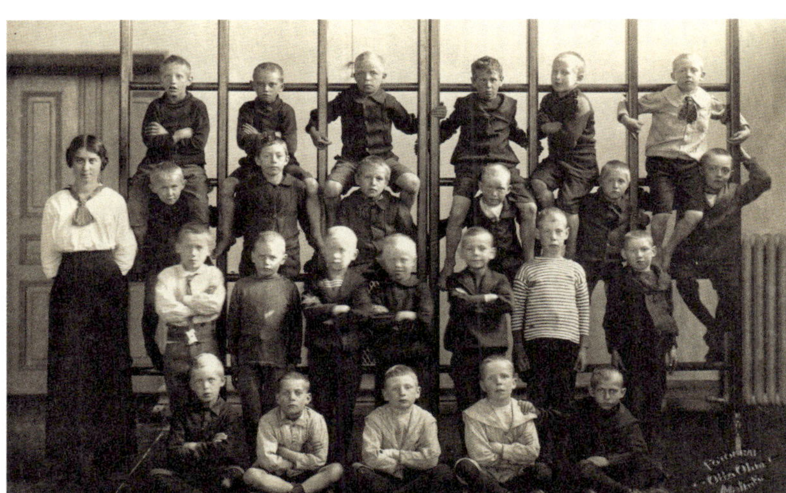

Hannah Jönsson with one of her classes, 1920s

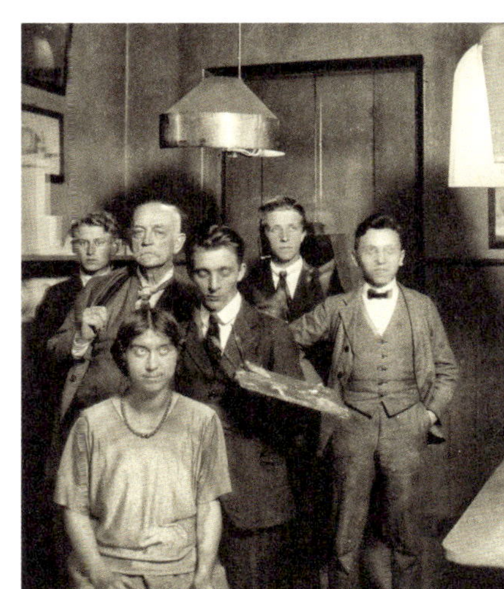

Fredrik Krebs (second from left) and his students, with Hannah Jönsson in the foreground, c. 1917–1920

entry into the war, Sweden and its neighbor Norway remained neutral. Hannah Jönsson thus only experienced the First World War from a distance. With its seventeen million victims, the war also showed in a terrible way the extent to which industrialization and modernization had changed how war was conducted.

+++ Germany Waves the White Flag. Kaiser Abdicates. Revolution in Berlin. Armistice Talks Underway. Delegates Blindfolded and Taken to Foch +++ **Daily Mail, November 11, 1918**

The First World War also simultaneously brought about a reorganization of political relationships. Three empires—the Austro-Hungarian, the Ottoman, and the German—dissolved and were superseded by eleven new nation states with a, for the most part, republican form of government. Constitutions with basic rights such as freedom of speech, expression, and assembly were adopted; the circle of individuals qualified to vote expanded to include broader segments of the population—including, gradually, women: Finland and Norway were European trailblazers in 1906 and 1913, and in 1919 Sweden followed, meaning that Hannah Jönsson was able to cast a vote in the general elections there two years later. Her sympathies, judging by her own statements, lay with the Socialist Workers' parties. With their position against the war, their protests against the shortage of supplies, and their commitment to workers' rights, they were increasingly able to win votes toward the end of the First World War.

1917

The first seizure of power by socialists in Europe took place in Russia in 1917 after the fall of the Tsar. In the "Red October" of the same year, the Bolshevists under Vladimir I. Lenin managed to seize power in a military putsch. In neighboring countries, with Russia's support, communist parties also came into power. In 1922, they joined forces to create the Union of Socialist Soviet Republics (USSR). The success of communism in Eastern Europe provoked a division of the leftist political wing into communist and socialist-democratic parties in numerous countries in the early 1920s. Such political rifts were, however, limited in comparison with the tensions between socialist, liberal, conservative, nationalistic, and fascist groups.

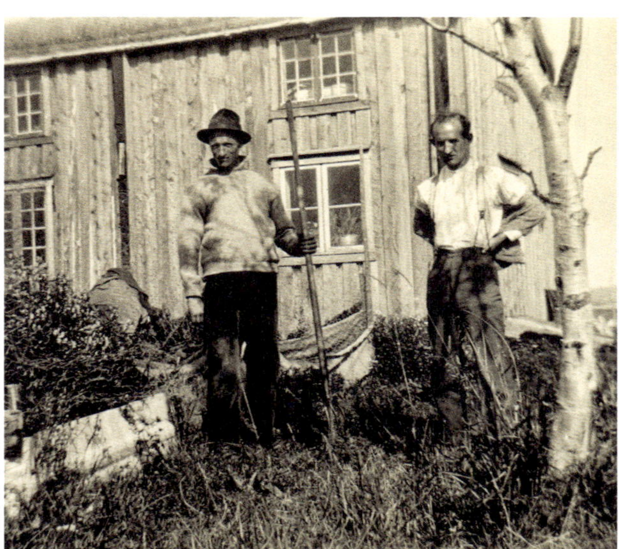

Hans Ryggen with Hannah's cousin Emil Nilson in front of their house "Rønnan" in Ørlandet, 1920s

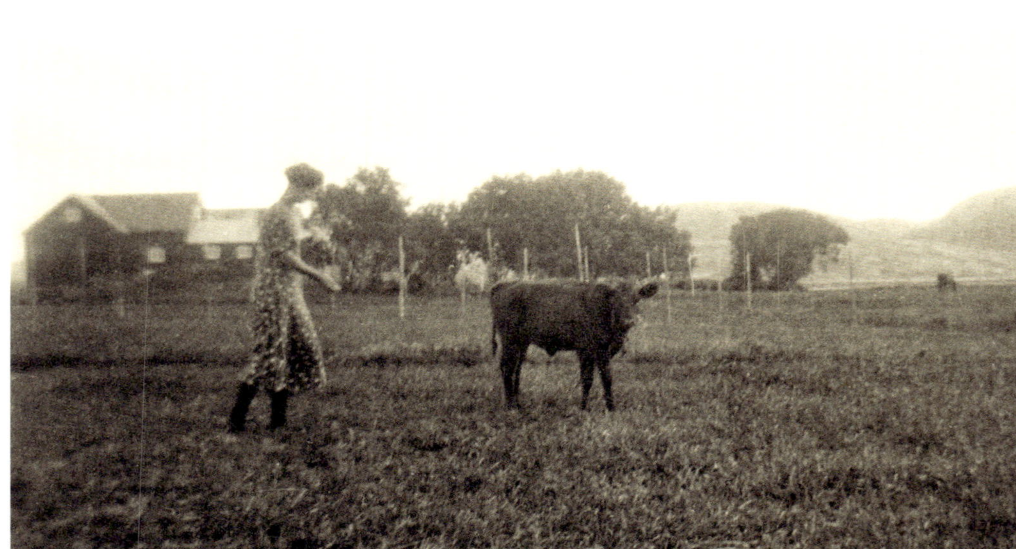

Hannah Ryggen with the family's cow in the field, 1920s

1922 Such idealistic battles were fought with particular vehemence in the still young Weimar Republic, which was established under social democratic leadership; Hannah Jönsson traveled there in 1922. On the recommendation of her teacher, Krebs, she spent the summer months in Dresden in order to study the extensive art collection of the Gemäldegalerie Alte Meister. Presumably she also moved in the surroundings of the contemporary art scene, which was influenced by the artists of the Dresdner Sezession. During her stay, she got to know the Norwegian painter Hans Ryggen, who was the same age as her. She also spent a period of time with him in Munich, where she visited the Alte Pinakothek.

After Hannah Jönsson returned from Germany, she and Hans Ryggen got engaged; they were married in Oslo in September 1923. Hans came from a family of small farmers that lived in Ørlandet, a coastal settlement about 100 kilometers northwest of Trondheim. He built a house for himself and Hannah on a nearby block of land. Until the dwelling was completed, Hannah Ryggen continued to work as a teacher in Malmö, supporting the construction with her income. She finally moved to Norway in March 1924, and gave birth to a daughter, Mona, in May.

The family lived simply: the house was only fifty square meters, and had no connection to running water or electricity. On around five hectares, the Ryggens were able to cultivate fruit and vegetables and keep some livestock such as geese, chickens, sheep, and a cow. Thus they were able to provide for themselves almost self-sufficiently; they obtained some money from the sale of livestock and agricultural products, as well as from the sale of Hans Ryggen's paintings and the dyeing courses run by Hannah Ryggen for a short while. Such forms of subsistence farming were frequently found in Norway until well into the twentieth century. Far removed from any romantic notions of farming, life on the small farm was hard work: "We were struggling desperately to pay debts, feed and clothe ourselves, and for what we actually felt our lives were meant to be in this world..."

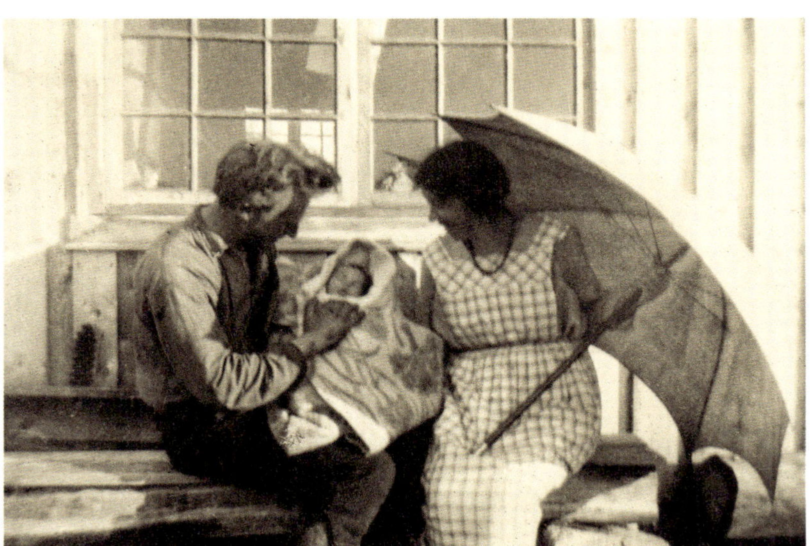

Hans and Hannah Ryggen with their newborn daughter Mona, 1924

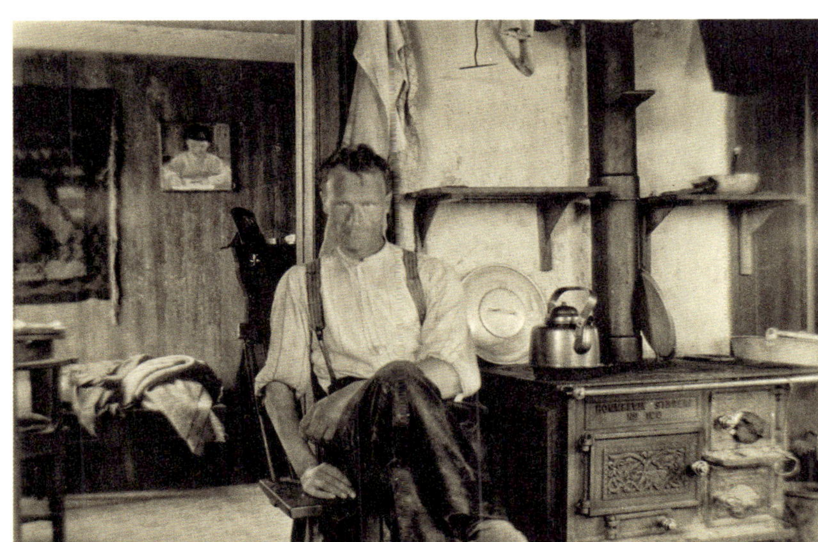

Hans Ryggen in the kitchen of their house, with the living room in the background, 1920s

In the time that remained, Hans and Hannah Ryggen dedicated themselves to their art. Following her return from Dresden, Hannah had decided to stop painting and to weave instead. She had probably already learned the fundamentals of the technique in a course in Nääs near Göteborg in 1916, as well as in a weaving course at a housekeeping school in Lund, shortly before she had moved to Norway. She learned everything else on her own. A first exhibition of her works along with paintings by Hans and woodcarvings by his brother Arne was held at the Lund Konstmuseum in 1926. Additional opportunities to present Hannah Ryggen's work to the public were provided by an annual exhibition in Trondheim in 1930, where she exhibited in the section for arts and crafts, as well as by the Foreningen Brukskunst (Association of Applied Art) in Oslo (1931/32). She first received greater attention in 1933 as a result of an exhibition at the Trondhjems Kunstforening (Trondheim Art Society).

1926

1929

It was at this time that the effects of the global economic crisis, which had spilled over to Europe like a wave after the collapse of the New York Stock Exchange in 1929, reached Norway. The withdrawal of loans from America became noticeable first in the financial sector, and then in industry. As of 1931, production and world trade drastically collapsed. The crisis led to mass unemployment and the social impoverishment of large sectors of the population. In Norway, the unemployment rate in some occupations was up to forty percent. The situation was most dire for workers and farmers, particularly small farmers, which included the Ryggen family. Many farmers and fishermen were forced to go into debt; farms were sometimes consequently sold off in forced auctions, amounting to a complete loss of livelihood. Hannah Ryggen lamented the distress of such people with her 1933 tapestry *Fiske ved gjeldens hav* (*Fishing in the Sea of Debt*).

+++ Huge Selling Wave Creates Near-Panic as Stocks Collapse +++
Washington Post, October 23, 1929

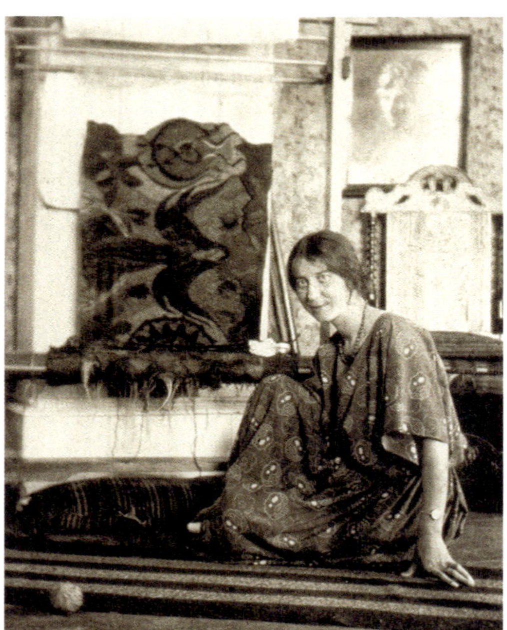

Hannah Ryggen in front of the loom, working on *Evas Datter* (*Eve's Daughter*), Malmö, 1922

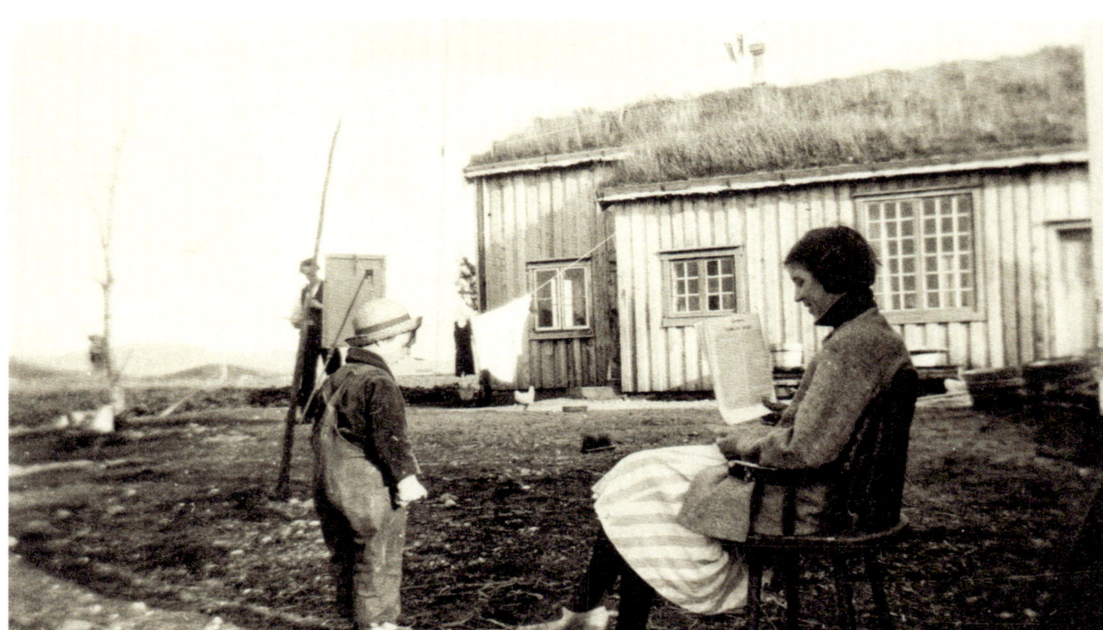

The Ryggen family in front of their house. Hans is painting in the background, Hannah and Mona are in the foreground, 1920s

The "Great Depression" brought a change of atmosphere along with it: the original openness to liberal-democratic governments drained away in light of their apparent failure; instead people hoped for swift solutions from more radical ideologies. The fact that the Soviet Union managed to experience an upswing in industry during the global economic crisis increased the attractiveness of the communist model. Fascism also benefited from the crisis and in the 1930s experienced a considerable rise in popularity transnationally. Benito Mussolini coined the still new term with his dictatorial regime imposed in Italy in 1922: it included a personality cult around an almost superhuman leader of the nation, the aestheticizing of political spectacle as well as the penetration of the ideology into all areas of life.

1933

Mussolini was, in many respects, the godfather of Adolf Hitler's self-conception as well as the program of the German National Socialist Workers' Party that he led—a party that was able to rely on considerable support among the population when Hitler was appointed as chancellor on January 30, 1933. Within only a few weeks, he had transformed the Weimar Republic into a dictatorship. Even though the leadership of the newly established "Third Reich" was still given the external guise of a democratically legitimated government, the true face of the regime was revealed in how it dealt with its opponents. The mistreatment and murder of members of the opposition as well as the withdrawal of basic rights and the ever-increasing violent persecution of the Jewish population caused dismay abroad. Germany was hence an especially terrifying example of how quickly a still fragile democracy could be transformed into a dictatorship, but this development was not an individual case among the newly established republics of Europe.

+++ Hitler chancelier! Flanqué de Von Papen et de Hugenberg, le chef des assassins fascistes préside le gouvernement de la terreur antiouvrière, de la misère et de la guerre +++ **L'Humanité, January 31, 1933**

While the fascist states pursued their political interests bolstered by mutual alliances, the great democratic powers proved to be hesitant in defending their values. When Mussolini, contrary to international law, invaded the East African Kingdom of Abyssinia (today Ethiopia) in October 1935 and systematically used poison gas against the military and civilian population there, the moral outrage was great, but the request for support that their emperor Haile Selassie brought before the League of Nations remained unanswered.

1936

Something similar took place the following year: in July 1936, conservative-monarchist forces under General Francisco Franco attempted to overthrow the socialist government in Spain. The militarily superior rebels were supported by the German Luftwaffe and Italian troops; the Republicans received assistance from an International Brigade established by the USSR. Although the brutality of the rebels—particularly regarding the total destruction of the city of Guernica by German aircraft— was condemned internationally, the great powers of France and Great Britain failed to intervene in the conflict. Five hundred thousand people died before Franco's dictatorship was successfully established in April 1939.

+++ Dans les ruines de Guernica. Les avions italo-allemands ont jeté des milliers de bombes sur la ville historique des Basques +++ **Ce Soir, April 29, 1937**

Hannah Ryggen commented uncompromisingly on all these events in her works throughout the 1930s. Highly topical and explosive, her works were repeatedly presented in exhibitions at Trondhjems Kunstforening and the Kunstnerforbundet (Artists' Association) in Oslo as of 1933. The Kunstindustrimuseet (Museum of Decorative Arts and Design) in Oslo purchased one of her works for the first time in 1935. The first international highpoints were the presentation of her work *Etiopia* (*Ethiopia*) in the Norwegian pavilion at the World's Fair in Paris in 1937 and in New York in 1939. Toward the end of the 1930s, the Ryggens' economic situation improved as a result of exhibition and teaching activities, as well as the sale of part of their land, which enabled them to pay off their debts.

1939

Even though the situation in Europe was tense, in 1939 the family planned an extended stay in France. After Hans and Hannah Ryggen opened an exhibition at the Kunstnerforbundet in Oslo in the spring, they picked up their daughter from relatives in southern Sweden with the plan to travel to Paris by bicycle. On May 1, they arrived in Copenhagen, where they were faced with the decision of whether they should continue their journey. But the apparent preparations of the Allies for a coming war made this seem like less than a good idea, so a few weeks later they began their journey back to Ørlandet.

The Allies had hesitated for a long time to provide a military response to Hitler's provocations, believing that they could avoid a war if they accommodated him to a sufficient extent: they thus tolerated the annexation of Austria to the German Reich in 1938 and accepted the annexation of the Sudetenland. Hitler, however, was not in the least interested in de-escalation; quite the contrary, the war was supposed to provide an opportunity to expand German *Lebensraum* toward the east. The German military began its attack on Poland on September 1 and overwhelmed the country within only a few weeks. They benefited in doing so from the non-aggression pact

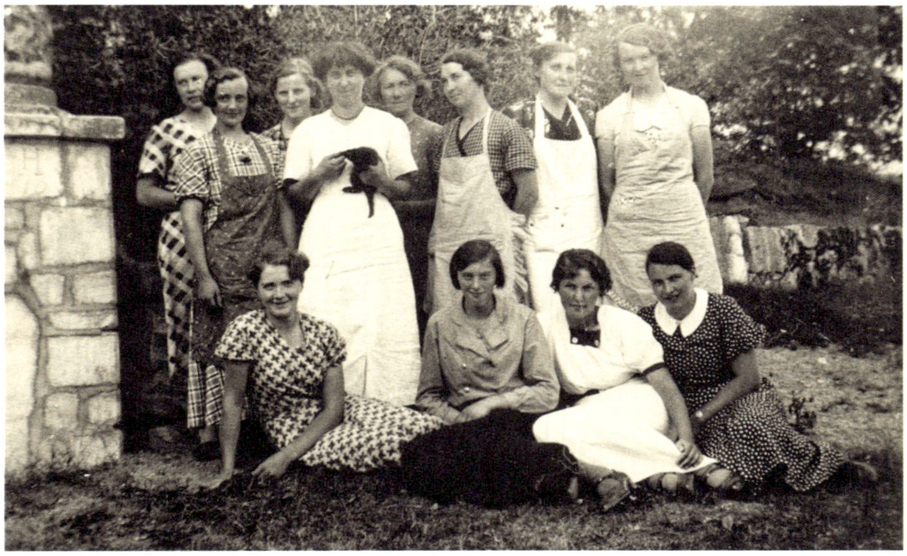

Hannah Ryggen (in the center, in a white dress) surrounded by the participants of her plant-dyeing course at Rein Abbey, 1936

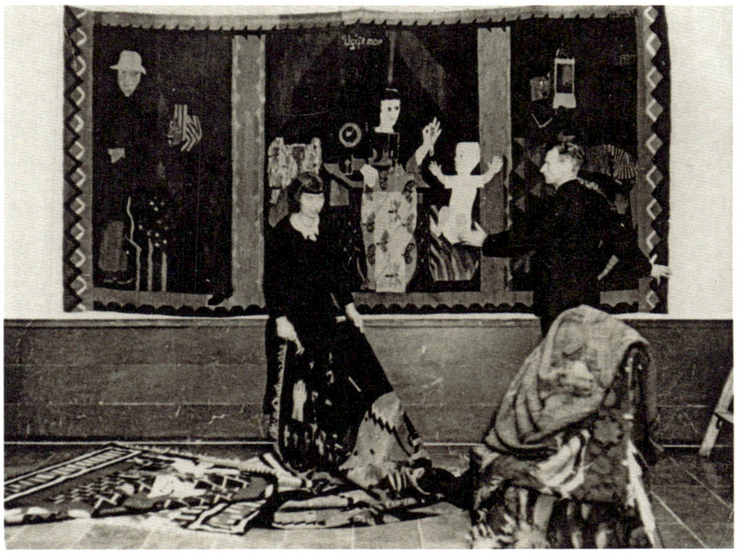

Hans and Hannah Ryggen mounting their joint exhibition at the Kunstnerforbundet (Artists' Association) in Oslo, 1939

that Hitler had signed with Stalin. As unlikely as this alliance between a fascist and a communist regime was considered from an ideological perspective, for the Soviet Union, it resulted in a welcome repartitioning of Eastern Europe, in which regions in Poland, Rumania, and Finland would be handed over to the USSR. For Hannah Ryggen, this collaboration denoted a betrayal of socialist values: “There needs to be a new banner in the world that doesn’t get dirty like the red one,” she wrote to a friend on December 6, 1939.

+++ Germans invade and bomb Poland. Britain mobilises +++ **Evening Standard, September 1, 1939**

1940

It was at this time that Mona began suffering seizures that would later be diagnosed as a form of epilepsy, but that were not treated correctly at the time. With a grant and the sale of Hannah Ryggen’s earlier work *Synderinnen* (*The Sinner*) from 1926 to the Nordenfjeldske Kunstindustrimuseum, her parents tried to come up with money for her treatment at a clinic in Copenhagen. In April 1940, however, these plans were shattered when the Wehrmacht attacked Norway and Denmark. The Scandinavian countries were of strategic interest due to their geographical location and resources such as iron ore. Sweden had already declared its neutrality at the beginning of the war. While Denmark surrendered after only a few hours of battle, the Norwegians put up resistance for a few weeks longer with the help of British troops. Ørlandet was also bombed in July 1940; in the years that followed, a German military airport would be created there, for whose construction Russian and Serbian forced laborers were used.

When the resistance collapsed, the king and the government fled to London; Norwegian collaborators in the fascist party Nasjonal Samling filled the political vacuum. But there was no broad support among the population for this collaboration: the resistance movement in Norway again and again took action against the German occupiers by means of civil disobedience, acts of sabotage, and attacks. The Germans responded by executing numerous individuals suspected of resistance—a policy of deterrence for which public figures were repeatedly made use of.

+++ Fiendtlighetene i Nord-Norge innstilt. Kongen og Regjeringa har forlatt landet? +++ **1ste Mai, June 10, 1940**

1944

The persecution of the Norwegian resistance intensified in the final year of the war. There was a wave of arrests by the German security police, in which Hans Ryggen was detained. In Hannah Ryggen’s absence, he was captured in May 1944 and brought to the prison camp in Faldstad near Trondheim, while his family was left in the dark about the reasons for and the consequences of his detention. In August, he was moved to the Grini police prison camp, from which Norwegian Jews and other prisoners were regularly deported to concentration camps in Poland and Germany. In comparison to other prisoners, Hans Ryggen was very fortunate: he remained in captivity until the end of the war, but did not have to do hard physical labor and was instead assigned to menial painting work.

Following the lightning-like victories achieved by the Wehrmacht in the initial years of the war, a turning point came in 1942 to 1943. The offensive against the former ally in the east, the Soviet Union, came to a halt and German forces were gradually pushed back by the Red Army. The Allied troops simultaneously advanced on the Western

Front with the support of the United States. At the end of April 1945, the troops met each other at Torgau on the Elbe River; the German Reich capitulated on May 8, 1945. A perfidiously systematized genocide, large-scale bombardments, scorched earth tactics, mass executions, and imposed famine had cost the lives of some fifty million people.

1945

+++ L'Allemagne vaincue! Capitulation sans conditions. Staline, Truman, Churchill et le general de Gaulle proclameront cet après-midi, à 15 heures la victoire +++
Le Parisien libéré, May 8, 1945

After the war, Hannah and Hans Ryggen allowed little time to pass before reviving their plan from 1939 of spending a few months in France. After Hannah opened a solo exhibition at Det danske Kunstindustrimuseum (today the Designmuseum Danmark) in Copenhagen, the family traveled on to France in September 1946 and rented a house in Bures-sur-Yvette, a few kilometers south of Paris, where they stayed until July 1947. Although Hannah Ryggen was not able to do any weaving at this time because her loom was located in Ørlandet, she gathered inspiration from the numerous museums in the French capital.

The postwar period cemented Hannah Ryggen's artistic reputation. In 1946, the Kunstnerforbundet in Oslo extended the duration of her solo exhibition due to the large numbers of visitors. In 1953, the Norwegian Nasjonalgalleriet (National Gallery) purchased her 1949 work *Henders bruk* (*The Use of Hands*), the first work of textile art that the museum incorporated into its collection, on the occasion of an exhibition at Oslo's Kunstnernes Hus. "Now I am a bona fide artist," Hannah Ryggen proudly wrote to her cousin. The following year she participated in an exhibition at the Petit Palais in Paris and, during 1955 to 1956, her art was included in a large traveling exhibition organized by the Smithsonian Institution; twelve of her works were shown in Chicago, Washington D.C., Seattle, and San Francisco, among other American cities.

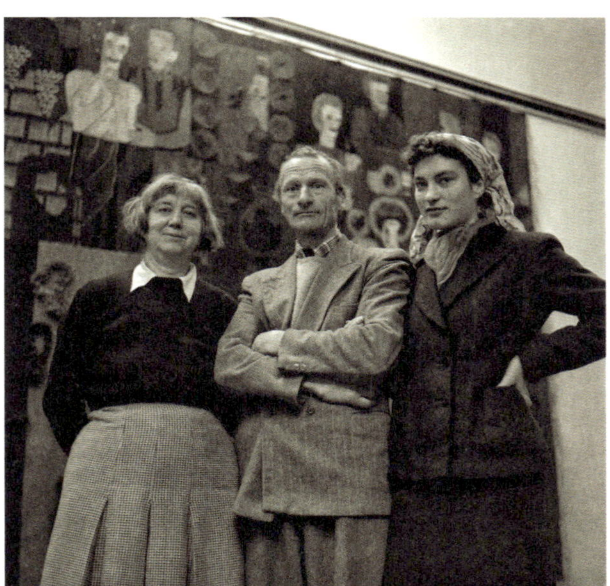

Hannah, Hans, and Mona Ryggen, portrait for the *Arbeider-Avisa* on the occasion of Hannah Ryggen and Ola Abrahamsson's exhibition at the Trondhjems Kunstforeningen, October 3, 1952

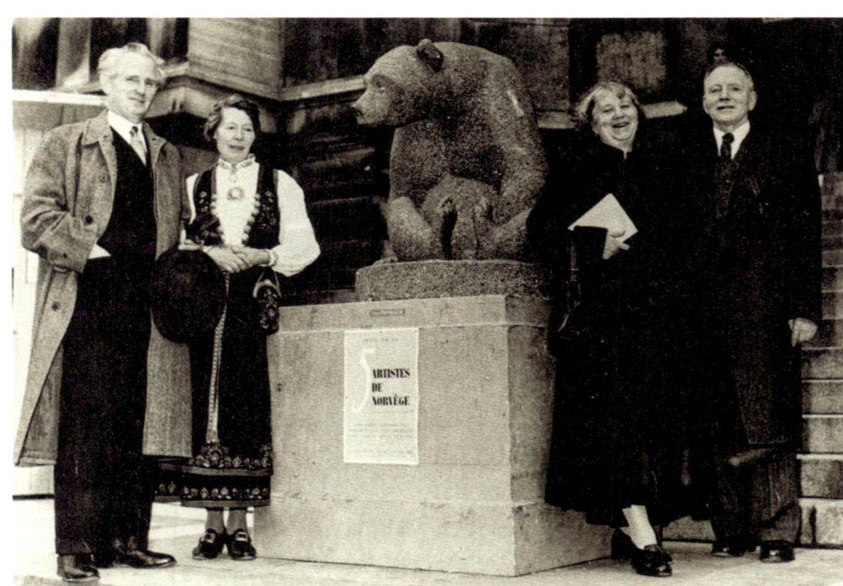

Erik Harry Johannessen, Anne Grimdalen, Hannah Ryggen, and Rolf Andvord at the opening of the exhibition *Cinq artistes Norvégiens at Petit Palais,* Paris, 1954

Although the war had come to an end, no true peace prevailed in Europe. Instead, the Western democratic bloc and the Eastern communist bloc confronted one another and reciprocally accused each other of aggressively implementing their respective ideological aims. By 1948, Stalin had expanded the Soviet Union's sphere of influence to include nearly all the countries lying between Russia and the Soviet zone of occupation in Germany. The United States in turn tethered Central and Western European countries to its market-oriented economic system by means of economic subsidies. Symbolically, the division of the world ran through Germany, which was divided into two countries in 1949.

1949

Amid concerns that the conflict might end in military action, twelve nations signed the North Atlantic Treaty, a defense alliance, on April 4, 1949. The communist states subsequently joined forces in the Warsaw Pact. By fall of the same year, the Americans were no longer the only ones to possess atomic weapons—the Russians had drawn level with them. A paradoxical balance of terror set in: if one side were to attack, the other would be in a position to retaliate in a timely manner; an escalation would have had devastating consequences for both sides. But, even though the war in Europe remained "cold," it was conducted in proxy wars such as the war between North and South Korea, from 1950 to 1953.

+++ Truman Says Russia Set Off Atom Blast +++

The Sun, September 24, 1949

In the 1950s, with works such as *Atomsen* (*Mr. Atom*), *Henders bruk* (*The Use of Hands*), and *Jul Kvale,* Hannah Ryggen positioned herself against the arms race between the two blocs. But private topics also entered her work more intensively again in the postwar years. In 1955, she was commissioned to produce three works for the newly erected headquarters in the Government Quarter of Oslo; one of the works would hang prominently in the entrance area of the so-called Highrise. The invitation occurred on the initiative of the architect Erling Viksjø, whom she had already gotten to know

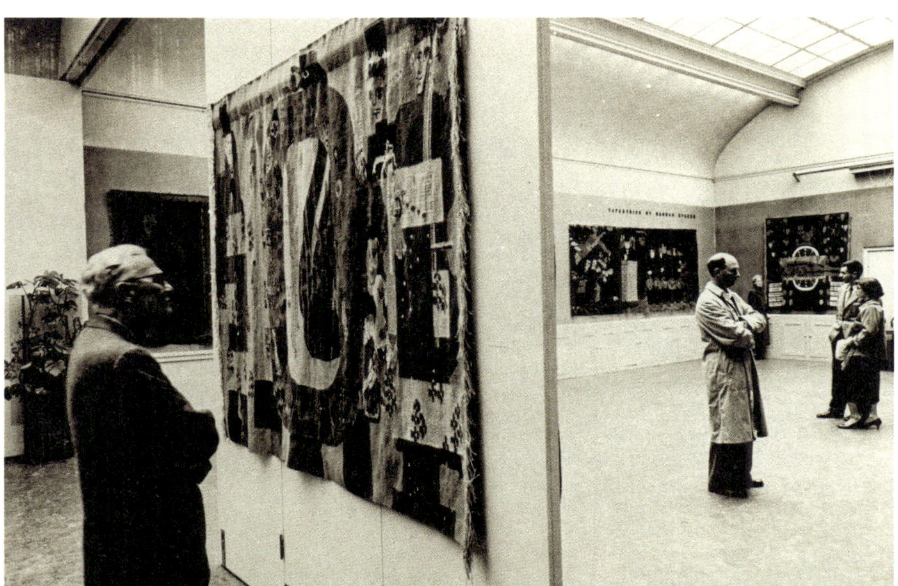

Hannah Ryggen's touring exhibition in the United States, San Francisco Museum of Modern Art, 1956

in 1943 in connection with a commission for a tapestry for a church in Oslo, which was ultimately not executed. But before she was able to begin, Hans Ryggen died on December 19, 1956. He had been diagnosed with tuberculosis in 1953 and, despite spending time at a sanatorium, had been unable to fully recover from the illness. After his death, Hannah Ryggen left Ørlandet and moved to Trondheim. There, she rented a studio with sufficient space for a larger loom, on which she produced the monumental work *Vi lever på en stjerne* (*We Are Living on a Star*) for the Highrise in 1958. The same year, she represented Norway at the World's Fair, and in 1959 Sweden awarded her the Prins Eugen Medaille in recognition of her outstanding artistic achievements in the field of arts and crafts.

1956

The Cold War reached its apex at the beginning of the 1960s. In August 1961, the conflict between the Soviet Union and the Western powers culminated in the construction of the "Anti-Fascist Protective Wall" around Berlin, as the SED government called the Berlin Wall. The following year, the Cuban Missile Crisis nearly resulted in the military escalation of the conflict: the USSR stationed intermediate-range missiles on Cuba, where Fidel Castro had just established a communist state—a direct threat to the United States, which demanded their immediate removal and threatened to make use of all available means of attack. Only after six tense days following Kennedy's ultimatum on October 22 was it possible to reach an agreement with the leader of the party and head of government Nikita Khrushchev.

1961

+++ ¡Alarma de combate! La nación en pie de guerra. Ordena el Primer Ministro Fidel Castro ante el peligro de la agresión dispuesta por Kennedy +++
Revolución (Extra), October 22, 1962

The shock over the narrowly averted nuclear catastrophe at least made the will to restrict the acquisition of nuclear armaments evident. The ossified ideologies of the Cold War were also shaken up. The student movement questioned Western guiding

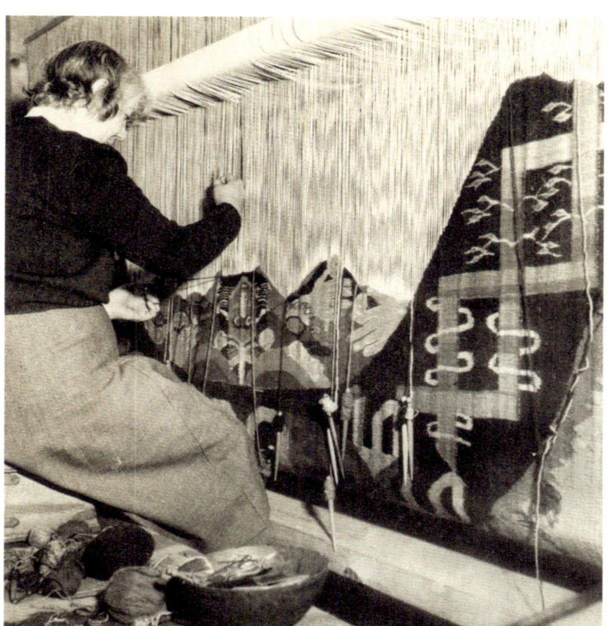

Hannah Ryggen working on *Vi lever på en stjerne* (*We Are Living on a Star*), c. 1957

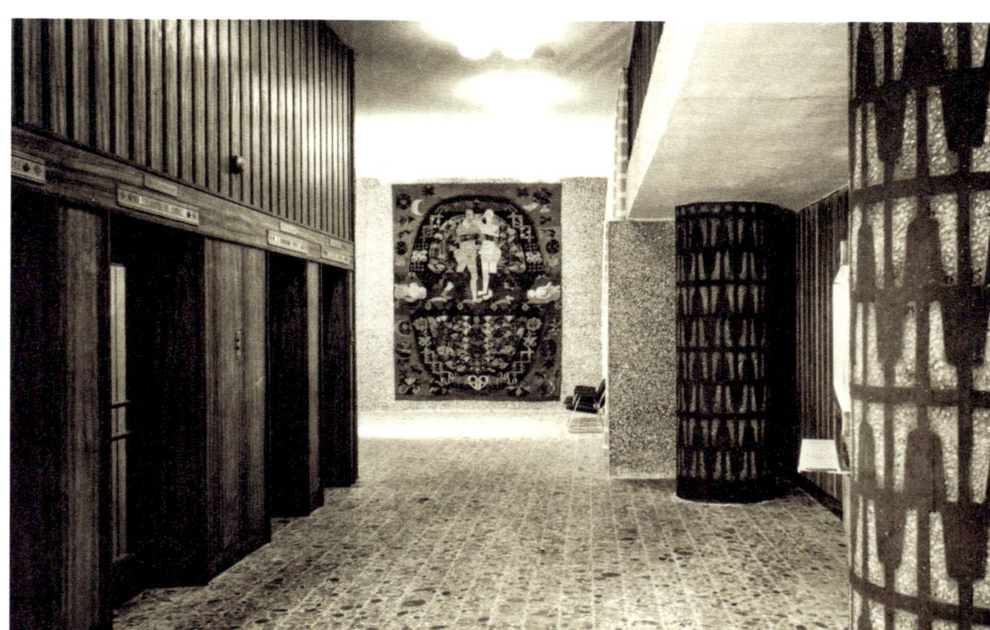

We Are Living on a Star hanging in the lobby of the Highrise building in Oslo's Government Quarter, 1958

principles such as capitalism and consumer society, and criticized the moral superiority that the West claimed for itself during the Cold War. American intervention in the civil war between the communist North and the Western-oriented South Vietnam came under criticism in particular. The exploitation of the conflict for the benefit of its own interests and the extensive use of chemical weapons against the civilian population provoked massive protest among the American population.

+++ 250,000 War Protesters Stage Peaceful Rally in Washington; Militants Stir Clashes Later +++
The New York Times, November 16, 1969

Hannah Ryggen continued her artistic positioning vis-à-vis current events by raising her voice against the Vietnam War with works such as *Blod i gresset* (*Blood in the Grass*) from 1966. The 1960s also brought important moments of recognition. In 1962, the Moderna Museet in Stockholm honored Ryggen with a large retrospective; in 1964, she represented Norway at the 32nd Venice Biennale with twelve primarily political works. The same year, she received an important commission (which was to be her last) from the University of Oslo, for whose council hall she created the seven-meter-long *Trollveggen* (*The Troll Wall*). The work was inaugurated two years later, on March 29, 1966. In 1964, the jury of the tradition-steeped *Høstutstillingen* (*Fall Exhibition*) in Oslo, which had been established in 1882, decided to present her works not in the section for textiles but in the painting section instead. In 1965, Ryggen's artistic achievements were honored by her being awarded Knight 1st Class of the Royal Norwegian Order of St. Olav. While continuing to live in Trondheim, that same year she donated seven major works to the Nordenfjeldske Kunstindustrimuseum. Hannah Ryggen died in Trondheim on February 2, 1970.

1970

Select Bibliography

Altrichter, Helmut and Walther L. Bernecker. *Geschichte Europas im 20. Jahrhundert.* Stuttgart: Kohlhammer W., GmbH, 2004.

Besier, Gerhard. *European Dictatorships: A Comparative History of the Twentieth Century.* Cambridge: Cambridge Scholars Publishing, 2013.

Brandt, Peter, Werner Daum, and Miriam Horn (eds.). *Der skandinavische Weg in die Moderne. Beiträge zur Geschichte Norwegens und Schwedens vom Spätmittelalter bis ins 20. Jahrhundert.* Berlin: BWV Berliner Wissenschafts-Verlag, 2016.

Jarausch, Konrad H. Out of Ashes: *A New History of Europe in the Twentieth Century.* Princeton: Princeton University Press, 2016.

Kuzma, Marta. *Hannah Ryggen* (100 Notizen – 100 Gedanken / 100 Notes – 100 Thoughts, vol. 67). Published on the occasion of dOCUMENTA (13), Kassel. Ostfildern: Hatje Cantz, 2012. Citation from p. 31.

Müller, Jan-Werner. *Das demokratische Zeitalter. Eine politische Ideengeschichte Europas im 20. Jahrhundert.* Berlin: suhrkamp taschenbuch wissenschaft, 2013.

Paasche, Marit. *Hannah Ryggen: Threads of Defiance.* London: Thames & Hudson, 2019. Citations from pp. 62, 104, 152.

Ustvedt, Øystein and Marianne Yvenes (eds.). *Hannah Ryggen: Weaving the World.* Exh. cat. Nasjonalmuseet Oslo, Moderna Museet Malmö. Cologne: Walther König, 2015.

Translation of foreign language quotes

1914 Murder of the Heir to the Throne Arch-Duke Franz Ferdinand and His Wife, the Duchess of Hohenberg. News That Will Profoundly Shake the Whole Monarchy Arrived Today from Sarajevo

1933 Chancellor Hitler! Flanked by von Papen and Hugenberg, the Leader of Fascist Murderers Heads a Government of Anti-Labor Terror, Misery, and War

1937 In the Ruins of Guernica. Italian-German Aircraft Drop Thousands of Bombs Over the Historical City of the Basques

1940 Hostilities Cease in Northern Norway. Have the King and Government Left the Country?

1945 Germany Defeated! Unconditional Surrender. Stalin, Truman, Churchill, and General de Gaulle Proclaim Victory at 3 p.m. this Afternoon

1962 Call to Battle! The Country Ready for War. Command of the Prime Minister Fidel Castro in Light of Kennedy's Threat to Attack

Untitled (*Self-Portrait*), 1970
Tapestry woven in wool and linen,
51 × 40 cm

Hannah Ryggen wove herself into quite a number of her tapestries, including her final work, which remained unfinished. Her self-portraits are a continual reminder of the importance of resolve and determination in being an artist, of never giving up, of scrutinizing oneself and one's work until one's very last breath. Being an artist is hard work, and it is something we should all value and respect. Art is both past and future.

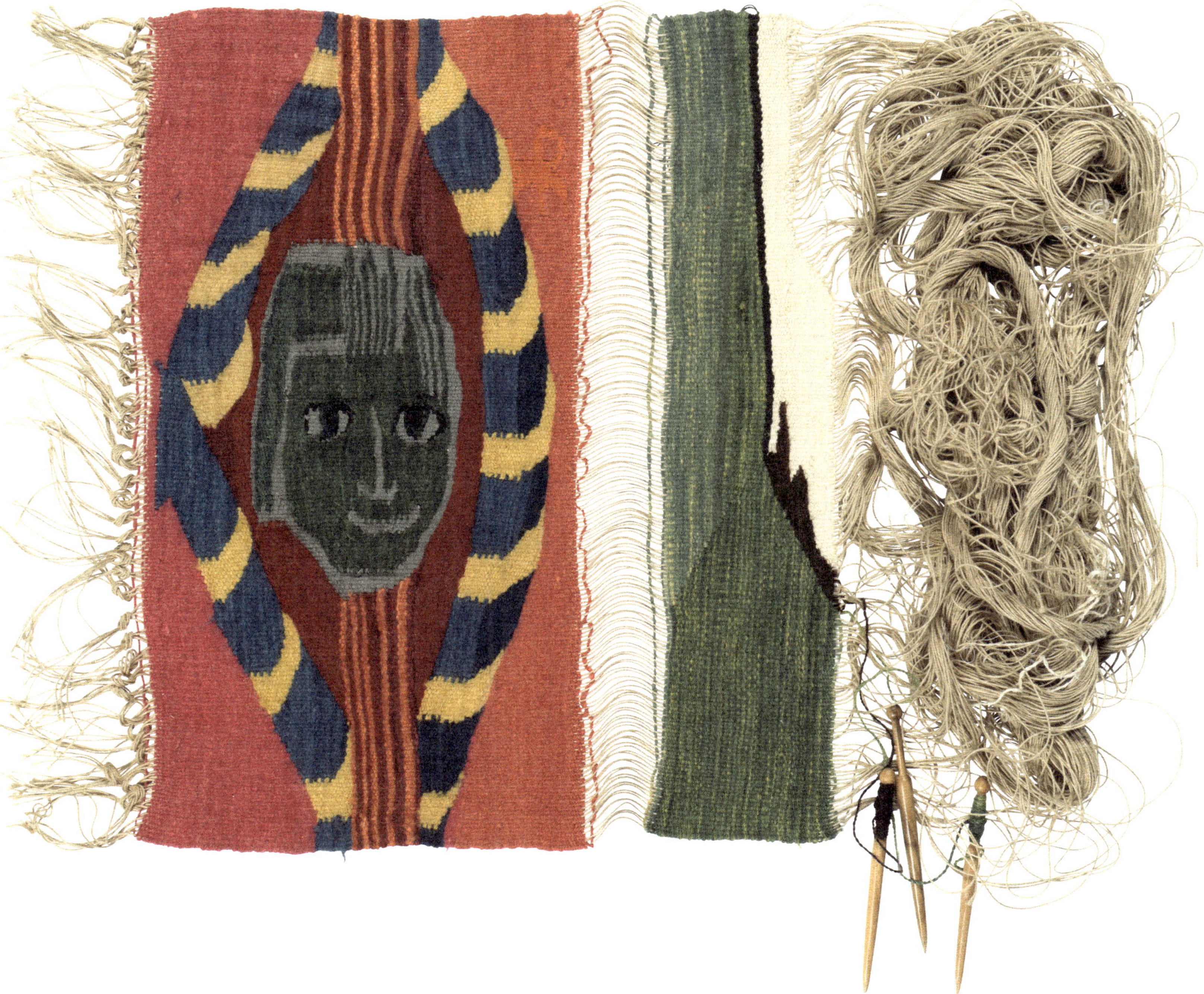

Exhibited Works

Synderinnen (*The Sinner*), 1926
Tapestry woven in wool and linen
190 × 222 cm
Nordenfjeldske Kunstindustrimuseum (National Museum of Decorative Arts and Design), Trondheim
Fig. pp. 68/69

Verhau (*The Squall*), 1928
Tapestry woven in wool and linen
160 × 153 cm
Ørland Public Health Association, Brekkstad
Fig. p. 93

Fiske ved gjeldens hav (*Fishing in the Sea of Debt*), 1933
Tapestry woven in wool and linen
145 × 185 cm
Private collection, Norway
Fig. pp. 34/35

Vi og våre dyr (*Us and Our Animals*), 1934
Tapestry in wool and linen
187.5 × 491 cm
Malmö Konstmuseum (Malmö Art Museum), Sweden
pp. 36/37

Etiopia (*Ethiopia*), 1935
Tapestry woven with pile in wool and linen
160 × 380 cm
Nordenfjeldske Kunstindustrimuseum (National Museum for Decorative Arts and Design), Trondheim
Figs. pp. 50–53

Gullammet Iselin (*The Golden Lamb Iselin*), 1935
Tapestry woven in wool and linen
184 × 140 cm
Private collection, Norway
Fig. p. 71

Drømmedød (*Death of Dreams*), 1936
Tapestry woven in wool and linen
235 × 273 cm
Nordenfjeldske Kunstindustrimuseum (National Museum for Decorative Arts and Design), Trondheim
Fig. pp. 38/39

Ugift mor (*Unwed Mother*), 1937
Tapestry woven in wool and linen
190 × 375 cm
The Röhsska Museum of Design and Craft, Gothenburg, Sweden
RKM 67-1956
Figs. pp. 72/73, 75

Liselotte Herrmann halshuggen (*Liselotte Herrmann Decapitated*), 1938
Tapestry woven in wool and linen
187.1 × 154 cm
Nordenfjeldske Kunstindustrimuseum (National Museum for Decorative Arts and Design), Trondheim
Fig. p. 41

Livet glir forbi (*Life Slides By*), 1939
Tapestry woven in wool and linen
190 × 185 cm
Private collection, Norway
Fig. p. 95

6. oktober 1942 (*6 October 1942*), 1943
Tapestry woven in wool and linen
175 × 419.5 cm
Nordenfjeldske Kunstindustrimuseum (National Museum for Decorative Arts and Design), Trondheim
Figs. pp. 42/43, 45

Grini, 1945
Tapestry woven in wool and linen
191.5 × 168.5 cm
Trondheim kunstmuseum
Fig. p. 47

Schweden (*Sweden*), 1946
Tapestry woven in wool and linen
190 × 175 cm
Private collection, Norway
Fig. p. 49

Mors hjerte (*Mother's Heart*), 1947
Tapestry woven in wool and linen
190 × 186 cm
Nordenfjeldske Kunstindustrimuseum (National Museum for Decorative Arts and Design), Trondheim
Figs. pp. 81, 83

En fri (*A Free One*), 1948
Tapestry woven in wool and linen
190.2 × 188 cm
Nordenfjeldske Kunstindustrimuseum (National Museum for Decorative Arts and Design), Trondheim
Fig. p. 97

Trojansk hest / Picassoteppet (*Trojan Horse / Picasso tapestry*), 1949–56
Two tapestries woven in wool and linen
190 × 320 cm (overall dimensions)
Owned by the Norwegian state, Office of the Prime Minister
Figs. pp. 99–101, 103

Henders bruk (*The Use of Hands*), 1949
Tapestry woven in wool and linen
192.5 × 208.5 cm
The National Museum of Art, Architecture and Design, Oslo
Fig. pp. 76/77

Hjemlige guder (*Homely Gods*), 1951
Tapestry woven in wool and linen
94 × 192 cm
DNB Art Collection, Norway
Fig. pp. 84/85

Atomsen (*Mr. Atom*), 1951
Tapestry woven in wool and linen
170 × 190 cm
Telenor Art Collection, Norway
Fig. p. 79

Dikt av T.S. Eliot (*Poem by T. S. Eliot*), 1952
Tapestry woven in wool and linen
194 × 165 cm
Nordenfjeldske Kunstindustrimuseum (National Museum for Decorative Arts and Design), Trondheim
Fig. p. 109

Jul Kvale, 1956
Tapestry woven in wool and linen
200 × 190 cm
Nordenfjeldske Kunstindustrimuseum (National Museum for Decorative Arts and Design), Trondheim
Fig. p. 57

Vi lever på en stjerne (*We Are Living on a Star*), 1958
Tapestry woven in wool and linen
400 × 300 cm
Nordenfjeldske Kunstindustrimuseum (National Museum for Decorative Arts and Design), Trondheim
Figs. pp. 110/111, 113

Bærestolen (*The Sedan Chair*), 1959
Tapestry woven in wool and linen
167 × 195 cm
Department of Museums and Art, City of Stockholm
Figs. pp. 104/105, 107

Blod i gresset (*Blood in the Grass*), 1966
Tapestry woven with pile in wool and linen
240 × 290 cm
KODE – Art Museums and Composer Homes, Norway
Fig. pp. 10/11

Sisyfos (*Sisyphus*), 1966
Tapestry woven in wool and linen with fringes
96 × 66 cm
Courtesy of STANDARD (OSLO)
Fig. p. 55

Untitled (*Self-Portrait*), 1970
Tapestry woven in wool and linen
51 × 40 cm
Nordenfjeldske Kunstindustrimuseum (National Museum for Decorative Arts and Design), Trondheim
Fig. p. 127

This catalog is published in conjunction with the exhibition

Hannah Ryggen
Woven Manifestos

Schirn Kunsthalle Frankfurt
September 26, 2019 – January 12, 2020

Editors
Marit Paasche, Esther Schlicht

Editing
Johanna Laub, Marit Paasche, Esther Schlicht

Publication Management
Antonia Lagemann, Anuschka Berthelius

Work Texts
Marit Paasche

Copyediting
Sarah Quigley

Translation
Amy Klement (German–English)
Katia Stieglitz (Norwegian–English)

Graphic Design
Sibylle Ryser, Basel

Production Management
Corinna Pickart

Separations
Reproline mediateam, Unterföhring

Printing and Binding
Kösel, Altusried-Krugzell

Paper
Salzer Design white

Typeface
Arnhem, Brown

Cover Illustration
Hannah Ryggen, *Trojansk hest* (*Trojan Horse*), 1949–1956, detail

Quote on Cover
Letter from Hannah Ryggen to Tora Sandal Bøhn, December 2, 1946, NTNU University Library, Trondheim

A member of Verlagsgruppe Random House GmbH
Neumarkter Strasse 28 · 81673 Munich
Prestel Publishing Ltd., 41–17 Wells Street, London W1T 3PD
Prestel Publishing, 900 Broadway, Suite 603, New York, NY 10003

A CIP catalog record for this book is available from the British Library.

ISBN 978-3-7913-5926-7
(English trade edition)
ISBN 978-3-7913-6970-9
(English museum edition)

ISBN 978-3-7913-5925-0
(German trade edition)
ISBN 978-3-7913-6969-3
(German museum edition)

Printed in Germany

MIX
Paper from responsible sources
FSC® C013736

Verlagsgruppe Random House
FSC® N001967

www.prestel.com

Photo Credits

Photo: Uta Freia Beer (p. 18, fig. 7)

Photo: Valentin Boure / Stavanger kunstmuseum (p. 61, fig. 2)

Photo: Dag Fosse / KODE (pp. 10/11)

Photo: Jørn Hagen (p. 95)

Photo © Jiri Havran (p. 26, figs. 15–18)

Photo: Steffen Wesselvold Holden (p. 93)

Photo: Mikael Lammgård (p. 30, fig. 19, pp. 72/73, 75)

Photo: Gregor Lorenz, Zschorlau (p. 18, fig. 6)

Photo: The National Library, Oslo (p. 64, fig. 7)

Photo: Thor Nielsen (p. 30, figs. 21/22, pp. 42/43, 45, 50–53, 81, 83, 110/111, 113, 127)

Photo: Schrøderarkivet / Sverresborg (p. 122, fig. on left)

Photo: Göran Sehlstedt; courtesy of the Department of Museums and Art, City of Stockholm (pp. 104/105, 107)

Photo: Anders Sundet Solberg (pp. 38/39, 41, 57, 61, figs. 3–4, p. 64, fig. 6, pp. 68/69, 97, 109)

Photo: Øystein Thorvaldsen (pp. 99–101, 103)

Photo: Øystein Thorvaldsen; courtesy of Henie Onstad Kunstsenter. Private owner (p. 23, fig. 12, pp. 34/35)

Photo: Trondheim kunstmuseum (p. 47)

Photo: Thomas Tveter (pp. 84/85)

Reproduced by unknown photographer / Malmö Art Museum (pp. 36/37)

Hannah Ryggen: Woven Histories, installation view, 2017 © Modern Art Oxford. Photo: Ben Westoby (p. 79)

© Munchmuseet, Oslo (p. 23, fig. 14)

© National Museum of Art, Architecture and Design, Oslo. Photo: Andreas Harvik (p. 61, fig. 1), Børre Høstland (p. 30, fig. 20, pp. 49, 71), Jaques Lathion (p. 23, fig. 13, pp. 76/77)

NTNU University Library, Trondheim. Photo: Karl Teigen (p. 124, fig. on right)

NTNU University Library, Trondheim. Photo: unknown (pp. 15, 18, figs. 8–10, p. 23, fig. 11, pp. 115–118, 120, 122, fig. on right, pp. 123, 124, fig. on left)

Courtesy of STANDARD (OSLO), Photo: Vegard Kleven (p. 55)